Nigeria at Fifty

Nigeria, Africa's most populous and biggest democracy, celebrated her fiftieth year as an independent nation in October 2010. As the cliché states, 'As Nigeria goes, so goes Africa'. This book frames the socio-historical and political trajectory of Nigeria while examining the many dimensions of the critical choices that she has made as an independent nation. How does the social composition of interest and power illuminate the actualities and narratives of the Nigerian crisis? How have the choices made by Nigerian leaders structured, and/or have been structured by, the character of the Nigerian state and state-society relations? In what ways is Nigeria's mono-product, debt-ridden, dependent economy fed by 'the politics of plunder'? And what are the implications of these questions for the structural relationships of production, reproduction and consumption?

This book confronts these questions by making state-centric approaches to understanding African countries speak to relevant social theories that pluralize and complicate our understanding of the specific challenges of a prototypical postcolonial state.

This book was published as a special issue of the *Journal of Contemporary African Studies.*

Ebenezer Obadare is an Associate Professor of Sociology at the University of Kansas, Lawrence, USA. He is the co-editor of *Encountering the Nigerian State* (Palgrave-Macmillan, 2010). A MacArthur Foundation Research and Writing grant awardee, Dr. Obadare's articles have appeared in *African Affairs, The Journal of Modern African Studies, Development in Practice, Politique Africaine, Africa Development, African Identities*, and the *Review of African Political Economy.*

Wale Adebanwi is an Assistant Professor in African-American and African Studies at the University of California, Davis in the United States. He is the co-editor of *Encountering the Nigerian State* (Palgrave-Macmillan, 2010). A recipient of the MacArthur Foundation Research and Writing grant, Adebanwi's articles have appeared in the *Journal of Historical Sociology, The Journal of Modern African Studies, Ethnic and Racial Studies, Media, Culture and Society, Review of African Political Economy, Citizenship Studies* and the *Journal of African History.*

Nigeria's modern history can be described as the twinning of hope and disaster. In this volume, composed to commemorate the country's golden jubilee, Ebenezer Obadare and Wale Adebanwi warn that Nigeria runs the risk of "exploding or imploding at any point" given the large number of unresolved national problems. Yet, the editors of this important book affirm that "Nigeria still contains within her the transformational possibilities and human potentialities which can be mobilized, harnessed and leveraged by a new kind of leadership".

Students of African politics will delight in this volume of essays by leading academics and the many insights it provides on the Nigerian predicament of political instability and stunted development.

Professor Richard Joseph
John Evans Professor of Political Science, Northwestern University.

Nigeria at Fifty

The Nation in Narration

Edited by
Ebenezer Obadare and Wale Adebanwi

Routledge
Taylor & Francis Group
LONDON AND NEW YORK

First published 2011
by Routledge
2 Park Square, Milton Park, Abingdon, Oxon, OX14 4RN

Simultaneously published in the USA and Canada
by Routledge
711 Third Avenue, New York, NY 10017

Routledge is an imprint of the Taylor & Francis Group, an informa business

First issued in paperback 2012

This book is a reproduction of the *Journal of Contemporary African Studies*, vol. 28, issue 4. The Publisher requests to those authors who may be citing this book to state, also, the bibliographical details of the special issue on which the book was based.

British Library Cataloguing in Publication Data
A catalogue record for this book is available from the British Library

ISBN13: 978-0-415-60840-4 (hbk)
ISBN13: 978-0-415-82887-1 (pbk)

Typeset in Times New Roman
by Taylor & Francis Books

Disclaimer
The publisher would like to make readers aware that the chapters in this book are referred to as articles as they had been in the special issue. The publisher accepts responsibility for any inconsistencies that may have arisen in the course of preparing this volume for print.

Contents

Notes on Contributors

Wale Adebanwi is Assistant Professor of African-American and African Studies at the University of California, Davis, in the United States. He holds two PhDs, the first in Political Science from the University of Ibadan, Nigeria, and the other in Social Anthropology from the University of Cambridge, United Kingdom. A MacArthur Foundation Research and Writing grant awardee, Dr. Adebanwi has published essays in peer-reviewed journals such as *Citizenship Studies*, *Ethnic and Racial Studies*, *Journal of Historical Sociology*, *Journal of African History*, *Journal of Modern African Studies*, and *Review of African Political Economy*. He is co-editor (with Ebenezer Obadare) of *Encountering the Nigerian State* (Palgrave-Macmillan, 2010).

Afe Adogame holds a PhD in History of Religions from the University of Bayreuth in Germany. Prior to his appointment in 2005 to the lectureship in World Christianity, he was Teaching and Senior Research Fellow at the Department for the Study of Religion and Institute of African Studies, Bayreuth University from 1995–1998 and from 2000–2005. He was also a lecturer in the Department of Religions, Lagos State University, Nigeria between 1998 and 2000. His current research interests include religion in the new African diaspora, religious transnationalism, religion and youth, and religion in prison. One of his most recent publications is (co-edited) *Religion crossing boundaries: transnational religious and social dynamics in Africa and the new African diaspora*, Leiden: E.J. Brill (2010).

Adekunle Amuwo, the former Head of the Department of Political Science at the University of Ibadan, Nigeria and ex-Chair of Politics Department at the University of the North (now University of Limpopo), South Africa, is currently Professor of Political Science and International Relations in the School of Politics, University of KwaZulu-Natal, Howard College Campus, Durban, South Africa. His multi-faceted research interests include International Political Economy, Governance, Comparative Politics, Democratisation and Integration, and Francophone Africa. He is the author of *Civil society dynamics in Francophone Africa: A case study of Benin Republic, 1990-2008* (2009) and co-editor of *Civil society, governance and regional integration in Africa* (2009).

Axel Harneit-Sievers, Director, East Africa/Horn of Africa Regional Office, Heinrich Böll Foundation, is a historian and political scientist specializing in African and development studies. He completed his PhD in 1990 and his "habilitation" in 2002 at Hannover University. He taught African History at Hannover, Hamburg and Humboldt University (Berlin). Between 1993 and 2001, Axel Harneit-Sievers worked as research fellow at the Center for Modern Oriental Studies in Berlin, for the Institute of African Studies in Hamburg (1999) and for the German Society for International Development in Bonn (2001). He has published extensively on the economic, social and political history and development of Africa, with a focus on Nigeria.

Darren Kew (PhD Tufts University) is Associate Professor of Conflict Resolution at the University of Massachusetts, Boston. He studies the relationship between conflict resolution methods and democratic development in Africa. Much of his work focuses on the role of civil society groups in this development. He also monitored the last three Nigerian elections and the 2007 elections in Sierra Leone. Professor Kew is the author of numerous works on Nigerian politics and conflict resolution, including the forthcoming volume: *Democracy, conflict resolution, and civil society in Nigeria* (Syracuse University Press).

Ebenezer Obadare is an Associate Professor of Sociology at the University of Kansas, Lawrence, USA. He holds a PhD in Social Policy from the London School of Economics and Political Science, where he received the Department of Social Policy's Richard Titmuss Best PhD thesis prize (2005). A MacArthur Foundation Research and Writing grant awardee, Dr. Obadare's articles have appeared in leading Africanist journals, including *African Affairs*, *The Journal of Modern African Studies*, *Development in Practice*, *Politique Africaine*, *Africa Development*, *African Identities*, and *Review of African Political Economy*. He is the author of *Africa between the old and the new: The strange persistence of the postcolonial state* (UNCW, 2008) and coeditor (with Wale Adebanwi) of *Encountering the Nigerian State* (Palgrave Macmillan, 2010).

Cyril I. Obi is Senior Researcher, and Leader of the Research Cluster on Conflict, Displacement and Transformation, Nordic Africa Institute, Uppsala, Sweden. He is also an Associate Research Professor, on leave from the Nigerian Institute of International Affairs.

Eghosa E. Osaghae, Professor of Comparative Politics, has been Vice-Chancellor of Igbinedion University, Okada, Nigeria since September 2004. His research interests are in the areas of ethnicity, federalism and state politics in Africa. He has published extensively on these subjects in books and journals, and is currently engaged in research on conflict mobility in West Africa.

Rotimi Suberu is currently a faculty member in politics and international relations at Bennington College, Vermont, USA. Previously, he was professor of political science at the University of Ibadan in Nigeria. He is the author of *Federalism and ethnic conflict in Nigeria* (Washington, DC: United States Institute of Peace Press, 2001), numerous book chapters and articles in journals such as *The Journal of Modern African Studies*, *African Affairs*, *Journal of Democracy*, *Commonwealth and Comparative Politics*, *Current History*, and the *Journal of International Development*.

Acknowledgements

The current volume would not have been possible without the support of a number of people and our respective educational institutions. First, we would like to express our sincere appreciation to the co-editor of the *Journal of Contemporary African Studies*, Professor Roger Southall, who responded warmly to the idea of a special edition to commemorate the 50th anniversary of Nigeria's independence, suggested possible thematics, and worked with us right through the peer review and editing process. His professionalism, epitomised by his promptness and efficiency, helped considerably in lightening an otherwise heavy editorial burden. We are also deeply indebted to the efficiency and commitment of Nova de Villiers, the JCAS Administrator, for her technical editing.

Second, we would like to express our gratitude to our distinguished contributors, both for honouring our invitation, and responding to our frequently irrational deadlines. This volume is as much a product of our unreasonable demands, as it is of their unaffected equanimity.

The preparation of this volume (and indeed our scholarship in general) has benefitted immeasurably from the excellent collegial environment we have enjoyed in our respective institutions. Wale Adebanwi would like to thank the entire faculty and staff of the Programme in African American and African Studies at the University of California, Davis, USA, for their support. He is especially grateful to the Programme Chair, Professor Milmon F. Harrison, and Professor Moradewun Adejunmobi, for the special interest they have taken in his work.

Ebenezer Obadare is indebted to the faculty and staff of the Department of Sociology, University of Kansas, Lawrence, USA, for their support for this and other projects. For their generosity with their time, and for their particular interest in his work, he wishes to thank Professors Bill Staples, Joane Nagel, and Robert Antonio. Finally, we wish to thank Heinrich Böll Foundation (Nigeria) for their support for the Special Issue.

Ebenezer Obadare and Wale Adebanwi

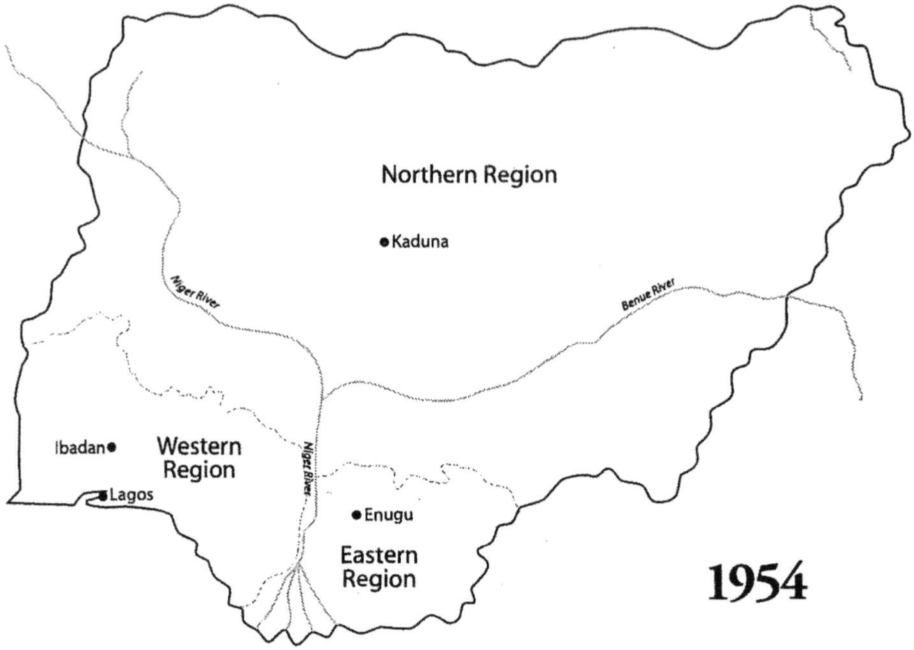
Northern Region
Kaduna
Niger River
Benue River
Ibadan
Western Region
Lagos
Niger River
Enugu
Eastern Region

1954

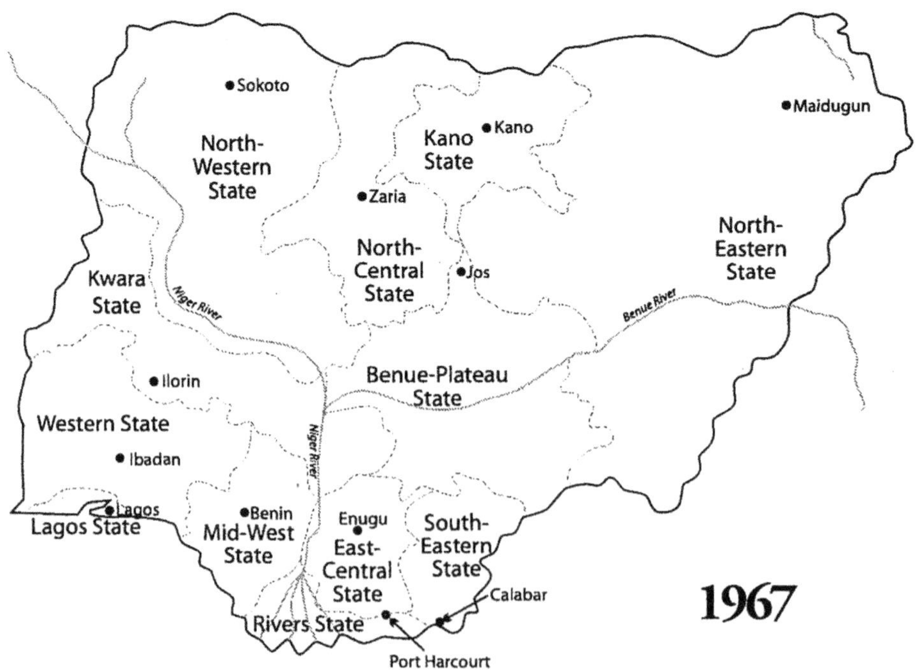
Sokoto
North-Western State
Kano
Kano State
Maidugun
Zaria
North-Eastern State
North-Central State
Jos
Kwara State
Niger River
Benue River
Ilorin
Benue-Plateau State
Western State
Niger River
Ibadan
Lagos
Lagos State
Benin
Mid-West State
Enugu
East-Central State
South-Eastern State
Calabar
Rivers State
Port Harcourt

1967

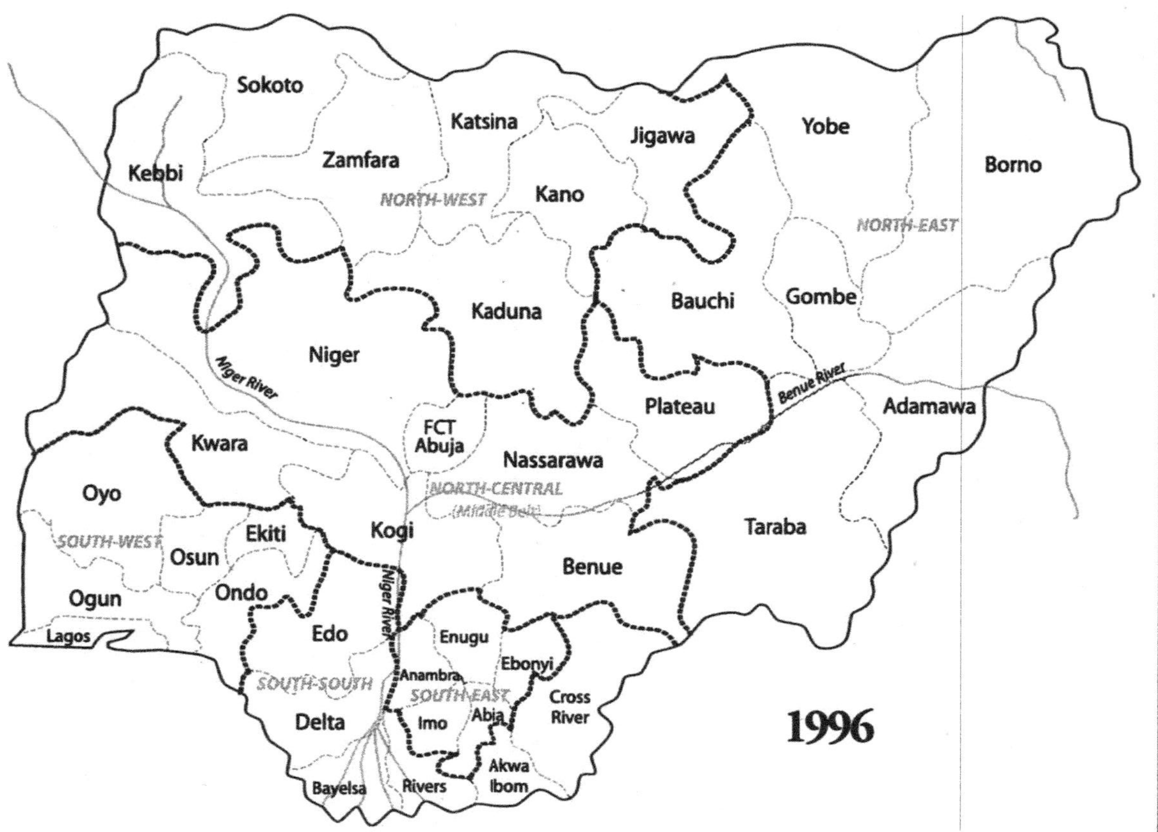

Maps reproduced from Rotimi Suberu, 2001. *Federalism and ethnic conflict in Nigeria*, xxii–xxiii. Washington, DC: United States Institute of Peace Press. Adapted with permission from Ekeh, P.P. 1997. *Wilberson conference on Nigerian federalism,* 68–69. Buffalo, NY: Association of Nigerian Scholars for Dialogue.

Introducing Nigeria at fifty: the nation in narration

Wale Adebanwi[a] and Ebenezer Obadare[b]

[a]*Department of African-American and African Studies, University of California, Davis, USA;* [b]*Department of Sociology, University of Kansas, Lawrence, USA*

Nigeria, Africa's most populous democracy, celebrates her 50th year as an independent nation in October 2010. As the cliché states, 'As Nigeria goes, so goes Africa'. This volume frames the socio-historical and political trajectory of Nigeria while examining the many dimensions of the critical choices that she has made as an independent nation. How does the social composition of interest and power illuminate the actualities and narratives of the Nigerian crisis? How have the choices made by Nigerian leaders structured, and/or been structured by, the character of the Nigerian state and state-society relations? In what ways is Nigeria's mono-product, debt-ridden, dependent economy fed by 'the politics of plunder'? And what are the implications of these questions for the structural relationships of production, reproduction and consumption? This collection confronts these questions by making state-centric approaches to understanding African countries speak to relevant social theories that pluralise and complicate our understanding of the specific challenges of a prototypical postcolonial state.

The giant as Lilliput

Nigeria offers a magnificent template for examining the chronic schizophrenia that characterises the African postcolonial state and the resulting social (de)formations that (re)compose, and are, in turn, (re)composed by, the state. Although rigged against reason and rhythm from its very conception and inception, Nigeria ironically, contains perhaps the greatest combination and concentration of human and natural resources that can be (re)mobilised in creating an African power state with a capacity to stand at the vortex, if not the centre, of continental revival and racial renewal. This paradox raises a fundamental question: Why have the socio-economic and political *actualities* of, and in, Nigeria, been historically (permanently?) subversive of her *potentialities*?

The momentous occasion of the country's 50th anniversary as an independent nation-state on 1 October 2010 is an interesting historic juncture to confront this question.[1] The anniversary calls for rethinking Nigeria in a way that is reflective of, yet challenges, the general and generalised pathologies of contemporary prototypical postcolonial formations. As Africa's most populous and biggest democracy – and one of its most fractious – *understanding* Nigeria continues to recommend itself as an important process of understanding the entire African postcolonial enterprise (Obadare 2008; Obadare and Adebanwi 2010).

A cliché states, 'As Nigeria goes, so goes Africa'. Three months after Nigeria's independence in 1960, the 17th African colonial creation to gain independence, America's *Time* magazine (5 December 1960, 20) predicted: 'In the long run, the most important and enduring face of Africa might well prove to be that presented by Nigeria'. It was a part-condescending and part-exoticising narrative of the 'ragged rectangle [country] the size of Texas and Oklahoma combined' (complete with a new Prime Minister, Abubakar Tafawa Balewa, dressed in 'native' regalia on the magazine's cover) and one perforated by the (il)logics of Cold War politics within which the magazine placed the 'moderating' role of Nigeria in Africa and the world under Balewa. This was apparently in contradistinction to the 'imperialistic elbowing' of Ghana under Kwame Nkrumah and the 'heedless plunge into Marxism' of Guinea under Sékou Touré (ibid). The then newly-independent country was presented as having 'entered the world community without the noisy birth-pangs of ominous warnings of its determination to avenge ancient wrongs (ibid). Four decades later, as Karl Maier attests (2000), the basis of this prism and optimism, while understood, could be queried:

> When the British lowered the Union Jack and freed a land they had ruled for less than a century, Nigeria was the focus of great optimism as a powerful emerging nation that would be a showcase for democratic government. Seen through the Cold War prism through which the West and particularly the United States viewed the emerging nations, Nigeria was a good guy – moderate, capitalist and democratic.

In what may seem like an ironic combination of the country's *actual* potential with the specific role designed and wished for her by the Western powers, *Time*, while acknowledging that Nigeria, at independence, 'stands [as] a giant among Lilliputians', affirmed that 'Nigeria's sober voice urging the steady, cautious way to prosperity and national greatness seems destined to exert ever-rising influence in emergent Africa' (ibid, 201). Yet, the magazine conceded that despite Nigeria's 'favourable omens', her 'burdens are awesome'.

After five decades of turbulent *nationhood*, the exaltations, lamentations, limitations, simplifications, exaggerations and the contradictions of *Time's* 1960 prognosis can be read as representative of what was to become of one of Africa's most significant states – both in internal and external contexts. What Nigeria is, what she has (or should have) become, and what she (or should) represent(s) are important nodal points in the total consideration of a scholarly review of Nigeria as she celebrates half a century of postcolonial existence. As a nation space, we attempt to (re)examine Nigeria in this volume, in the context of how – to use Wole Soyinka's words (Soyinka 1996, 109, emphasis added) – 'it provides for or deprives [her] *inmates* of the means to life, self-worth, and productive existence'.

This volume attempts to confront some of the key questions and analyse some of the important nodes in the overall attempt to comprehend a country which, though still standing, is generally assumed as having *fallen* (Maier 2000). Nigeria is the predicted 'Giant' that has become a disappointing, even aggravating 'Lilliput' – or, what Eghosa Osaghae (1998) calls a 'crippled giant'. Undeniably, at independence, there was as much evidence of the potentials of Nigeria to be an African success story as there was of her becoming a grand failure. While it is true that 'When Africa discarded the bonds of colonial rule, few could have imagined the depths to which

Nigeria... would sink a generation later', ... '(w)ith the benefits of hindsight, it is clear that such optimism [as indicated by *Time* magazine] was naive' (Maier 2000). In retrospect, it was perhaps nigh impossible for Nigeria, 'the bastard child of imperialism' (ibid), like many other African nation-states, to succeed. As Lord Frederick Lugard, the first British Governor-General of 'united' Nigeria, stated, 'when we are discussing the past of Britain, I always tell [my African friends]: yes, but it was all done in the interest of Britain, not of Africa'[2] (Perham 1960, 48).

Claims, contentions, considerations

A fractious and contentious politics, even in peace times, defined the colonial project which resulted in the creation of Nigeria – between the 'natives' and 'subjects', on the one hand, and between them and the metropolitan power (Britain) and its agents, on the other. The amalgamation of the Southern and Northern Protectorates, both peopled by more than *200* disparate ethnic groups,[3] to form a united Nigeria in 1914, which was choreographed by Lugard, was described by one of the nationalist leaders, Sir Ahmadu Bello, the first premier of the Northern Region and Sardauna of Sokoto, as the 'Mistake of 1914'. Chief Obafemi Awolowo, first premier of the Western Region, for his part, concluded that Nigeria was 'a mere geographical expression' (Awolowo 1947). Many have since concluded that Awolowo's observation 'remain[s] true, but [even] more so' (Watts 2003, 26). As revealed in John Paden's classic work, in the 1960s, as Nigerians and the leaders of the fractious groups and emergent political parties struggled not only for independence but also to gain leverage over and above one another, two leading definers of Nigeria's political future, one from the north (Bello) and the other from the south, Dr. Nnamdi Azikiwe, the first premier of the Eastern Region (and later the first ceremonial president of Nigeria), also traded barbs on whether the differences among Nigeria's many regional/ethnic/religious groups should be forgotten or understood. Azikiwe, the pan-Africanist nationalist and perhaps the finest orator in Nigeria's political history who helped to galvanise a critical generation towards a dialectical (dis)engagement from and with (global and racial) imperial politics, had insisted that, as 'subjects' of a newly emerging modern nation-state, Nigerians must 'forget' (perhaps, efface) the differences rooted in past and continuing ethnic, ethno-regional, religious and cultural *subjecthood*, while evolving into a new form of 'higher', collective, modern, and national citizenship. Ahmadu Bello had countered in an (in)famous exchange between the two – reportedly after a forum for negotiating the bases and structures of post-independent Nigeria – that, rather, what Nigerians must do was not to forget or transcend, but to 'understand' (and perhaps permanently honour) these differences.

What impact have the variant approaches of Azikiwe and Bello regarding the differences among Nigeria's composite groups had on the practical political life of Nigerians after five decades? The contentions and conclusions, which are reflected in the historic battles fought at different times for the Nigerian state, under different guises, with different weapons and on different platforms – ethnic, ethno-regional, religious, democratic, class, etc. – have, in the last 50 years, produced interesting dynamics in the continuous formation of what we know today as Nigeria. It is interesting that a country seen at independence as one with a 'sober voice urging the steady, cautious way to prosperity and national greatness' (*Time*, 5 December 1960,

21) now struggles at the end of the first decade of the twenty-first century with what is perceived by some critics as the 'end of [her] history' (Soyinka 1997).

Michael Watts (2003, 26), in a frontal analysis of the Nigerian crisis from the perspective of governmentality, argues that 'any construction of a robust, meaningful, national identity requires' a 'rigorous survey of the social body' (Clifford 2001, 114), so as 'to determine its makeup and nature'. But because Nigeria has consistently avoided a fundamental and *politically honest* 'rigorous survey' – whether at the level of census, through elections, the many constitutional conferences, or the much-trumpeted controversial 'sovereign national conference' – Watts concludes that 'What we have, in other words, is not nation building . . . but perhaps its reverse; the 'unimagining' (contra Benedict Anderson, that is) or deconstruction of a particular sense of national community' (ibid). As an '*unimagined community*', Nigeria reminds us of Nicos Poulantzas's (1978) important postulation that *forging* unity or common national destiny from history and territory requires 'a historicity of a territory and a territorialisation of a history' (ibid). While the 'historical authenticity' of any given territory would include both negative and positive *histories*, the positive must *overwhelm* the negative – both in the ways the territory is generally historicised and the specific ways in which it is encountered as what Ernest Renan (1882) famously called a 'daily plebiscite'; otherwise, a territory remains a 'mere geographical expression', while a history would be largely composed of glorified narratives of infamies.

In the struggle to create a more just, more equitable and more democratic polity than was inherited from the British, Nigeria has experimented with all sorts of political systems, ideologies, economic policies and even cultural paradigms. Under a leadership and political elite that is deficient in many respects, Nigeria has fought a civil war to save and transcend 'the mistake of 1914', survived serial bloodletting in the attempts to understand religious, ethnic and regional differences, and emerged from several years of brutal, even homicidal, military rule (Table 1).

It has also mobilised national democratic hope and aspirations – even racial glory – and simultaneously dashed them cruelly many times over. Yet, as an

Table 1. Chronology of regimes in Nigeria since 1 October 1960

Name of Head of Government	Period	Regime Type
Abubakar Tafawa Balewa	1 October 1960–15 January 1966	Elected Civilian
General Aguiyi J.T. Ironsi	15 January 1966–29 July 1966	Military
General Yakubu Jack Gowon	29 July 1966–29 July 1975	Military
General Murtala Muhammed	July 1975–13 February 1976	Military
General Olusegun Obasanjo	13 February 1976–1October 1979	Military
Shehu Usman Aliyu Shagari	1 October 1979–31 December 1983	Elected Civilian
General Muhammadu Buhari	31 December 1983–27August 1985	Military
General Ibrahim Babangida	27August 1985–27 August 1993	Military
Ernest Oladeinde Shonekan	27 August 1993–17 November 1993	Unelected Civilian
General Sani Abacha	17 November 1993–8 June 1998	Military
General Abdulsalam Abubakar	8 June 1998– 29 May 1999	Military
Olusegun Obasanjo	29 May 1999–29 May 2007	Elected Civilian
Umaru Musa Yar'Adua	29 May 2007–5 May 2010	Elected Civilian
Goodluck Ebele Jonathan	5 May 2010–	Elected Civilian

important political formation, Nigeria remains a national, even if fractured, aspiration towards the formation of a commonwealth that makes important global statements. Thus, the aspiration – or critical need – to ensure a *Jacobin* (absolute, total, or uncomplicated) coincidence between state and people to mobilise the national sentiments (soul), without which, Renan argues, a 'community of interest' can only be a 'body' (*-politic*), but not a nation, pervades Nigeria's colonial and postcolonial history.

It is, therefore, important to understand why and how the current challenges of Nigeria and the hopes and aspirations that continue to hold her together, despite the darkest political astrologies, are historically rooted. The work in this collection represents the most recent thinking from a distinguished group of scholars on how the past, present and future of Nigeria mix and mesh in the (re)production of a particular instance of postcolonial mess. The contributors frame historical, structural and agential trajectories that make the examined current practices and realities understandable. On this basis, they have projected into the future of a country whose *common* future as a united polity has been dismissed as much by the American security community, as well as by many of its frustrated citizens. Why does such a stupendously rich country, a potential 'Giant of Africa' as Nigerians have since grown tired of describing their country, invite such dark prognoses and invidious conclusions?

The idea of hope in the context of hopelessness is one of the defining sketches of Nigeria's history. Some Nigerians – never suffering humility even in the middle of humbling historical realities that have humiliated them and turned their country into a simultaneous tragedy and joke – boast that the British, primarily, and other European powers and, and ultimately, the United States, saw the country's great potential early, and, therefore decided, through a combination and coordination of measures, to ensure that Nigeria was (is?) never able to realise it. They would press further that the realisation of the full potential of a putative African power state would obstruct, if not subvert, the strategic interests of the Euro-American powers for global domination.

The British, the country's former colonial overlords, this line of argument goes, started this 'imperial conspiracy' by handing over power during the process of decolonisation to the least competent fraction of the emergent national elite. They have since consistently ensured support for this incompetent, and even semi-criminal elite, ensuring in the process that the resources and human capacities that could have been mobilised in building and sustaining a powerful African state that can challenge the West's strategic interests in many parts of the continent are dissipated and even corrupted.

While this reading and the resultant externalisation of national guilt points to the colonial origins[4] and external dimensions of the Nigerian crisis, and it would also seem to dismiss local capacities and agencies as well as the failure of the inherent promises of the Nigerian nation-state. But it raises a broader question: Are internal (local) social forces absolutely at the mercy of external factors and global hegemonic fixes and forces?

This question has been taken up by many scholars writing about Africa in general or/and writing about specific African polities. While it is incontestable that the Nigerian crisis is a particular manifestation of historical dynamics dominated by the colonial experience, what Nigerians – the elite and the masses; classes and social forces and so on – have made of that heritage ought to drive the analyses of present and future possibilities, if we are not to be called upon to give up on this *nation-state-in-formation*. One of the leading African theorists of the postcolonial formation, Achille Mbembe, fleshes out this challenge by posing the question of African agency – even within the 'lines of fragility ... precariousness, the fissures in contemporary African life' – in this way: '(H)ow could what is be no more, how could it give birth to something else?' (*Eurozine*, 9 January; Mbembe 2008, 11). He continues that the central purpose of his famous book, *On the postcolony* (2001) is to serve as 'a way of reflecting on the fractures, on what remains of the promise of life when the enemy is no longer the colonist in a strict sense, but the 'brother'?... (I)t is concerned with memory only insofar as the latter is a question, first of all, of responsibility towards oneself and towards an inheritance' (Mbembe 2001).

In the specific case of Nigeria, the contributors here confront the *responsibility* that the colonial *inheritance* – and, perhaps, other forms of precolonial inheritances – imposes on Nigerians and how the various formations, groups and individuals, including leaders and other key actors, have pressed their (*non*)agency in reaction to this *inheritance*. The varying and varied conception and perception of this responsibility-inheritance nexus is also critical to understanding the choices that Nigerian leaders and social formations have made in the 'vague belief in common destiny' (Adejumobi 2009, 404) which characterises the Nigerian project – as reflected in the statements of the leaders captured above.

The tears of God: a pre-history of the postcolonial problematique

> There is absolute higgledy-piggledy – economic collapse, political commotion, wars, social dislocation, tsunamis, etc., etc. – in the world and all nations of the world decide to meet God in Heaven to ask for when their great tribulations would come to an end. Every single country that comes before God does so in sublime supplication and with torrents of tears, pleading for knowledge of when its problems would end. The Almighty obliged each country, telling it when all would be well. Some got 10 years, others were promised 25 years, others about 50 years. When Nigeria staggers before the Almighty to ask God for when her problems would be over, God bursts into tears....[5]

The theoretical puzzle that the African postcolony has induced and the paralysis that often results from the many policy initiatives which have been designed to address the pathological and perennial problems of African states are sometimes mirrored in lay humour. Indeed, as a few instructive works on the African social formation have shown (Mbembe 2001; Obadare 2009; Tcheuyap 2010), where '(d)ebauchery and buffoonery readily go hand in hand' and where people 'by their laughter, kidnap power and force it, as it by accident, to examine its own vulgarity' (Mbembe 2001, 108), 'nation-building will not be incompatible with laughter, buffoonery and carnival life which all liberate postcolonial subjects from various anxieties' (Tcheuyap 2010, 25). Thus, there are 'correlations between the political, the social [and the economic] and the comic' in a continent *distinguished* by its tragicomedies.

Jokes are serious things, and placing the comic in the heart of the tragic has implications for class and social stratification (see the contribution by Amuwo below for a class reading of the Nigerian crisis). As Aristotle long ago contended, and as Mikhail Bakhtin (1984) has also explained, historically, ridicule is monopolised by the 'inferior' or the 'subaltern' (ibid, 29). Thus, 'the power to laugh, and the right to be laughed at' is assumed to be the 'minimal constituent of subaltern people who never miss an opportunity to entertain themselves'. On the other hand, tragedy is the terrain and (ill)luck of the powerful and the 'superior' – the high classes. However, this binary overlooks the complexities of the interplay of comedy and tragedy in actually-existing postcolonial life. We can briefly problematise the relationship of comedy and tragedy in the African postcolony as follows: First, while ridicule may be the 'weapon of the weak', that is, the 'inferior', in public life and public *play*, the ridiculous and the ridiculed are often the powerful and the superior. Still, tragedy, *contra* Bakhtin, is indeed most mirrored in the *actual* lives of the *ridiculing* masses of the African postcolony. Therefore, in a sense, ultimately, and perhaps, fundamentally, the joke is on the *laughing* masses. This is in spite of the fact that the joke is *against* power and the powerful classes.

Indeed, the joke about the intractable and perpetual nature of the Nigerian crisis – as a mirror of postcolonial crisis – which, in the narrative above, forces God to burst into tears, is reflective of the dark prognosis on the African condition which is yet to be resolved by decades of sundry ideological, philosophical, theoretical and policy options. The postcolonial *problematique* has survived all of its care-takers or care-givers.

From the earliest era of European encounter, Africans and Africanist scholars have tried to understand the nature of the location of the black people and Africans, in particular, in the historical and global order. From pan-Africanism, through the different manifestations of racial/continental philosophical and theoretical responses to the black/African condition such as 'negritude' and 'neo-colonialism', scholars and lay theorists have tried to understand Africa's historical experiences and the misfortunes of the continent in modern times. While the early decades of the twentieth century in Africa, when the colonial enterprise was fully consolidated, became the sharpest historical context for the attempted resolutions of the experiences and misfortunes of Africa, the departure point in global history could be dated to the 'long' sixteenth century in Western Europe[6] (McGowan and Smith 1978, 180).

The late independence era and the first two decades of the post-independence era led to the embrace of all sorts of 'isms' and paradigms by scholars for understanding the African condition and proffering solutions. Many of such 'isms' (Marxism, Communism, Capitalism, Socialism, African Socialism and so on) and their resulting paradigms (such as the modernisation and dependency theses), were eventually abandoned when they became not only obsolete, but deficient in capturing the African crises and presenting workable templates for solutions. All had attempted to 'explain past history and make relevant policy recommendations to Third World leaders' (McGowan and Smith 1978, 179). Even the capitalist mode of economic and political organisation, which has survived the ideological and historical struggles, has adopted a 'cooler' name of neoliberalism.

As the focal point of analysis moved from 'grandiose' frames and frameworks, the language of 'world system' (Wallerstein 1974, 1980, 1989) was replaced with the language of 'globalisation'. The practices and structures of the 'system'[7] also changed under *globalisation* – even though fundamental outcomes remained largely devastating in the African political and social formations, which were increasingly identified and captured in the scholarship within the specificities of the postcolony.

As a new global era, or what Francis Fukuyama (1992, 46) controversially declared as the 'end of history' – in which, 'we have trouble imagining a world that is radically better than our own, or a future that is not essentially democratic and capitalist'[8] – is inaugurated, different scholars have attempted to capture and explain the totality of the postcolony (Mbembe 2001; Chabal 2009). Some have examined its specific and critical aspects (Obadare and Adebanwi 2010; Comaroff and Comaroff 1991, 1997; Diamond 1987, 1988; Osaghae 2005; Lindberg 2003; Le Vine 1980; Bratton 2007; Bratton and Van de Walle 1994). Others have taken explicit historical approaches, while some have attempted to locate the postcolonial crisis within the structures and strictures of globalisation, neoliberalism, Cold War, imperialism, colonialism, etc. (Comaroff and Comaroff 2000; Amuwo 2009a). Some others still adopt historic-dialectical entry-points (Amin 1972, 1975, 1996; Shivji 1975, 1976, 1992; Rodney 1981; Mamdani 1976) pointing to the overall nature and dynamics of imperialism, colonialism and global capitalism or to the (resultant) postcolonial (dis)order. An instance of the last is the literature on the leadership or elite formations that the overall nature and dynamics of imperialism, colonialism and global capitalism have produced (Osaghae 1991; Kirk-Greene 1991; Nyamnjoh and Rowlands 1998).[9]

There are also countless policy approaches with regard to, or within, Africa, that feed off, or are consequences of, both the ideological and theoretical debates over the previous two centuries in the modern Euro-American world. These include the neoliberal approach, organised around the Structural Adjustment Programme (SAP) and its associated rolling-back-the-state thesis (Olukoshi 1992; Adejumobi 2003) and the contrasting *liberal-radical* investments in 'social forces', such as labour, youth (Obadare 2007; Ukeje 2006; Adebanwi 2005a; Gore and Pratten 2003), student movements (Adejumobi 2000), and women (Ukeje 2004; Tripp 2002; Mama 1995). All of this is captured in the theory and practices of 'civil society' (Obadare 2005b); the (African) 'home-grown' *Utopias*, including partnerships with other global bodies such as the Lagos Plan of Action (for the Economic Development of Africa, 1980–2000) and the Lome Convention of 1975 to its contemporary manifestations such as the rechristened African Union, the New Partnership for Africa's Development (NEPAD), and United States of Africa (USA) discourses (Adejumobi 2009). Others link global and local encounters in historical or contemporary contexts. But all these are not necessarily mono-factoral analyses. Also, there are several lay approaches by past leaders – such as Kenya's Jomo Kenyatta, Nigeria's Nnamdi Azikiwe and Obafemi Awolowo, Ghana's Kwame Nkrumah, Tanzania's Julius Nyerere – to understand the bases or foundation of Africa's condition with matching ideological-political proposals on 'what is to be done'. To draw two instances: one, Nkrumah argued that colonialism was the 'last stage of imperialism'. He presented 'consciencism' as both an ideology that could be 'pivotal to decolonisation' and as a method of 'African national liberation' (McClendon 2003). His intention was 'an African text in socio-political philosophy' (ibid). Second, for Nyerere (1973), 'Ujamaa', that is 'African socialism', which he located at the level of individuals, was a 'socialist attitude of mind'. This ideology, which Nyerere argued, did not 'define the institutions which may be required to embody it in a modern society', could be used to reject 'the capitalist attitude of mind which colonialism brought into Africa . . . [and] the capitalist methods which go with it' (ibid) – such as individual ownership of land.

Despite all this, the African state seems to have defied all solutions. Goran Hyden (2006, 1) emphasises what he calls the 'untamed nature' of the continent. Thus, '(s)peaking rationally' about the African postcolony, as Achille Mbembe (2001, 1) correctly notes, 'is not something that has ever come naturally'. This is, of course, made even more difficult by the sorry contemporary picture of Africa. As the first decade of the twenty-first century comes to an end, Africa is plagued with a limitless list of negatives: civil wars, armed conflicts, different forms of social violence, sub-human poverty, famine, the ravages of diseases, including AIDS-HIV, cholera, malaria fever, polio, etc, economic crises and collapse, political crises, including the uses of democratic means for autocratic ends, travesties of all forms in the name of elections, the crisis of citizenship and indigeneity, inter-faith and inter-ethnic and inter-racial violence, lack of access to basic modern amenities by the largest proportion of populations within the different national boundaries, and many more. These ills continue to constitute the African postcolony as 'a source of terror, astonishment, and hilarity, at once' (Mbembe 2001, 15).

For all the grievous nature of the totality of the African condition we cannot give in to what has been described as 'Afropessimism', or 'the nihilism of despair and surrender' (Mbembe 2006, 150), which homogenises the 'postcolonial space as one uniform site of dysfunctionality' (Adesanmi 2004). On the contrary, while drawing a largely justifiable, continental pattern, we need to pay attention to the eclectic particularities of the postcolonial experience in Africa, discern its specificities in different polities and regions, and identify the mixes, paradoxes and contradictions that these (re)produce in the context of Africa's insertion in the global order.

We suggest, however, that despite the 'continuous tension between comparability and contextuality' (Hyden 2006, 3), these differences, specificities, and contradictions do not make scholarly identification of continental patterns of 'dysfunctionality' impossible. While some of the scholarly conclusions can be contested, we cannot dismiss 'the politics of the belly' (Bayart 1993), the 'disorder as political instrument' (Chabal and Daloz 1999), 'the criminalisation of the state' (Bayart, Ellis, and Hibou 1999), 'prebendalism' (Joseph 1987), 'predation' (Lewis 1996), 'the politics of suffering and smiling' (Chabal 2009), 'resource curse' (Humphreys, Sachs and Stiglitz 2007), 'the perils of belonging' (Geschiere 2009), and similar approaches that capture specific aspects of the totality of the contemporary African formation. However, what has been challenged by African/ist scholars is the reluctance, if not refusal, evident in some of these perspectives, to historicise these experiences properly, and to recognise that they are critical dimensions of a global-local and historical-structural totality. As such, a few of these perspectives often appear as sophisticated descriptions of actualities which are not correctly *enframed* within the fundaments of the ideological-historical-practical (in)capacities for social transformation in the contemporary African postcolony.

The *dis*order-as-a-system-of-order thesis that governs many approaches to African realities often misses the historical nature of the order that the positive Other – that is, the social forces committed to the transformation, or, at least, reformation – has been attempting, before and since independence, to impose on the African state. Yet, that the result of the struggle has been less than satisfactory or even visible must be conceded. Nigeria is a great template for examining some of these challenges and the failures of ameliorative, reformist or transformational politics.

The abstractions and attractions of (non-)violent realities

Nigeria is essentially a creation of colonial violence. The consolidation of colonial violence and metropolitan arbitrariness is sharply emphasised by the amalgamation of the Northern and Southern (British) Protectorates, executed without consultation with the 'natives' or 'subjects'. The (dis)credit for this naming of the country goes to Dame Flora Louisa Shaw, journalist, writer and eventual wife of colonial Nigeria's first colonial Governor-General, Lord Frederick Lugard. Shaw, in her travels to British colonies as a correspondent for *The Times* of London, had imagined a global territorial expansion of the British Empire into which 'natives' and others would be incorporated to enjoy the benefits of British 'civilisation'. She and the man she married constituted complementary faces of British global hegemony. While in classic Gramscian mode, Lugard was the more openly forcible (violent) side of that hegemonic coin; Shaw was its non-forcible (discursive) side. Incidentally, she was also close to two other men who, along with Lugard, represent the most significant elements of the materialist basis of the metropolitan violence exported to Africa by the British: Cecil Rhodes, businessman, mining magnate and founder of the diamonds company, De Beers, and one whose racist legacy constitutes part of the challenging inheritance of Southern Africans today; and George Goldie, Rhodes's parallel on the west coast of Africa, who helped to 'pacify' many parts of what eventually became Nigeria and ran the Royal Niger Company – which preceded and eventually encouraged full colonial imposition.

It was Shaw, in her essay in *The Times* of London on 8 January 1897, who suggested that Goldie's Royal Niger Company Territories, an 'agglomeration of pagan and Mahomedan States', now acquired as British Protectorates on the Niger River, be named 'Nigeria'. Before the British forces advanced on the African kingdoms, chiefdoms, clans, sultanates and settlements, employing metropolitan fire to acquire forcible and, eventually, non-forcible consent, Lugard, based on his experience in Hong Kong, had identified the duality of violence and non-violence in the imposition and consolidation of power. He knew the *methods* in (and of) foreign imposition.

In articulating the 'Methods of ruling native races' in his seminal book, *The dual mandate in British tropical Africa* (1922), Lugard displays his brilliant understanding of the conflation of power and commerce and the mobilisation of the interface of the 'modern' and the 'traditional' towards achieving colonial domination. He argues:

> If *continuity* and *decentralization* are ... the first and most important conditions in maintaining an *effective administration*, *cooperation* is the key-note of success in its application... co-operations between the Government and the commercial community, and, above all, between the provincial staff and the native rulers. Every individual adds his share not only to the accomplishment of the ideal, but to the ideal itself. Its principles are fashioned by his quota of experience, its results are achieved by his patient and loyal application of these principles, with as little interference as possible with native customs and modes of thought. (Lugard 1922, 193)

In his methodical and detailed layout of how this hegemonic project was to be worked out and sustained, even Gramsci would have marvelled at the Machiavellian instincts of the English soldier turned administrator. Yet, the Machiavelli in Lugard did not adhere strictly to the rules of colonial rule which he so ably enunciated wherever the exception (as means) served the end, which was successful domination. Where the British found no suitable 'traditional' institutions to implement the project of economic and political domination, they invented one. Where the consolidation of Islam, say in the Fulani north, would impede the 'Enlightenment' pretensions of the Metropole woven around Christianity, the (Christian) faith was abandoned to its fate. In bonding the British interest with the (re)versioned interests of the Fulani aristocrats in power in much of what became northern Nigeria to create an Anglo-Fulani power bastion (described by Lugard as a 'community of interest'), Lugard pressed that 'the personal interests of the (Fulani) rulers must rapidly become identified with those of the controlling Power (the British)' so that the surviving 'forces of disorder' are unable to 'distinguish between them', while 'the rulers [would] soon recognise that any upheaval against the British would equally make an end of them' (Lugard 1922, 195).

In spite of the great challenges that this new form of rule faced in the colony of Lagos where there were many educated people, and in the Southern Protectorates in general, particularly among the Igbo whose acephalous society was largely destroyed to make way for 'Indirect Rule', the 'Dual Mandate' was largely successful. It imposed the British mandate, on the one hand, as the supreme Order in the colonial space and also imposed the sultan and the emirs in the Northern protectorates – and to some extent, the obas, obis, etc. in the Southern Protectorates – as the supreme agents of that supreme Order.

The structural inequities, injustices and fatal errors that were inherent in this colonial project as part of the divide-and-rule tactics and the strategies of domination of imperial Britain became fundamental challenges that Nigeria would not recover from for almost a century after the amalgamation and five decades after independence was achieved. His Majesty's Government had come to the conclusion that 'it would be to the great advantage of the countries known as Southern and Northern Nigeria that they should be amalgamated into one government, conforming to one policy and mutually co-operating for the moral and material advancement of Nigeria as a whole (Lugard 1914, in Kirk-Greene 1968).

The *Lagos Weekly Record* (Editorial, 1 February 1919), one of the manifestations of the 'advancement' of the emergent modern civic space in Lagos, had, in February 1919, captured the attitude of much of Southern Nigeria to the British 'invention' in general and Lugard's particular role, by describing the latter's administration as an 'inglorious' one 'which constitutes not only a standing disgrace to the cherished traditions of British colonial policy in West Africa but also a positive libel upon the accepted principles of British culture'. The newspaper dismissed the 'founder' of colonial Nigeria as 'a hopeless anachronism'. What does this say for what was *founded*?

But the 'standing disgrace' would seem to have stood firm since then, despite the best efforts of many activists, journalists, politicians, social forces, including labour unions, youth groups, students groups, town unions, religious groups and others to humanise the colonial space and ensure the evolution of a postcolonial entity that would be 'the pride of the black race'.

From the decolonisation period when Nigeria's many ethno-linguistic groups, forced to operate under the shadows of a tripartite ethno-regional groupings (Hausa-Fulani in the Northern Region, Igbo in the Eastern Region, and Yoruba in the Western Region), started the struggle for ascendancy and/or accommodation, the question of power has remained central to understanding the crisis of the invented nation-state, Nigeria. Since then, there have been different attempts to re-write and right Nigeria's history against the backdrop of its colonial inheritances and imbalances. As both the manifest and the latent violence of foreign imposition receded in the late 1940s and 1950s, the different ideological, ethnic, religious and civic forces organised themselves into groups to define the parameters of national engagement in the emerging nation state. As these forms of organising transformed from their 'anti-imperialist' bases to take on a 'pro-independence' footing, constitutional talks were the much-vaunted primal mode of bilateral (British and Nigerian) engagement.

Despite the tensions, broadly cast along northern (largely Islamic, 'traditional') bloc against southern (largely, Christian, 'modern') bloc, or western (Yoruba) versus eastern (Igbo) regions, the British and the emergent leaders of the key regions managed to ensure a precarious balance. At the same time, an inchoate, 'veto power' was granted to the behemoth northern region, and inscribed into the constitutional and democratic processes of the emergent federation.

As the (assumed) common enemy retreated to the metropolis between 1952 and 1960, most Nigerians and key political parties organised largely along ethno-regional lines (NCNC (National Council of Nigeria and the Cameroons), NPC (Northern People's Congress), AG (Action Group), NEPU (Northern Elements Progressive Union), etc). The (im)balance that was reached at independence produced a federal government that was an alliance between the dominant party in the northern region (NPC) as the senior partner, and the dominant party in the eastern region (NCNC), as the junior partner. The NCNC, which had started as the most pan-Nigerian, and the most ideologically radical, had ended up as the 'junior' partner to the last party to be formed, and the least eager for independence. It was a contradiction that would become a permanent reflection of Nigeria's deep political flaws. The fact that these political parties and ethno-regional blocs were principally organised around key leaders further *complexified* the Nigerian crisis and made it susceptible to implosion around the egos and personal agendas of the leaders which were extended over group/party agendas and ideologies (see Osaghae 1998 and in this volume).

In less than two years after independence, the tenuous agreements designed to craft a national understanding could no longer sustain the strain. Personal, ideological, political, cultural and ethno-regional and ethno-religious tensions started to break out. Its first major theatre was the Western Region of Nigeria where the internal crisis of the ruling Action Group and the Western Region Government, launched by ideological differences, personal ambitions and the manoeuvres by the leaders of the dominant party in the federal government, the NPC, led to the treason trial of its leader, Chief Obafemi Awolowo, by the federal government. That was preceded by the declaration of a state of emergency in the eastern region. Awolowo was later sentenced to jail in 1963. When the premier of the region and Awolowo's successor, and now political adversary, Chief Samuel Ladoke Akintola, leading the new Nigeria National Democratic Party (NNDP), was proclaimed the winner of massively rigged regional elections in 1965, the region imploded in what was described as 'Operation *Wetie!*' (Douse it!). The rump of the masses of the region, led by youths, reacted with violence to the electoral theft (Anifowose 1982). In less than one year after this, Nigeria's First Republic unravelled.

On 15 January 1966, the soldiers struck. From that point, a specific form of local *politicised* violence – not unrelated to, even if sometimes in opposition to, the old metropolitan and now neo-colonial apparatuses of political violence – re-defined itself as an elaborate instrument of organising for and against power. It would be impossible, from the point at which a state of emergency was declared in the Western Region, for the *relations of (ex)change* of political power to be carried out or facilitated without manifest or latent *violence* in Nigeria. Whether that violence consolidates, re-establishes or attempts to break existing violence; whether it is practised as a military coup or counter-coup, a civil uprising or ethno-regional, inter-ethnic, inter-faith or political violent clashes, hegemonic or counter-hegemonic suppression, oppression or revolt, pro-democratic, student and workers' riots or election violence, police killings, pogrom, rebellion or civil war, Nigeria has become a permanent *state of emergencies* – with hardly any means, method, or institutions for efficiently addressing emergencies beyond more violence.

However, from the January 1966 putsch executed by young soldiers of mostly Igbo extraction with a revolutionary zeal under the leadership of Major Chukwuma Kaduna Nzeogwu, which was eventually seized by 'reactionary' forces and then later reversed by the counter-coup of July 1966 led by young northern soldiers, attempts to violently reconstitute and/or *de-constitute* Nigeria have always failed. Yet, civil reformative efforts have consistenly nudged the country towards a fairer and more just system (see Suberu's essay in this volume) more than every such violent challenge to the status quo..

Yet, it can be argued that, the fundamental inadequacy of these institutional, policy and super-structural gestures are made evident by the continued resolve of many groups within the polity to use violence as a critical method of venting frustrations and to point to the inequities that have been lodged in the federal equation from inception. One critical concept that demonstrates the fact that the *idea* of Nigeria is yet unsettled is that of citizenship. Fifty years after independence, what it means to be a *citizen* of Nigeria remains unclear and attracts constant challenges in political, economic, social, religious, gender, communal and territorial terms (Ekeh 1972; Taiwo 2000; Egwu 2003; Alubo 2004; Adebanwi 2005b, 2009). An almost absurd example of this is the recent issue regarding Nigerians living in the area known as Bakassi in the south-east of the country, who, only in the fourth decade of the nation state's independent existence, realised that they were no longer living within the Nigerian territorial space, and that to be able to continue to be identified as Nigerians, they had to leave their 'ancestral homes' – and move *into* Nigeria. In a legal tussle with interesting historical details, the land was ceded to Cameroon in a case decided by the International Court of Justice at The Hague. The disputed oil-rich area – it was gathered in the middle of the acrimonious debate within Nigeria – had been ceded by the General Yakubu Gowon regime in the late 1960s to Cameroon to secure her support in holding down the eastern region of the country which was fighting to secede.

The violent protests, and eventually, the killings of people of eastern origin, principally in the northern parts of Nigeria, preceding and following the July 1966 counter-coup by northern soldiers (code-named 'Araba', Hausa for 'separation') which overthrew the regime of Major General J.T.U. Aguiyi Ironsi, was the immediate context that led to the declaration of the secessionist Republic of Biafra and the Civil War that was fought for 30 months between 1967 and January 1970.

The civil war remains perhaps the greatest signifier of what many assume to be the irreconcilable nature of the world views and the aspirations of the component parts of the Nigerian *union*. It was on the basis of this assumption – and its 'realities' as captured and constantly expressed by the various groups within the country – that Lieutenant-Colonel Chukwuemeka Odumegwu Ojukwu announced, on behalf of the people of the Eastern Region of Nigeria on 30 May 1967, the total dissolution of 'all political ties between us and the Federal Republic of Nigeria'.

Two years into the war, on 1 June 1969 in the 'Ahiara Declaration' or 'The Principles of the Biafran Revolution', Ojukwu elaborated the external and internal bases of the crisis that had consumed the Nigerian union from the perspective of the secessionist republic. Some of these sentiments have survived the 'reconciliation' that supposedly followed the collapse of Biafra, despite the fact that such sentiments make functional national unity clearly impossible. States Ojukwu (1969):

> Nigeria was a classic example of a neo-colonialist state, and what is left of it, still is. The militant nationalism of the late forties and early fifties had caught the British imperialists unawares. They hurried to accommodate it by installing the ignorant, decadent and feudalistic Hausa-Fulani oligarchy in power. For the British, the credentials of the Hausa-Fulani were that not having emerged from the Middle Ages they knew nothing about the modern state and the powerful forces that now rule men's minds. Owing their position to the British, they were servile and submissive. The result was that while Nigerians lived in the illusion of independence, they were still in fact being ruled from Number 10 Downing Street. The British still enjoyed a stranglehold on their economy.

Before the civil war, Major Isaac Adaka Boro, who became one of the pioneers of minority rights activism in Nigeria, led the first armed insurrection on 23 February 1966 where the Niger Delta Volunteer Force (NDVF) publicly declared its intention to re-draw the map of Nigeria violently. The NDVF, constituted mainly by the Ijaw, was defeated in 12 days. Even though the July 1966 coup led by Colonel Murtala Muhammed was also mobilised around splitting the north from the rest of Nigeria, the soldiers were quickly advised against the folly of their armed exuberance, principally by the British.

In another of the compulsive ironies of the Nigerian story, both Major Boro and Colonel Mohammed, who had led different ethno-sectional armed insurrections against the composition of the Nigerian federation, were to become heroes of maintaining and sustaining Nigeria. Mohammed led the second Infantry Division during the war to defeat Biafra, while Boro, earlier jailed for treason, was pardoned and then enlisted in the fight against Biafra. After helping to 'liberate' oil-rich Niger Delta area from Biafra, Boro was killed in 1968.

However, the dissatisfaction to which Boro and Murtala earlier gave vent, the inequities (both perceived and real) which are the causes and consequences of these, and the ironies, contradictions and paradoxes of the struggles to them, have survived both symbolic comrades-in-arms. It is therefore important to realise the place of violence in the attempt to re-order the consolidated (Dis)Order that was imagined, crafted, and imposed by metropolitan/imperial/colonial violence.

Examining the place of violence is critical because, despite its continued failure to re-order Nigeria successfully, (dis)organised violence is a major vector for the understanding of the Nigerian polity and its many dimensions. Thus, when another group of young soldiers, mainly of Middle-Belt and Niger Delta (southern) extraction, attempted on 22 April 1990, to again challenge the 'balance of terror' by overthrowing what Major Gideon Gwarzo Orkar described as a 'dictatorial, corrupt, drug-baronish, evil men sadistic, deceitful, homosexually-centred, prodigalistic, unpatriotic' regime of General Ibrahim Babangida (1985–1993), it became again clear that despite all the pretensions of the ruling class, the country remained a potential victim of disintegrating forces which could not continue to live within a 'mere geographical expression' and a territorial 'mistake'. The failed 'Orkar coup' was not only the bloodiest in terms of those executed as a result of the coup (Ihonvbere 1991), but was also the most significant expression of the unsustainable nature of the structural imbalances of the Nigerian federation.

A reflection of this was the announcement by the coup-plotters of the excision of five core Hausa-Fulani northern (also Muslim-dominated) states of Sokoto, Borno, Katsina, Kano, and Bauchi from the Nigerian federation. The 'aristocratic class' in these states, alleged the coup plotters, 'even though they contribute very little economically to the well being of Nigeria', has a history:

> replete with numerous and uncontrollable instances of callous and insensitive dominatory [*sic*], repressive intrigues by those who think it is their birth-right to dominate till eternity the political and economic privileges of this great country to the exclusion of the Middle Belt and the South (Ihonvbere 1991, 616).

While the angry plotters exhibited critical limitations which simplified a complex reality,[10] they nonetheless bloodily emphasised the crisis of nationhood in Nigeria. The execution of almost 70 officers for their complicity in the coup and the imprisonment of many others could not disguise the fundamental issues that the failed coup raised. In many ways, Orkar's rhetoric was only another version, if less sophisticated, of the rhetoric of Nzeogwu in the January 1966 coup, of Boro in the February 1966 insurgency, of Colonel Odumegwu Ojukwu in May 1967, and of the several other groups that have sought through physical or verbal violence to contest the Nigerian union.

The several casualties of the violent conflicts, crises, and contestations of the structural and ideological composition of Nigeria em*body* the crisis of the putative African Giant. They humanise the statistics that sometimes compose the political and social tragedies; they popularise the unending struggle for an egalitarian polity that is big enough to contain all and functional enough to work for all Nigerians of whatever ethnicity, region, religion, class or gender.

Leadership, religiosity, citizenship and insurgency: critical readings

Writing in the dawn of the French Revolution, Montesquieu had contended that, at the birth of new polities, leaders mould institutions, whereas afterwards institutions mould leaders. How did the nature and character of post-independent leadership and the political elite determine the fate and fortunes of Nigeria?

Like the rest of Africa, Nigeria 'has long been saddled with a poor, even malevolent, leadership: predatory kleptocrats, military-installed autocrats, economic illiterates, and puffed-up posturers' (Rotberg 2004, 14). Under these leaders, Rotberg advances:

> Infrastructure … has fallen into disrepair, currencies have depreciated, and real prices have inflated dramatically, while job availability, health care, education standards, and life expectancy have declined. Ordinary life had become beleaguered: general security has deteriorated, crime and corruption have increased, much needed public funds have flowed into hidden bank accounts, and officially sanctioned ethnic discrimination – sometimes resulting in civil war – has become prevalent (ibid).

Using the famous conclusion of Chinua Achebe, the author of *Things fall apart*, that 'the trouble with Nigeria is leadership', as a departure point, Eghosa Osaghae (in this volume) reviews the conceptual and theoretical debates on leadership in Africa and links them to how the general and specific experiences within African polities (re)produce different *practices* of leadership. Doubtless, the kinds of leaders that Nigeria has (re)produced are reflections of why the country is the way it is after 50 years of self-rule. As Wole Soyinka (1996, 14–5), specifically notes in the case of General Sani Abacha, many of these leaders, particularly those who have held the highest offices in the land have 'no *idea* of Nigeria [and] no *notion* of Nigeria' as a spatial and structural instrument of the construction, expansion and popularisation of egalitarian social life. Thus, from Lugard (in the colonial era) and through Balewa (in the immediate postcolonial era) to President Goodluck Jonathan (in the present), Nigeria's largely unfortunate history can be written around the tunnel vision of its leadership.

In this vein, the 'privatisation of power', its trivialisation, exoticisation and canonisation, in which leaders are either self-constructed and/or are popularly accepted as spiritual-secular exceptions is one of the most critical socio-political phenomena in Nigeria. Osaghae correctly notes how 'contemporary charismatic legitimation' in Nigeria is 'further reinforced by the rise of fundamentalist religious movements' from the 1980s, with the new pentecostal churches' leaders becoming *diviners* of sorts who routinely recognise and locate the 'divine will of God' in the 'God sent' leaders. As is to be expected, members of the contemporary Nigerian power elite appropriate and mobilise the spiritual symbols, pillars, and legitimation that are invented by those that Afe Adogame (in this volume) describes as 'religious celebrities and charlatans'.

Fundamentalist Islam, as Osaghae argues, is one mode of challenging this collaboration between spirituality and the regular order of political power in Nigeria. Leadership tenets in this context, which Adogame described as a 'puzzling terrain', has, Osaghae suggests, 'rested on an anti-system, anti-secularism radicalism that brooked only what adherents believed to be puritan Islam'. Thus, the question of access to power and space has had to contend with the emergent 'dramatisation of religion' which has resulted in 'the increasing visibility and mobility, contestation and instrumentalisation of religion' (Adogame, in this volume) which have 'engendered ambivalences of peace and violence, cohesion and conflict, functionality and dysfunctionality' that threaten Nigeria's corporate existence (see also Obadare 2005a).

The question of structure and agency runs through the analyses of all the contributors to this volume. This is not surprising given the attention that all the contributors pay to the role of political leadership (Osaghae), religious leaders (Adogame), social forces (Amuwo), and other key agents in the (re)construction and (de)mobilisation of the agential templates, and the institutions, and structural contexts, such as the political economy (Amuwo 2009b), federalism (Suberu), religion and religious representation (Adogame) and the petroleum industry (Obi), which have determined Nigeria's fortunes in the last five decades.

While Osaghae surmises that 'although there is a great deal of consensus on elite hegemony, domination and determinism, the transitional and transformatory circumstances of [Nigeria] ... have made counter-elite politics and elite overthrow a fairly popular moulder of politics'. Such 'non-systemic interventions', he concludes, 'often end up as forced entries into, and processes of reconstituting, the elite ranks'. Against the backdrop of the structural properties of the Nigerian union and the historical experience under the 'strategic improvisers', Osaghae presses that 'the focus and diagnosis of leadership problems' must 'move away from the individual and personal parameters of charismatic legitimation to the democratic institutional correlates of leadership'.

Federalism is one such key democratic structural correlate (of leadership) which has been historically debated and was eventually accepted in Nigeria as a potential solution to the challenges of ethno-regional diversity, resource accumulation and distribution, citizenship, individual rights and collective responsibility. Suberu (in this volume) reassesses the evolution, performance, problems and prospects of Nigerian federalism with a view to promoting a more balanced federalist debate which started about one and half decades before Nigeria was granted independence. In his authoritative review of the federalist debate in Nigeria and the lay articulation and responses to the structures and practices of federalism since 1954, Suberu's article is more eclectic than most scholarly interventions and more optimistic than most lay contributions. While arguing that federalism remains 'a reasonably viable and successful mechanism for managing inter-group conflict and preventing ethno-political disintegration', Suberu suggests that the other potentials of this 'structural solution' to Nigeria's problems, such as its potential role in promoting democratic and economic development have been 'largely neglected or de-prioritised'.

Cyril Obi's contribution does not take for granted the resources on which the elements of Suberu's structural solutions are based. He argues that, 'by using the fiscal instrument to centralise political and oil power, the federal government [has] effectively subordinated the constituent units/regions or states to its post-war hegemonic national unity project', while the ordinary people of the oil-bearing communities, have 'remained marginalised from the ownership and control of the oil produced from their region'. Their sense of grievance is made worse 'by federal neglect, widespread impoverishment and increased oil-related environmental degradation'. Thus, the 'overdeveloped distributive capacities' of the centre have been strengthened by the extractive nature of the economy (Watts 2003, 15) and not by common consent or mutual solidarity. This has produced, what Obi (this volume) describes as 'fractional [and fratricidal] struggles for the control of ... federal power and the sharing of oil revenues has remained a source of political instability'.

While the 'resource curse' thesis[11] (Auty 1993; Soares de Oliveira 2007; Duruigbo 2005; Humphreys, Sachs, and Stiglitz 2007) [12] is most poignant in the Niger Delta, its evidence is spread over the length and breadth of Nigeria. 'Disorder and profit, far from being antithetical, mutually complement and strengthen each other' (Mbembe 2000, 280), despite the 'politics of local resistance ... directed at blocking further alienation, expropriation and environmental degradation, and forcing through a mass project of restitution and self-determination' (Obi 1997, 137), these being evident of low-intensity warfare in the Niger Delta (Obi 2009; Ikelegbe 2001; Ukeje and Adebanwi 2008). The latest phase of the insurgency in the Niger Delta, where the struggle against injustice led by the militants cross-cut with activities of *criminals*, has led to the turning, in Watts' (2003, 7) words, of 'adversity into advantage', even while some 'seek the cleansing power of violence, both figuratively and literally, as a means to bring about the New Jerusalem' (Mbembe 2006, 150). It is within disorder or adversity that many social actors in Nigeria have derived profit and advantage, thus jeopardising 'what is clearly the nation's major opportunity to climb into higher levels of prosperity' (Ascher 1999, 16).

The outcome of the oil wealth, therefore, becomes a reflection of the cruel joke that foreshadowed the crisis. A story has it that in the late 1950s, the economic minister in Nigeria said to the prime minister, 'I have some good news and bad news'. The prime minister asks for the good news and is told that the country has just discovered vast reserves of petroleum. The prime minister is happy. He says, 'Well, this is great. We can accelerate income growth. What could the bad news possibly be?', he asks. The reply is, 'The bad news is that we have just discovered vast reserves of petroleum' (cited in Duruigbo 2005, 1).

The activities of armed groups in the 'ungovernable' spaces of the Delta, such as the Niger Delta People's Volunteer Force (NDPVF), the Niger Delta Vigilante (NDV) and the Movement for the Emancipation of the Niger Delta (MEND), in confrontation with 'the evil twins of authoritarian governmentality and petro-capitalism' (Watts 2003, 15), involve the struggle to *(a)mend* Nigeria. In light of this, the conclusion that 'In the global geopolitics of hydrocarbons', 'new oil frontiers coincide, paradoxically, with one of the most clearly marked boundaries for state dissolution in Africa' (Mbembe 2000, 279) rings very true.

Perhaps the most controversial argument advanced by Suberu in reviewing five decades of Nigeria's independence is that 'the challenge of federal reform is not to fundamentally reconfigure or restructure current institutional structures', but how to create and nurture robust institutions of democratic and economic development, including electoral and anti-corruption reforms which will 'reinforce and enhance current federal processes for cauterising ethnic instability'(see also Suberu 1990, 2001, 2009). He is characteristically subtle in his dismissal of the transformational standpoint in Nigeria's politics. First, he brackets out violent and exclusionary-centrifugal forces, some of which insist on further decentralisation of the polity into autonomous zones of ethno-linguistic or even religion clusters, or, indeed, the dissolution of the Nigerian federation; second, he flags a critical polarity that has marked the historic struggle on how to ensure that Nigeria fulfils her supposed 'manifest destiny', between the 'reformist' and the 'transformational' theses and politics; third, he indirectly challenges the political economy perspective (Amuwo in this volume) that assumes the structural (global and local) deformities which over-determine the economics and feed the politics of postcolonial Nigeria cannot be egalitarian and popular as long as it remains untransformed; lastly, he favours the *structural* (institutional) argument in the understanding of the Nigerian crisis, challenges and solutions, far above the *agential* argument.

Suberu assumes that the fundamental question of power – addressed in the late 1940s and early 1950s through the then *radical* proposal of a federal arrangement – has been, and will be, settled through the structural devolution of the same. This is where the transformational thesis (scholarly and lay) might: (i) provide radical limits to *reformatory* hopes and dreams concerning Nigeria; (ii) further problematise the question of power; and (iii) broaden horizontally, and expand vertically, the debates about Nigeria's future. This is important, not only in the context of the old attempts to dissolve the federation through force of arms or civil uprising, but the present (represented by the Ijaw and other Niger Delta militants, the open and secret secessionist movements in Igbo and Yoruba regions, including the OPC and MASSOB) and future attempts that would feed off dissatisfactions with the Nigerian union. These latter agents and groups have already rejected the elite consensus on the 'distributive mechanism' on which the current federalist hopes, both fiscal (resource mobilisation, distribution and allocation) and political (regarding citizenship, indigeneity, and membership of the Nigerian state), are built. When the fact that – as Cyril Obi notes – the 'exclusive power over oil rents [is] the ultimate prize[d] of political contestations' is thrown into the federal equation of extractive and non-productive economy, the basis of contestatory politics comes into bold relief.

Adekunle Amuwo's dialectical approach to 'the political economy of Nigeria's fractured state since juridical independence' helps us to further understand the challenges of the possible solutions to the problems of nationhood. Amuwo's organising thesis is that Nigeria was 'programmed to implode' – or, perhaps, explode – in its structural composition by the British because of 'all the booby traps of a lopsided federal system and a mono-cultural economy' which 'a largely venal and rickety oil economy has all but entrenched'. In linking local and global structural problems (such as neo-colonialism, transnational capital, lopsided federalism) with agential questions (such as elite formation, leadership crisis, social struggles), in the 'use of the state as an instrument of resource and power accumulation', Amuwo articulates the predicaments of the Nigerian ruling elite over the last 50 years. These are, first, how to 'deal with salient external and internal forces such as the imperatives of trans-national capitalism'; second, how to ensure coherence between the sometimes conflicting interests, whims and caprices of the members of the 'dominant military-political-business complex'; and third, how to dominate and domesticate 'the anti-imperialist and anti-capitalist political struggle of the popular, but dominated classes'.

We want to suggest that Amuwo and Suberu point to some of the ironies and paradoxes that Nigeria's historical experience raises in the context of providing solutions and pathways to the future. While Suberu, understandably, might seem to occlude the possibilities of transformational means, while siding with reformatory politics at the same time, he favours 'transform[ing] the current revenue sharing system from a mechanism for dividing the spoils of national oil wealth ... into an instrument for efficient and equitable economic governance'. Such a 'reformist' agenda, as proposed by Suberu, will be clearly *transformational*, in that it will cruelly damage, if not destroy, the *rules of the game* as it is currently played in Nigeria, break the material basis of the sustenance of the system *as it is*, with local and external implications for the 'oil flows', breach the 'elite consensus' which was crudely rendered by a former Federal Minister of Internal Affairs, Chief Sunday Afolabi, as 'come and eat', and ultimately, empower the citizens, civil society and democratic forces in their struggle to *popularise* the basis of, and *humanise*, power in Nigeria. As Chabal and Daloz (1999, 14) ask, 'Why should the African political elites dismantle a political system which serves them so well?'

The paradox in Amuwo's case has to do with what, he argues, is 'the obfuscation of the class character of the state, society and politics' in Nigeria since independence 'by the glittering light of ethnicity'. While it is true, as Larry Diamond (cited by Amuwo) argues, that the 'major political conflicts' in the Second Republic (1979–1983) were 'generated not by ethnic cleavages but by party, ideological and class interests', thus, pointing towards what some scholars might describe as the 'epi-phenomenal' nature of ethnicity (Sklar 1963; Diamond 1983), the ways in which, in everyday political life, class and ideological standpoints have been woven around such identities as ethnicity, region and religion, raise important puzzles for emancipatory and transformational politics in Nigeria. The result is that, while, on the one hand, class and ideological interests that are detrimental to the 'national', collective interests of Nigerians and the Nigerian state are championed, defended and enacted on the bases of ethnic, ethno-regional and/or religious ideals and interests; on the other hand, class and ideological interests which are grounded in egalitarian, just and equitable politics are dismissed and discredited on the bases of ethnicity, ethno-regional politics and/or religion.

However, while the prognosis is dim, the historical fissures occasioned by counter-elite and popular (subaltern) politics have often created the conditions for possible improvements and perhaps hopes for transformation of Nigeria. For example, the struggles of the pro-democracy movement after the annulment by Babangida of the 12 June 1993 presidential elections presumed to have been won by Basorun M.K.O. Abiola (Haynes 2003; Omoruyi 1999; Diamond, Kirk-Greene and Oyediran 1997; Kew this volume), and against the subsequent medieval cruelties imposed on Nigeria under General Sani Abacha, attempted to resolve the fundamental question of power through democratic means. Unfortunately, this resolution was not only deferred, but aborted as reactionary forces reinvented themselves after the sudden death of Abacha in June 1998 and recruited a former military head of state, General Olusegun Obasanjo, to help stave off the forces of transformation that were coalescing around the democratic movement when Nigeria returned to democratic rule in 1999. Subsequently, democratic organisations have struggled since 1999 to widen the parameters of social engagements with the crisis of nationhood and its social consequences.

For his part, Kew offers a subtle and intriguing re-interpretation of what he describes as Nigeria's 'neopatrimonial paradox'. His basic approach is to rethink the totality of the country's postcolonial history using as narrative milestones the many unsuccessful elections for which, rightly or wrongly, the country has become infamous. He contends that there is a basic and seemingly inextricable connection between Nigeria's persistent failure to organise credible elections (a failure that has become more apparent since the atypically credible vote of 12 June 1993) and the inability of the governing elite to evolve and organise politics around an assumed 'Social Contract'. In the immediate post-independence era, Kew suggests, Nigeria enjoyed an 'ethnic contract' under which members of the ruling elite felt some obligation to care for the public interests of their ethnic constituents. Frail even at the best of times, by the end of the 1980s, that sense of obligation had completely eroded, giving way to a more personal neopatrimonial culture of politics. Part of the explanation for the erosion, Kew continues, is the incursion of the military into politics and its infusion into civil society of a mode of governmentality which, in the name of trans-ethnicity, casually aborted old structures of patronage. As a result, Nigeria is currently marooned in a no-man's land between an 'Ethnic Social Contract' and a 'National Social Contract'. A relatively transparent election could help spring the country from its trap and launch it on the path to democratic transformation, but then, such are the stakes in an oil-based rentier economy that the ruling elite cannot countenance a surrender of its political privileges. Just as in the early days of independence, Nigeria continues to live under constant fear of a devastating military putsch.

Conclusion: The festering sore of a continent

What does the future hold in stock for Nigeria? What might we reasonably expect, given the structural and agential properties of the total organisation of her political economy, the dynamics of identities, and how these are 'intricately linked with the virulent competition for national resources', 'representation in governance and the modalities for sharing political offices' (Adogame, this volume)?

We like to suggest that Nigeria has to be approached as a totality, in vertical and horizontal terms, in its historical and dialectical dimensions, in order to articulate fully its grand opportunities and its fatal vulnerabilities. In spite of her fundamental challenges, Nigeria still contains within her the transformational possibilities and human potentialities which can be mobilised, harnessed and leveraged by a new kind of leadership working in consonance with social forces and the mass of the people, to forge a workable, liveable polity that would be the pride of the continent. Yet, despite the elite consensus to the contrary, Nigeria also runs the risk of exploding or imploding at any point given the sheer absence of any rooted, overarching, popular basis for sustaining the union. If she unravels, particularly if she violently snaps, the Nigerian space may well be the bloodiest of all human tragedies the world has witnessed in modern times. Every other human tragedy the world has known in the post-Second World War, from the unravelling of the Democratic Republic of Congo to the genocide in Rwanda, may become limited compared to the immensity of 150 million souls searching for a straw to life.

In using the Niger Delta to reflect on 'governmentality and development', Watts (2003, 26) has concluded that the socio-political and economic dynamics centred on oil 'have produced an unimagined community on which the question of Nigeria's future hangs'. Earlier, analysing 'two expressions of subaltern identity politics' (one Islamic, the Maitatsine movement, in the north and the other, environmentalist-minoritarian, the Movement of the Survival of the Ogoni People, MOSOP, in the south), Watts (2001, 97) uses the notion of 'public secret' in pointing to the paradox that is 'widely understood but yet not spoken; a secret that everyone knows'. That secret is 'the very fiction of Nigeria as a Nation' (for how the press reflects this, see Adebanwi 2002). He cites the perspective of Fernand Braudel who argues that 'any nation can have its being only at the price of forever being in search of itself'. Nigeria, Watts mournfully declares, 'has barely begun that search' (Watts 2001, 109).

For Nigeria, after *50* years of false nationhood, the secret is now totally out. While the late 1980s and 1990s democratic struggle attempted to further expose this falsehood and force the hegemonic forces into a reconciliation with an unenviable history, Soyinka articulated the popular position that Nigeria could not continue on the terms on which she was being run with any hope of surviving as a corporate entity in the twenty-first century. Soyinka's articulation of this deserves to be quoted at length:

> Neither the tenacity of state repression nor the longevity of an illusion is adequate to guarantee an eternity to nationhood whose foundations are unsound and whose

> super-structures, however seductive, are constantly stressed as much by the incubus of collective memory as by the dynamics of human development, both the quantifiable aspects and the intangible. I believe that the human mind can encompass this recognition in an original, revitalizing way, enabling us to map, literally, new directions that redress the history of societies and humanize the destiny of their peoples (Soyinka 1996, 143).

The process of redressing the history of 'modern' Nigeria so as to ensure that the country survives as a corporate entity and becomes a nation state worthy of the allegiance of her citizens remains controversial. Osaghae argues here that 'a paradigm shift and identification of the imperatives of institutionalised leadership' would be critical to the 'new directions' that Soyinka points to. Osaghae warns about the perils of 'messiah-nic' leadership, but still emphasises the crucial role of leadership in Nigeria's history. Meanwhile, Suberu (this volume) favours the consolidation and expansion of the 'federal architecture', which he argues 'exhibits several features [which are] judicious'. However, he pushes for the redressing of the 'fundamental defects in the country's constitutional framework', so as to overcome the 'precarious balance' on which the Nigerian federation subsists. To transform Nigerians from subjects to citizens within the next half a century, Amuwo argues that 'a radical and revolutionary approach' will be needed. Relying on the dictum that 'no problem can be solved with the mindset that created it', Amuwo's proposal would fit the insistence by some social forces for the total demobilisation of the (colonial and postcolonial) logics on which Nigeria was founded in favour of the reconstitution of the country through a *genuine* national conference (most probably sovereign).

For Obi, the prospects of the achievement of the hopes expressed by Amuwo particularly, and Osaghae and Suberu in different forms, 'may be difficult', yet they cannot be 'entirely foreclosed'. He refocuses the possible solutions on the structural-agential nexus that the other contributors variously identify and analyse. The emergence of a visionary and committed ruling elite and leadership capable of forging a new equitable social contract between the Nigerian state and its citizens, within a popular-democratic and an equitable participatory framework, which Obi advances, may be the way to contest and perhaps falsify the 2005 prediction of the United States National Intelligence Council that Nigeria may witness 'outright collapse as a nation-state within the next 15 years', dragging down much of the rest of West Africa, if not also some parts of Central Africa.

Fifty years hence, will this prediction on the perils and paradoxes of the Lugardian enterprise in the heart of Africa read like anachronistic nonsense, or will a much feared 'Nigerian Armageddon' have consumed the biggest territorial concentration of black people in the world?

Notes

1. See Table 1 for a chronology of Nigerian political regimes from 1 October 1960 to date.
2. Lugard, in typical Empire-speak, had been economical with the truth as Governor-General of Nigeria, claiming that the amalgamation was in the best interest of Nigerians. Thus he iterated on the occasion of the declaration of the constitution of the Colony and Protectorate of Nigeria on 1 January 1914 that 'so far as it lies, I shall not spare myself nor find any work too hard or arduous, if I can thereby advance the true interests of this country and of each individual person in it, whatever his [sic] race or creed, or however humble his [sic] rank' (Lugard 1914, in Kirk-Greene 1968, 266).
3. The latest figure is 374.

4. Bogged down in controversial 'culturalist' arguments, Chabal and Daloz dismiss the 'fundamentality' of colonialism, or, what might be called the 'colonial determinism', that is popular among many radical scholars and lay commentators in the understanding of postcolonial crises in Africa. They more or less blame Africans exclusively and squarely for their plight, given 'the significance of continuities in political practice from the pre-to the postcolonial period' (Chabal and Daloz 1999, 11). This view, of course, grossly underplays the ways in which the colonial imposition radically changed the relations of (re)poduction in Africa by forcing the countries in the continent into global structures of exchange with implications for every sphere of life in the colonies. Ekeh (1975, 1990) and Mamdani (1994), among others, have provided fascinating ethnographic evidence that contests the trivialisation of the fundamental destabilisation caused by colonialism and its continuous effects.
5. One of the many popular jokes about the Nigerian crisis. Other forms substitute Africa for Nigeria.
6. As McGowan and Smith (1978, 180) correctly note, this critical stage of history started with the Spanish 'discovery' of the Americas in the 1490s, which ending in the 1648 Peace of Westphalia, 'established the classical state system.... based upon the principles of capitalist production and state-building that may be said to have continued to this day'. The implications for the modern state-system remain particularly relevant to the African (Nigerian) experience, particularly as it reshaped Africa's history forever.
7. Wallerstein (1974) acknowledges that 'A world-system['s]... life is made up of the conflicting forces which hold it together by tension and tear it apart as each group seeks eternally to remold it to its advantage' (229). He later conceded that, in the post-Cold War era, the 'system' faces 'systemic crisis' (Wallerstein 2006, 81).
8. The literature in response to Fukuyama's extravagant claims is prodigious. See, for instance: Burns (1994). In response, Fukuyama (1995) later claimed, unconvincingly, that the latter 'confused' the 'empirical part' and the 'normative part' of his thesis and 'their proper relationship'.
9. Kirk-Greene's 1991 famous article is a signal example of the literature on the political leadership and personal rule in Africa which is extended in the literature of neo-patrimonialism and clientelism.
10. Such as substituting the so-called 'aristocratic class' in the Hausa-Fulani north with the entire ethno-regional group, ignoring the fact that many Hausa-Fulani people are native to other states in the north of Nigeria, and the fact that what has been described as the 'pan-Nigeria bazaar of buccaneers' transcends mono-ethnic lenses.
11. For a critical limitation of this thesis, see Mitchell (2009, 400) who argues that 'Failing to follow the oil itself, accounts of the oil curse diagnose it as a malady located within only one set of nodes of the networks through which oil flows and is converted into energy, profits and political power – in the decision-making organs of individual producer states'.
12. Mainly because of 'the detachment of the oil sector from domestic political and economic processes and the non-renewable nature of natural resources' (Humphreys et al. 2007, 4).

References

Adebanwi, W. 2002. The Nigerian press and the idea of Nigerian nation. In *Nigeria in the twentieth century*, ed. F. Toyin, 143–156 . Durham, NC: Carolina Academy Press.
Adebanwi, W. 2005a. The carpenter's revolt: youth, violence and the reinvention of culture in Nigeria. *Journal of Modern African Studies* 43, no. 3: 339–65.
Adebanwi, W. 2005b. Contesting exclusion: the dilemmas of citizenship in Nigeria. *The African Anthropologist* 12, no. 1: 11–45.
Adebanwi, W. 2009. Terror, territoriality and the struggle for indigeneity and citizenship in Northern Nigeria. *Citizenship Studies* 13, no. 4: 349–63.
Adebanwi, W., and E. Obadare, eds. 2010. *Encountering the Nigerian state.* New York and London: Palgrave-Macmillan.
Adejumobi, S. 2000. *Structural adjustment, students' movements and popular struggles in Nigeria, 1986–1996*. Stockholm, Sweden: Nordiska Africa Institute.
Adejumobi, S. 2003. Globalisation and Africa's development agenda: From the WTO to NEPAD. DPMF Occasional Paper, no. 12, *Development Policy Management Forum*, Addis Ababa.
Adejumobi, S. 2009. Popular participation and Africa's development agenda: projecting a citizen-based United States of Africa. *Politikon: South African Journal of Political Studies* 36, no. 3: 403–22.
Adesanmi, P. 2004. Of postcolonial entanglement and durée: Reflections on the francophone African novel. *Comparative Literature* 56, no. 3: 227–42.
Alubo, O. 2004. Citizenship and nation making in Nigeria: New challenges and contestations. *Identity Culture and Politics* 5, nos. 1–2: 135–61.
Amin, S. 1996. The challenge of globalization. *Review of International Political Economy* 3, no. 2: 216–59.
Amin, S. 1972. Underdevelopment and dependence in black Africa: historical origin. *Journal of Peace Research* 9, no. 2: 105–20.
Amin, S. 1975. Accumulation on a world scale. *Journal of Contemporary Asia* 5, no. 4: 478–83.
Amuwo, A. 2009a. Towards a new political economy of the Niger Delta question in Nigeria. *Politikon* 36, no. 2: 237–57.
Amuwo, A. 2009b. The political economy of Nigeria's post-military elections, 1999–2007. *Review of African Political Economy* 36, no. 119: 37–61.
Anifowose, R. 1982. *Violence and politics in Nigeria: the Tiv and Yoruba experience.* New York: Nok Publishers International.
Ascher, W. 1999. *Why governments waste natural resources: policy failures in developing countries.* Baltimore and London: The Johns Hopkins Press.
Auty, R. 1993. *Sustaining development in mineral economics: the resource curse thesis.* London: Routledge.
Awolowo, O. 1947. *Path to Nigerian freedom.* London: Faber & Faber.
Bakhtin, M. 1984. *Rabelais and His World.* Trans. Helene Iswolsky. Bloomington: Indiana University Press.
Bayart, J.-F., S. Ellis, and B. Hibou. 1999. *The criminalization of the state in Africa.* Oxford: James Currey.
Bratton, M. 2007. Formal versus informal institutions in Africa. *Journal of Democracy* 18, no. 3: 96–110.
Bratton, M., and N. Van de Walle. 1994. Neopatrimonial regimes and political transitions in Africa. *World Politics* 46, no. 4: 453–89.
Burns, T., ed. 1994. *After history? Francis Fukuyama and his critics.* Lanham, Maryland: Rowland and Littlefield.
Chabal, P. 2009. *Africa: the politics of suffering and smiling.* London: Zed.
Chabal, P., and J. Daloz. 1999. *Africa works: disorder as political instrument.* Bloomington and Indiana: Indiana University Press.
Clifford, M. 2001. *Political genealogy after Foucault: savage identities.* London: Routledge.
Comaroff, J., and J. Comaroff. 1991. *Of revelation and revolution, volume 1: Christianity, colonialism, and consciousness in South Africa.* Chicago: University of Chicago Press.
Comaroff, J., and J. Comaroff. 1997. *Of revelation and revolution, volume 2: the dialectics of modernity on a South African frontier.* Chicago: University of Chicago Press.

Comaroff, J., and J. Comaroff. 2000. Millennial capitalism: first thoughts on a second coming. *Public Culture* 12, no. 2: 291–343.
Diamond, L. 1983. Class, ethnicity, and the democratic state: Nigeria, 1950–1966. *Comparative Studies in Society and History* 25, no. 3: 457–89.
Diamond, L. 1987. Class formation in the swollen African state. *The Journal of Modern African Studies* 25: 567–96.
Diamond, L. 1988. *Class, ethnicity, and democracy in Nigeria: the failure of the first republic.* Syracuse, New York: Syracuse University Press.
Diamond, L., A. Kirk-Greene, and O. Oyediran. 1997. *Transition without end: Nigerian politics and civil society under Babangida.* Boulder, CO: Lynne Rienner.
Duruigbo, E. 2005. The World Bank, multinational oil corporations, and the resource curse in Africa. *University of Pennsylvania Journal of International Economic Law* 26, no. 1: 1–67.
Egwu, S. 2003. Ethnicity and citizenship rights in the Nigerian federal state. In *Federalism in Africa: The imperative of democratic development, Vol. II*, ed. A. Gana and S. Egwu. Trenton, NJ and Asmara, Eritrea: African World Press.
Ekeh, P. 1972. Citizenship and political conflict: A sociological interpretation of the Nigerian crisis. In *Nigeria: dilemma of nationhood*, ed. J. Okpaku. Westport: Greenwood.
Ekeh, P. 1975. Colonialism and the two publics in Africa: A theoretical statement. *Comparative Studies in Society and History* 17, no. 1: 91–112.
Ekeh, P. 1990. Social anthropology and two contrasting uses of tribalism in Africa. *Comparative Studies in Society and History* 32, no. 4: 660–700.
Fukuyama, F. 1992. *The end of history and the last man.* New York: Free Press.
Fukuyama, F. 1995. Reflections on the end of history, five years later. *History and Theory* 34, no. 2: 27–43.
Geschiere, P. 2009. *The perils of belonging: Autochthony, citizenship, and exclusion in Africa and Europe.* Chicago, IL: University of Chicago Press.
Gore, C., and D. Pratten. 2003. The politics of plunder: The rhetorics of order and disorder in Southern Nigeria. *African Affairs* 102: 211–40.
Haynes, J. 2003. Mobilizing Yoruba popular culture: Babangida must go. *Africa* 73, no. 1: 77–87.
Humphreys, M., J. Sachs, and J. Stiglitz, ed. 2007. *Escaping the resource curse.* New York: Columbia University Press.
Hyden, G. 2006. *African politics in comparative perspective.* Cambridge: Cambridge University Press.
Ihonvbere, J. 1991. A critical evaluation of the failed 1990 coup in Nigeria. *The Journal of Modern African Studies* 29, no. 4: 601–26.
Ikelegbe, A. 2001. Civil society, oil and conflict in the Niger Delta region of Nigeria: ramifications of civil society for a regional resource struggle. *The Journal of Modern African Studies* 39, no. 3: 437–69.
Joseph, R. 1987. Democracy and prebendal politics in Nigeria: The rise and fall of the second republic. Cambridge: Cambridge University Press.
Kirk-Greene, A. 1968. *Lugard and the amalgamation of Nigeria: A documentary record.* London: Frank Cass.
Lagos Weekly Record. 1919. Editorial 1 February 1919.
Le Vine, V. 1980. African patrimonial regimes in comparative perspective. *The Journal of Modern African Studies* 18, no. 4: 657–73.
Lewis, P. 1996. From prebendalism to predation: The political economy of decline in Nigeria. *The Journal of Modern African Studies* 34: 79–103.
Lindberg, S. 2003. It's our time to 'chop': Do elections in Africa feed neo-patrimonialism rather than counter-act it? *Democratization* 10, no. 2: 121–40.
Lugard, F. 1922. *The dual mandate in British tropical Africa.* Edinburgh: W. Blackwood and Sons.
Maier, K. 2000. *This house has fallen: Nigeria in crisis.* Boulder, CO: Westview.
Mama, A. 1995. *Beyond the masks: Race, gender, and subjectivity.* London: Routledge.
Mamdani, M. 1976. *Politics and class formation in Uganda.* New York and London: Monthly Review Press.
Mamdani, M. 1994. *Citizen and subject: Contemporary Africa and the legacy of late colonialism.* Princeton, NJ: Princeton University Press.

Mbembe, A. 2000. At the edge of the world: Boundaries, territoriality and sovereignty in Africa. *Public Culture* 12, no. 1: 259–84.
Mbembe, A. 2001. *On the postcolony*. Berkeley: University of California Press.
Mbembe, A. 2006. On the postcolony: A brief response to critics. *African Identities* 4, no. 2: 143–78.
Mbembe, A. 2008. What is postcolonial thinking? *Eurozine*, 9 January.
McClendon, J.H. 2003. Nkrumah's Consciencism as philosophical text: Matters of confusion. *Journal on African Philosophy* 3: 1–13.
McGowan, P., and D. Smith. 1978. Economic dependency in black Africa: An analysis of competing theories. *International Organization* 32, no. 1: 179–235.
Mitchell, T. 2009. Carbon democracy. *Economy and Society* 38, no. 3: 399–432.
Nyamnjoh, F., and M. Rowlands. 1998. Elite associations and the politics of belonging in Cameroon. *Africa* 68, no. 3: 320–37.
Obadare, E. 2005a. A crisis of trust: History, politics, religion and the polio controversy in northern Nigeria. *Patterns of Prejudice* 39, no. 3: 265–84.
Obadare, E. 2005b. Second thoughts on civil society: The state, civic associations and the antinomies of the public sphere in Nigeria. *Journal of Civil Society* 1, no. 3: 267–81.
Obadare, E. 2007. White-collar fundamentalism: Interrogating youth religiosity on Nigerian university campuses. *The Journal of Modern African Studies* 45: 517–37.
Obadare, E. 2008. *Africa between the old and the new: The strange persistence of the postcolonial state*. Wilmington, NC: University of North Carolina.
Obadare, E. 2009. The uses of ridicule: Humour, 'infrapolitics' and civil society in Nigeria. *African Affairs* 108, no. 431: 241–26.
Obadare, E., and W. Adebanwi. 2010. Excess and Abjection in the Study of African State. In *Encountering the Nigerian state*, ed. W. Adebanwi and E. Obadare. New York and London: Palgrave-Macmillan.
Obi, C. 1997. Globalisation and local resistance: The case of the Ogoni versus Shell. *New Political Economy* 2, no. 1: 137–48.
Obi, C. 2009. Nigeria's Niger Delta: Understanding the complex drivers of violent oil-related conflict. *Africa Development* XXXIV, no. 2: 103–28.
Ojukwu, C.O. 1969. The Ahiara declaration: The principles of the Biafran Revolution. Speech delivered on June 1.
Olukoshi, A. 1992. *The politics of structural adjustment in Nigeria*. London: James Currey.
Omoruyi, O. 1999. *The tale of June 12: The betrayal of the democratic rights of Nigerians (1993)*. London: Press Alliance Limited.
Osaghae, E. 1991. A re-examination of the conception of ethnicity in Africa as an ideology of inter-elite competition. *African Study Monographs* 12, no. 1: 43–60.
Osaghae, E. 1998. *Crippled giant: Nigeria since independence*. London: C. Hurst.
Osaghae, E. 2005. The state of Africa's second liberation. *Interventions* 7, no. 1: 1–20.
Perham, M. 1960. *Lugard: The years of authority 1898–1945*. London: Oxford.
Poulantzas, N. 1978. *State, power, socialism*. London: NLB.
Renan, E. 1882. Qu'est-ce qu'une nation? Conférence faite en Sorbonne, le 11 Mars.
Rodney, W. 1981. *How Europe underdeveloped Africa*. Washington, DC: Howard University Press.
Rotberg, R. 2004. Strengthening African leadership: There is another way. *Foreign Affairs* 83, no. 4: 14–8.
Shivji, I. 1975. Peasants and class alliances. *Review of African Political Economy* 2, no. 3: 10–8.
Shivji, I. 1976. *Class struggles in Tanzania*. New York and London: Monthly Review Press.
Shivji, I. 1992. The politics of liberalization in Tanzania: The crisis of ideological hegemony. In *Tanzania and the IMF: The dynamics of liberalization*, ed. H. Campbell and H. Stein. Boulder, CO: Westview.
Sklar, R. 1963. *Nigerian political parties*. Princeton, NJ: Princeton University Press.
Soares de Oliveira, R. 2007. *Oil and politics in the Gulf of Guinea*. New York: Columbia University Press.
Soyinka, W. 1997. The last despot and the end of Nigerian history? In *An embarrassment of tyrannies*, ed. W. Webb and R. Bell. London: Gollancz.
Soyinka, W. 1996. *The open sore of a continent: A personal narrative of the Nigerian crisis*. New York, Oxford: Oxford University Press.
Suberu, R. 1990. Political opposition and inter-governmental relations in the second Nigerian republic. *Commonwealth & Comparative Politics* 28, no. 3: 269–87.

Suberu, R. 2001. *Federalism and ethnic conflict in Nigeria*. Washington, DC: United States Institute of Peace.

Suberu, R. 2009. Religion and institutions: Federalism and the management of conflicts over Sharia in Nigeria. *Journal of International Development* 21, no. 4: 547–60.

Taiwo, O. 2000. Of citizens and citizenship. In *Constitutionalism and national question*. Lagos: CENCOD.

Tcheuyap, A. 2010. Comedy of power, power of comedy: Strategic transformations in African cinemas. *Journal of African Cultural Studies* 22, no. 1: 25–40.

Time. 1960. Nigeria: The black rock. *Time*, 5 December: 20–23, 25–6.

Tripp, A. 2002. Women's movements and challenges to neopatrimonial rule: Preliminary observations from Africa. *Development and Change* 32, no. 1: 33–54.

Ukeje, C. 2004. From Aba to Ugborodo: Gender identity and alternative discourse of social protests among women in the oil delta of Nigeria. *Oxford Development Studies* 32, no. 4: 605–17.

Ukeje, C. 2006. Youth movements and youth violence in Nigeria's oil delta region. In *Global perspectives on youth conflict and resilience*, ed. C. Daiute, Z. Beykont, C. Higson-Smith and L. Nucci, 289–304. New York: Oxford University Press.

Ukeje, C., and W. Adebanwi. 2008. Ethno-nationalist claims in Southern Nigeria: Insights from Yoruba and Ijaw nationalisms since the 1990s. *Ethnic and Racial Studies* 31, no. 3: 563–91.

Wallerstein, I. 1974. *The modern world-system, vol. I: Capitalist agriculture and the origins of the European world-economy in the sixteenth century*. New York and London: Academic Press.

Wallerstein, I. 1980. *The modern world-system, vol. II: Mercantilism and the consolidation of the European world-economy, 1600–1750*. New York: Academic Press.

Wallerstein, I. 1989. *The modern world-system III. The second era of great expansion of the capitalist world-economy, 1730–1840s*. San Diego and London: Academic Press.

Wallerstein, I. 2006. Globalization or the age of transition? A long-term view of the trajectory of the world-system. In *Globalization and after*, ed. S. Dasgupta and R. Kiely New Delhi: Sage.

Watts, M. 2001. Violent geographies: Speaking the unspeakable and the politics of space. *City and Society* XIII, no. 1: 85–117.

Watts, M. 2003. Development and governmentality. *Singapore Journal of Tropical Geography*. 24, no. 1: 6–34.

The limits of charismatic authority and the challenges of leadership in Nigeria

Eghosa E. Osaghae

Vice-Chancellor Igbinedion University, Okada, Nigeria

Charismatic legitimation theory emerged in the 1960s as a framework for analysing the rise of personal leadership in developing countries. The theory fitted in quite well with the roles that post-independence leaders who had built large followership in the struggles for independence were expected to play in nation building and economic development. The failure to meet these expectations and, in particular, the development of charismatic legitimation into personality cults and unaccountable authoritarian rule has however led to critical reviews of the theory. This article reviews the theory in the light of the Nigerian experience and argues that given the character of the country's elite effective and accountable leadership cannot be left to the preferences and choices of leaders no matter how exemplary, messianic, heroic, or revolutionary they may be. The article makes a case for installing the requisite institutional correlates that are consonant with democracy, rule of law and accountability and capable of restraining the tendencies towards the personalisation of political power.

The nature of the leadership question

The point of departure for this article is the argument made by scholars and public commentators alike that 'the trouble with Nigeria' is leadership (Achebe 1983). The problem is commonly defined in terms of the failure of leaders to deliver on the promises and challenges of independence, appropriate political culture, good governance, economic development and national cohesion despite the country's abundant material and human resources. This statement of the problem, which takes its cues from a normative framework that demands outstanding and extraordinary leadership qualities on the part of those aspiring to or holding top elective and appointive positions and therefore places greater premium on personal attributes than institutional correlates, is typical of the circumstances that have made charismatic legitimation involving heroic, messianic, strongman and revolutionary frames and forms of leadership dominant in many developing countries.

The attributes attached to and expected of so-called good leadership include altruism, patriotism, moral uprightness (especially one based on conspicuous religiosity in the case of Nigeria), sense of historical mission, comprehension of developmental challenges and how to overcome them, courage, boldness and determination. In Nigeria, the leadership question has often been posed in terms of a seemingly endless search for 'good' leaders, a propensity that for a long time encouraged military interventions in the country. In the 50 years between 1960 when the country became independent and 2010, there were a total of 19 heads of state and government. Although only eight of these were military officers, the period was dominated by military rule, which accounted for over 30 of the 50 years. The dominance is even more when it is considered that the civilian regimes and leaders after the First Republic were installed by military governments and retained important elements of military governance including personnel and repressive tendencies. The large number of leaders is partly a manifestation of the elusive search for good leadership, a search that was made more serious by a popular perception that there has been a steady decline in the quality of leadership in the country over the years.

The failure to attain the expected levels of leadership provides a useful framework for analysing the problems of leadership in Nigeria. The question raised by the resulting gap approach is to explain why the levels of leadership in the country have fallen short of expectation. This requires an interrogation of the nature and character of the (political) elites around whom leadership revolves, but as a premise, it is necessary to situate properly the accent on expectations of outstanding personal qualities for leadership. The next section of this article does this in terms of the charismatic legitimation theory, which provides an appropriate framework for explaining the dominant conceptions of and approaches to leadership in developing societies. It is against this background that the rest of the article interrogates the character of the political elite for explanations of the gap between expected and actual levels of leadership.

Charismatic legitimation to the rescue

The circumstances of political development in Africa and the Third World, characterised, as the process has been, by turbulent *perennial* transitions, crises of legitimacy, national cohesion and stability, chronic conflicts and war, oppressive and exclusionary rule, pervasive poverty and economic underdevelopment, and subjection to global hegemony marginalisation, all of which have cumulated to incomplete state building and fragility, make leadership a critical factor in these societies. The foundations of what may be called messianic leadership paradigms were well laid in the historic struggles against colonialism and colonial rule, which are mostly analysed in terms of the heroics of nationalists. Subsequently, after independence, the huge disappointments of the runaway gap between rising expectations and actual performance of governments reinforced the wherewithal of heroic leadership as opposition politicians, military adventurists, revolutionaries, strong men and warlords capitalised on the frustrations of unfulfilled hopes and expectations to seize power and impose themselves on the people in the name of delivering 'strong' and redemptive leadership. Populist and revolutionary leaders such as Fidel Castro of Cuba, Abdel Nasser of Egypt, Muammar Gaddafi of Libya, General Murtala Mohammed of Nigeria and J.J. Rawlings of Ghana were some of the heroes of that era who all ended up being dictators. The democratisation or second independence struggles to liberate citizens and the state from the stranglehold of despots and authoritarian regimes marked another phase of the demands for exceptional and heroic leadership (Osaghae 2005). However, the rise of new social movements and civil society as the harbingers of what Cornwall and Coelho (2007, 1) call the new *participatory sphere* and main drivers of change in the democratisation struggles brought with it new parameters and imperatives of leadership (inclusion, rights, rule of law, transparency, oversight) that had the potential to promote accountable leadership based more on laws and institutions than heroics and personal initiatives.

The foregoing provides the context within which charismatic legitimation theory emerged as a major framework for analysing leadership issues in the Third World. The theory derives from Max Weber's ideal type of charismatic authority that hinges allegiance and support for leaders on their perceived extraordinary or supernatural leadership qualities (or gifts of grace) that enable them to provide answers to situational needs and positively affect the affairs of followers. According to Weber, charisma is more of a relational category than innate personal traits because 'it is recognition on the part of those subject to authority which is decisive for the validity of charisma'. On the basis of this, charismatic authority involves some kind of bond between the charismatic leader and followers.

Although charismatic authority is typically suffused in myths and mythologies about the leader's abilities, which is why it is more usually associated with religious leadership, it found resonance in many developing countries whose material conditions of abject poverty, deprivation, disempowerment, oppression, exclusion, as well as the interests and expectations of followers, invited leaders that possessed the qualities that made them hero, saviour, messiah or liberator and revolutionary (Beyer 1999; Jones 2001). In secular terms, traits such as 'sense of mission', oratorical skills, exemplary leadership, and boldness constitute the ingredients of charisma. Kothari (1988, 166) has constructed profiles of charisma from Gandhi and Nehru in India to include 'pace-setting personal example, a moral fervor based on indigenous symbols of identity, and a militant organizational style' (Gandhi) and 'Overriding personal symbolism, pedagogy and self-confidence' (Nehru). The Nigerian flavour, as enumerated by Achebe (1983, 10–45) include exemplary leadership, mental or intellectual rigour, patriotism, capacity for just rule, ability to treat every group equally, meritocracy and incorruptibility. Of particular note here are the 'moments of crisis', or 'communicative situations', which as Eisensadt (1968, 233) pointed out long ago, precipitate the emergence of leaders with 'radical vision(s) of systemic change'. At such moments as it were, charismatic leaders emerge to champion popular causes, stabilise turbulent situations and restore the confidence of citizens.

The initial setting for the theory was the identification by modernisation scholars of the critical roles of mass-following leaders that had emerged from the anti-colonial struggles as 'fathers of the nation' in the integration of the disparate groups that made up the so-called new states, legitimisation of the (as yet artificial and abstract) state, and subsequent mobilisation of economic development (Shils 1958; Wallerstein 1961). The key factor here was charismatic authority which, it was argued, offered the window to political integration through the transfer of loyalty to and support for the leader to the state. Thus, Claude Ake (1966, 1) defined charismatic legitimation as 'the process of creating loyalty for the new state through the personal influence of the charismatic leader'. The ultimate goal, of course, was the legitimation of the state, which for Ake was a matter of getting the citizen to regard the state 'as a genuine representative of his interests'. Since the charismatic leader already enjoyed the confidence of followers in this regard, it seemed that reproducing the state in the image of the leader, was one sure way of legitimising it. The failure of the first generation of charismatic leaders to play the roles expected for reasons that revolved around the privatisation of power should have invalidated charismatic legitimation theory, but it did not because the challenges faced by developing countries continued to demand heroic leadership (for a brilliant analysis of the wider applications of the theory based on a case study of post-Fidel Castro's Cuba, see Hoffmann 2009).

Elements of charismatic legitimation, especially the propensity towards personal, messianic and heroic leadership, are well ingrained and very much in evidence in Nigerian political culture. The country's historical narratives celebrate the heroics of the champions of anti-colonisation struggles including those such as Oba Ovonramwen of Benin and King Jaja of Opobo who led the initial resistance movements. But it was from the ranks of the nationalist leaders of the colonial period, especially the so-called 'founding fathers' of Nigerian nationalism that the foundations of contemporary charismatic legitimation were laid. The famous educated elites, who studied within the country and overseas, organised the various political associations, parties and nationalist movements that opposed colonial rule, and to whom power was transferred at independence, formed the bulk. The most notable of them included Herbert Macaulay, Funmilayo Ransom-Kuti, Nnamdi Azikiwe, Obafemi Awolowo, Ahmadu Bello, Tafawa Balewa, Michael Okpara, Margaret Ekpo, Alvan Ikoku, Eyo Ita, Udo Udoma, Ladoke Akintola, Adegoke Adelabu, K.O. Mbadiwe, Humphrey Omo-Osagie and Mbonu Ojike. These men and women dominated the national scene and had strong alliances with local notables and strongmen who controlled the grassroots and local politics.

The rise, acceptance and consolidation of the new men of power were suffused with charisma-related elements. By far the most notable of this was the 'cult' of mystifications about their extraordinary and supernatural abilities. Nnamdi Azikiwe was revered as a 'spirit' of sorts whose speaking abilities could not be matched by the Europeans. Like Azikiwe, Mbadiwe and Adegoke Adelabu had oratorical skills that captivated followers while radicals like Mbonu Ojike and Anthony Enahoro won support for defiant and militant mobilisation against the colonial regime. Obafemi Awolowo was the model of personal discipline, a born leader who, his followers believed, had the solutions to human needs. Such mystifications were laced with aristocratic, traditional and magical powers, which accorded well with the tradition-laden popular culture. This was certainly true for elites from the north who had aristocratic backgrounds, but others made their entries through chieftaincy titles and membership of powerful traditional secret societies.

Long after these founding fathers left the scene, they have remained the anchors of enduring charismatic legitimation. Successor politicians take their bearings from them and legitimise claims to leadership on the basis of being their disciples. Also, their children, families and associates have provided the pool for elite recycling and circulation, while in one case at least – that of Awolowo – an attempt at charismatic inheritance was made by his daughter who, when she contested the gubernatorial election in Lagos state in 1991, used the late chief's famous cap as a campaign symbol. These are the factors that underlie what have become the dominant patterns of leadership politics in Nigeria: the primacy of personality and personal qualities; the stranglehold of patrons and godfathers to whom electoral victories and political appointments are owed; and the endless recycling of elites as, across generations, top appointments at all levels of government are reserved for children, descendants and associates of founding and successor charismatic leaders. One good example is the Yar'Adua family of Katsina. The patriarch of the family, Alhaji Yar'Adua was minister of defence and one of the most powerful politicians in the First Republic. His son, General Shehu Yar'Adua was Chief of Staff Supreme Headquarters or deputy head of state between 1976 and 1979 and leading contender for the presidency in the 1990s. Shehu's brother, Musa Yar'Adua, was elected president in 2007 and following his exit from office on grounds of ill health, Shehu's son was appointed federal minister in 2010.

The failure of the first generation of leaders to meet the high expectations elicited by their charismatic bonds precipitated demands for alternative forms of heroic leadership. These mainly involved military officers who had to be at their populist, radical, revolutionary, redemptive or corrective best to justify overthrow of extant governments and mobilise support. The broadcast of the first military coup in the country, in which the idealistic majors that led the putsch denounced tribalism, nepotism, regionalism and corruption, and pledged to 'fight the enemies of progress' – the 10 percenters, homosexuals, feudal lords and the like – set the tone and agenda for subsequent coups which always seemed to renew hopes of redemption. In spite of the populist orientation of successive military governments, however, the military failed to show itself as a credible alternative to the civilian elite. The military leaders did not only continue along the paths of corrupt, personal, patron-godfather and elite recycling leadership, they propagated some of the worst correlates of charismatic legitimation including open-ended tenures and succession crisis. Nonetheless, the military did succeed in cumulatively reconstituting and reshaping the elite. In particular, the military created a new class of client elites in its own image, and it is a mark of how successful this project was that the civilian republics (1979–1983, 1991–1993 and 1999 afterwards) that were crafted by military governments were dominated by coalitions of retired military officers and their civilian clients (Adejumobi and Momoh 1995; Akinrinade 2006).

Contemporary charismatic legitimation in Nigeria was further reinforced by the rise of fundamentalist religious movements in the period beginning from the 1980s. Due to the concurrence of fundamentalism with the rise of economic decline, structural adjustment, state incapacitation, deadly conflicts and diminishing human security, it is commonly explained as part of the exit, voice and loyalty adjustments to increased hardship by large segments of immiserated citizens (Osaghae 1999). One strand of this involved Pentecostal churches whose fervent proselytes created a new code of leadership that revolved around the divine 'will of God'. Only 'God sent' and 'God fearing' leaders with messianic vision, it was believed, could provide good leadership and aspiring leaders were required to demonstrate such spiritual endowments and allied moral rectitude to garner support. Another strand involved fundamentalist Muslim sects like *el Zakzaky*, *Maitatsine*, *Izala* and *Boko Haram* whose leadership tenets rested on anti-system, anti-secularism radicalism that brooked only what adherents believed to be puritan Islam. The new leadership codes served to sustain and reinforce charismatic legitimation that was expected to decline with the ascendancy of civil society and focus on institution-building that hallmarked the democratisation struggles of the 1980s and 1990s.

The essence of charismatic legitimation discussed here is to demonstrate the relevance of the theory to understanding the nature of leadership in the developing world rather than a case for its appropriateness, not the least because of the fairly well known problems of charismatic authority. First, charismatic authority as used by Weber represents a fine type of authority which does not exist in a pure form, meaning that the existence or predominance of charismatic authority does not preclude the existence or development of other Weberian ideal types of authority, namely, legal-rational authority and traditional authority. In Nigeria certainly, all three types co-exist in ways that are both complementary and conflictual. The considerable influence wielded by traditional rulers and the resilience of traditional structures have provoked debates on how to accommodate traditional authority within constitutional orders. Politicians and power holders have also tapped into traditional authority to strengthen their support structures by acquiring chieftaincy titles and co-opting traditional rulers into government structures.

Secondly, to the extent that charismatic authority is conducive for the rise of strongmen, 'for life' father figures and personality cults that 'equate the leader with the nation' and brook no alternatives to 'the Leader' (Kothari 1988, 290–1), its predominance actually constitutes an obstacle to the development and strengthening of rational-legal norms and institutions, which are the hallmarks of modern statehood. Indeed, given the abysmal governance records of countries where personal rule has held sway, the need for strong democratic institutions and practices such as constitutional provisions, time limits on mandates and competitive elections that promote accountability, transparency and responsiveness, as well as the framework for disciplining leadership and succession to power cannot be overemphasised. These are additional to the more endemic problems associated with charismatic authority, including the elicitation of high and sometimes unrealistic expectations as well as the dangers of regime prolongation and succession disorders. The problem of elongation often arises because of the tendency of charismatic leaders not to abdicate 'even when water reaches its throat' (Robert Michels cited in Turner 2003, 7).

The leadership-elite nexus and the limits of charismatic legitimation

Our concern is, however, with the ways in which charismatic legitimation theory has been used to explain the fairly peculiar contexts and demands of leadership in the Third World rather than the problematics of the theory. It explains why the stakes and expectations of leadership tend to be high and why the focus has been on the qualities of individual leaders and what they are able to offer – rather than say the institutional correlates of leadership that promote effectiveness, accountability, inclusion, participation. By relating these to the perennial crisis and transformations that characterise the societies, charismatic legitimation theory differs in important ways from the perspectives championed by Bayart (1991) and Chabal and Daloz (2005) who attribute the predominance of so-called patrimonial legitimacy to the particularistic cultural and traditional foundations – or primitivity even – of African societies that are antithetical to modern statehood. But while the theory provides a useful framework for explaining the demands for and tendencies toward heroic, strong, personal and sit-tight leadership in developing countries including Nigeria, it does not explain the character of leaders and leadership, including their capabilities and actual performances. The latter are contextual historical and social formation variables that relate to the character of the elites – their values, social basis, levels of coherence and cohesion, recruitment mode, attitudes, motivations, orientations and so on – which differ from one country to another.

The centrality of the elites is on account of the fact that leadership is largely an elite affair, the elites being the tiny proportion of leaders in all spheres of society (economy, politics, military, bureaucracy, education, etc.) who exact disproportionate influences over collective action processes and dominate political processes through 'continuity, transformation and replacement' (Parry 2005, 2). There is also elite hegemony that assures its members of material reproduction and non-violent domination – the fact that the values and culture of society, especially those that relate to political economy and state organisation are a reflection of the propensities of the elite. Stated in such terms, it goes without saying that the quality of leadership and by extension the character of the state depend largely on the character of the elite. However, although there is a great deal of consensus on elite hegemony, domination and determinism, the transitional and transformatory circumstances of developing countries described earlier on have made counter-elite politics and elite overthrow fairly popular modes of politics also, though in the final analysis, such 'non-systemic' interventions (for example military coups and fundamentalist uprisings) often end up as forced entries into, and processes of reconstituting, the elite ranks.

Having provided what I consider to be a suitable framework for interrogating the nature of political leadership in developing countries and the centrality of elites in the process, the rest of the article focuses on the Nigerian case. Based on the gap approach outlined at the beginning, the question to be addressed is why the Nigerian elite has failed to provide the kind of leadership that matches the expectations elicited by charismatic legitimation. The correlates – some would say consequences – of leadership failure include the low levels of national cohesion (Nigeria remains one of the world's best examples of deeply divided societies where conflict tends to be endemic and intractable), economic development and human security (this in spite of being one of the world's leading oil-producing countries), and bad governance, political instability and state fragility. The correlates have become something of a vicious cycle as every downturn and crisis requires the elusive good leadership to overcome the challenges. And yet the diagnosis continues to locate leadership problems within personality constructs. Indeed, the explanations, which have ranged from absence of requisite values and qualities like love of country, moral uprightness, discipline, vision on the part of the elite to pervasive corruption and weak institutions, assign too much weight to individual leaders whose personal choices are considered the most critical factors of leadership.

While personal qualities and choices are important considerations and have proven to be quite decisive at critical junctures (they certainly were in the decolonisation and democratisation struggles and the Nigerian civil war), they are only necessary but not sufficient factors for good leadership. The experience with the first generation of political leaders in Nigeria, who led the country to independence, laid the foundations of charismatic legitimation and are generally regarded as the best leaders the country has had so far in terms of their patriotic zeal, discipline and morality, illustrates the point very well. In spite of their outstanding credentials, they constituted the bulk of those denounced by the coup plotters of January 1966, with the concurrence of the vast majority of disappointed citizens, as corrupt enemies of progress. According to Dudley (1982, 70), the problem of the elite at that time, which subsisted and even became worse in later years, was the pursuit of power as 'an end-in-itself and not a means to the realisation of some greater good for the community, and whatever the instrumentalities employed in the pursuit of power, such instrumentalities were legitimate ... the only possible kind of ethic [was] thus that of privatisation, the preoccupation of the individual with the personal rather than his social situation'. The privatisation of the pursuit and holdership of power produced the predominant forms of elite politics. It is against this background that this article makes the overall argument that the focus and diagnosis of leadership problems have to move away from the individual and personal parameters of charismatic legitimation to the democratic institutional correlates of leadership, which include norms and practices. In the words of Kothari (1988, 178), we have to move away from the 'crisis of leadership' to the 'crisis of institutions' as demanded by 'the whole framework of mediating between government and the people, the state and civil society, between technocratic think tanks and socio-cultural grassroots'. But first, what is wrong with the political elite, the segment from which leaders come?

The basis of the problem: Nigerian political elite and the crisis of leadership

The factors that underlie the leadership crisis in Nigeria are to be found in the character of the political elite. We shall interrogate this in terms of a number of mutually reinforcing attributes that diminish the capacity of the elite to match the high stakes of leadership. The first is that it is a colonial creation. The elite developed as a client and dependent class of global capital and has retained this character because of its unwillingness to tamper with the structure of the colonial state inherited at independence. That state, which is oppressive, exclusionary, authoritarian, non-accountable and yet to be meaningfully appropriated (owned) by citizens has, as one of its primary objectives, the preservation of the privileges of its power holders – first the colonisers and later the indigenous political elite. Ake (1985) reminds us that what took place at independence was a mere change of guards of one set of (colonial) oppressors by another (indigenous) set, while the state retained the trappings of a dependent peripheral formation. One consequence of this subsisting structure was that the individual and group rights of ordinary citizens (the famous natives of colonial narratives) continued to be emasculated. Another was that power holding and succession were susceptible to the interplay of powerful external forces. Indeed, beginning from the 1980s when structural adjustment programmes exposed the vulnerability of the country's political economy to external manipulation, one of the interesting ways in which globalisation played out in the popular perception was the belief that leaders have to be acceptable to powerful international forces to succeed and remain in office.

The second attribute of the Nigerian elite is its divisiveness. Although this is partly a consequence of the deep (ethnic, religious, geo-political) cleavages in the country, it is also well known that it is the elites that have mobilised – or manipulated – the cleavages to the dangerous levels of political salience, and have been major instigators of deadly conflicts. They have done so through the agencies of political parties, power blocs, clandestine cabals and mafias, religious, cultural and ethno-regional political associations, tribal unions and hometown associations, which give political competition the appearance of sectional, regional, religious and ethnic battles for supremacy and underlie allegations of domination, exclusion and marginalisation. One of the most powerful of these groups was the 'Kaduna Mafia', a clandestine – or mythical – association of the Northern elite or oligarchy similar to the Afrikaner Broederbond in South Africa. The mafia was believed to be the force behind so-called Northern domination, which was a major theme of Nigerian politics and the object of counter-mobilisation by other ethno-regional groups for a long time (Othman 1984; Takaya and Tyoden 1987; Olukoshi 1995).

Although the Kaduna Mafia and others like it, notably the Arewa Consultative Forum, Afenifere, and Ohaneze Ndigbo claim to be serving ethnic, regional and religious interests in seeking power, top political appointments, creation of states, greater share of the country's revenue, fighting injustice and redressing marginalisation, it is obvious that elites have been the main beneficiaries of group rights and privileges, and that the articulation of these larger and noble interests may actually be a smokescreen for class interests. This is not to deny the genuineness of the problems and rights demanded by aggrieved groups; what happens in some cases is that opportunistic elites simply hijack the grievances in furtherance of their own interests. In any case, the elites need the group pedestal to remain relevant in the bargaining game. These factors underlie the adoption of a federal system in the country, and have made continuous exchange, bargaining, pacting, settlement and power sharing expedient strategies for accommodating difference and building consensus. To its credit, the Nigerian political elite has been quite creative and relatively successful in managing diversity using such instrumentalities as a quota system, federal character principle, creation of more states and local governments, periodic reviews of revenue sharing formula, zoning and rotation of access to top political positions. Yet, the elites remain badly divided, ruling and opposition coalitions are fragile and tenuous, power holding and succession are chaotic, fiercely contested and unstable, and the survival of the country as one entity is threatened all the time. This paradox is explained by other underlying propensities of the elite which are discussed below.

Another important attribute of the political elite is its almost total dependence on the state for social and material reproduction. In the absence of a strong private sector – which is largely controlled by the state – the huge resources needed to maintain the big man status, oil patron-client networks and run for political office are sourced from state spoils and largesse in opportunistic ways that approximate primitive accumulation: 'politics of the belly' (Bayart 1993) and criminalisation of the state (Bayart et al. 1999). It is on account of this that the political elite has been described as pirate, rogue, parasitic and predatory. The ways and means of politics of the belly include the desperation to win elections, secure ministerial and other top government appointments, secure juicy contracts, licences and concessions especially in the all-important oil and gas sector, rent-seeking, embezzlement of funds and other criminal uses of public office for private gain and benefit. To all intents and purposes, it is those who control power and have access to its resources that have the wherewithal to function as powerful or influential political elites. Only a few of those who are shut out and in opposition are able to survive in the wilderness as it were, which largely accounts for the high rate of carpet-crossing to ruling and dominant parties by politicians (even incumbent state governors and legislators have had to join the survival game). In the face of the exclusionary winner-takes-all tendencies on the part of state power holders, the competition for access to and control of the state is fierce, war-like and 'do-or-die' as evident in the country's long history of military coups and counter-coups as well as violent and inconclusive elections.

Exclusionary politics, which is antithetical to the consensus-directed accommodation strategies outlined earlier, is usually propagated in the name of furthering supposedly ethnic, communal, religious and regional interests and identities. However, the fact that the benefits and privileges of domination and exclusionary rule have accrued disproportionately to the elites while the ordinary members and home areas of the groups have remained deprived and impoverished suggest that the claims to group power are a smokescreen for private interests. The classical example for this has to be the old Northern region which, in spite of the several years of so-called Northern domination especially under prolonged military rule, remains underdeveloped and impoverished and lags behind the supposedly marginalised south. Similarly, the deprivation, neglect and poverty of the oil-rich Niger Delta region have not been obviated by the fact that several sons and daughters from the region have held important federal and state appointments. The point is that is the coupling of the power of the elite with the power of the group is part of the ideological repertoire of the elite because the 'fruits of development have not reached the people, certainly not the worst affected among them, nor even those who have not so completely been marginalised or disenfranchised' (Kothari 1988, 178).

This leads to the next attribute of the elite, which derives directly from the culture of charismatic legitimation, namely, the propensity to privatise and personalise power and be autocratic rather than approach it as an accountable, common good, social contract variable. The corollary of this is the gross indiscipline of the elite manifest in the impunity of its members and their imperviousness to laid down rules and regulations. Although these tendencies would appear to be truer of a military regime, which Nwabueze (1994, 4) aptly describes as 'lawless autocracy, that is to say, a government not limited by law', lawlessness has been endemic to the governing elite in Nigeria. A major reason for this is the weakness of accountability norms and institutions, which is at once a consequence of the unresolved ownership crisis of the (colonial) state, the excesses of charismatic legitimation that encouraged personality cults, and the emasculation of the judiciary, legislature (which did not exist throughout the over 30 years of military rule) and other oversight institutions and civil society, including most notably the media.

The installation of democratic institutions has not resolved the problem of accountability as was expected because the efficacy of the franchise on which accountability ultimately hinges has been continuously diminished by flawed electoral precepts and processes. For the most part, the electoral leverage that political parties and politicians have depends on the amount of support given to them by strong men and women because to all intents and purposes, these are the people who secure and 'win' elections. It is rare to find an electoral victory that was not literally delivered by the strong men who control the constituencies. As it were, the outcomes of elections are pretty much pre-determined by the patterns of support by the 'kingmakers' and 'godfathers', and quite often elections end up working from the answers. Thus, even where elections are clearly rigged as affirmed by election observers and monitors as well as electoral tribunals that have had to sometimes cancel elections and upturn official results, the results are accepted, even justified, because they are secured by the powers-that-be and it is inconceivable that strongmen can lose their constituencies.

It is only when the strongman loses to rival strongmen that elections 'hot up' and become more violent. So, it is the big men, the super patrons that count, and politicians and political parties invest almost exclusively on buying and retaining their support. Of course, the big men do work very hard to validate their patron roles.

They actually 'buy' the votes and retain the services of the terror machines constituted by thugs, criminals and groups like motor park gangs and drivers unions whose internal operations thrive on violence. In some cases, they also have security agents on their payroll – many of them actually have police and other state security operatives as personal bodyguards. The following analysis in a national newspaper on the prospects of the incumbent governor of Oyo state getting re-elected is instructive:

> Following the death of Lamidi Adedibu [Governor Alao Akala's erstwhile political godfather], Akala became a political orphan. But he has now secured the endorsement of a new godfather, Chief Richard Akinjide . . . who proclaimed him as the candidate for the next poll. Akinjide, who is a less formidable political figure than Adedibu, has an ally in former Governor Victor Olunloyo, who supported the endorsement. However . . . Akinjide and Olunloyo *lack the structure to make things happen*
>
> (*The Nation*, Friday 30 April 2010, 13, emphasis added).

As it were, the prospects of the governor's re-election did not depend on how well he had performed in his first term as governor and how citizens of the state were going to vote, but on the structure the godfathers had 'to make things happen'. This had serious implications for accountability, which then had to be to the godfathers rather than the citizens.

Again, the experience of Governors Rasheed Ladoja and Alao Akala with the late Lamidi Adedibu, the strongman of Ibadan politics in Oyo state, and Chris Ngige with Chris Uba in Anambra state, provide interesting examples. One of the reasons publicly given by the late Lamidi Adedibu to justify the impeachment of Governor Ladoja in 2007 was the governor's failure to remit an apparently agreed portion of the statutory monthly revenue allocation from the Federation Account to Oyo state to him. Ladoja had to be punished for his stubbornness and selfishness since, as Adedibu argued, the governor 'corruptly' appropriated state revenues alone. Ladoja's successor, Alao Akala may have been less selfish and probably fairer to the godfather, but his failure to let the strongman have his way on appointments to key state government positions made him less accountable to the chief, and he had to pay the price for attempting to become autonomous, as the threat of impeachment loomed large until Chief Adedibu died in 2008. The case of Chris Ngige, who was allegedly forced to swear a secret oath of fidelity to his godfather Chris Uba at the notorious Okija shrine, was not too different, but this time, the godfather used his strong connections with the federal government and security forces to intimidate and eventually impeach the governor for intransigence over the sharing of Anambra state funds.

Remarkably, very few people or groups rose to the defence of the embattled governors, even when it was so glaring that they were being punished for 'fighting' 'corruption'. From what has been said so far, three reasons can be adduced for this. The first is that it was not really the votes of citizens that brought the incumbents into office. Indeed, in the 2003 and 2007 elections, legislative seats were won even before the party determined which candidates would run – the candidates were only known after elections had been won! Also, rather than the votes, the election tribunals and law courts assumed responsibility for determining the outcome of elections which were lost and won on technical grounds. In one interesting case involving the 2007 gubernatorial election in Rivers state, which was won by the ruling People's Democratic Party (PDP), the elected governor who actually contested the election lost the seat to another aspirant he had earlier defeated at the party primaries organised by the party to select its gubernatorial candidate. In effect, the governor that later emerged following a court ruling of the state did not participate in the election and was therefore not directly elected. Even if the governor was popular and people were willing to support him or her, lawlessness, violence and terrorism of politics are sufficient instruments of deterrence and exclusion. Indeed, these are deployed in large doses to keep the people including civil society at bay and ensure that political spaces remain the preserve of the strong and mighty. Shrines, rituals, cults and nocturnal meetings are also used to the same ends. Thirdly, partly because of the first two reasons, the whole business of electing people to government offices has been left to godfathers and those they bargain with, the point being that the corrupt character of exchange and reciprocity makes the elected politician accountable to the strongman rather than the citizens.

The final attribute of the Nigerian political elite, and one which summarises all that has been said so far and has prevented the elite and state from serving as agents of development, is its pervasive corruption. Several official inquiries and probes have revealed the incredibly high levels of rent seeking, fraud, embezzlement, bribery and kickbacks amongst public officials and politicians whose main motivation in seeking public office is to use it as a means of corrupt enrichment no matter the cost of doing so to the country and its citizens (Osaghae 1995). Again, it is easy to see how corruption breeds on the unresolved crisis of ownership of the state (whose relevance for many people consists only of what can be milked from it) on the one hand, and the weak bonds and structures of accountability on the other. Corruption does not, however, connote privatisation of public office for private gain, embezzlement and other negative pecuniary transactions that deprive society of much needed resources only. It also includes the manipulation and subversion of institutions, rules, regulations, procedures and laws, which is mostly evident in the flawed electoral process.

One of the less interrogated aspects of electoral corruption lies in what is commonly referred to in Nigeria as the culture of settlement. Typically, a politician running for office spends large amounts of money to bribe voters who get cash, rice, salt and other commodities through the strongmen and other core supporters, with the common understanding that the 'investment' will be recouped after election, an open cheque for the elected office holder to be corrupt. Having been paid off ('settled' as it were), the electorate loses the right to demand further accountability though a great deal depends on the level of settlement – higher settlements mean far less accountability and vice versa. Thus, in terms of performance, much more is expected of a governor who as a poor gubernatorial candidate did not have enough resources to settle corrupt debts prior to elections than one who paid his or her dues and settled in full and is expected to recoup the huge sums invested. Attempts by daring elected office holders to gain autonomy, overthrow their godfathers and become strongmen in their own rights have produced dangerous divisions and other high tension outcomes that in some cases led to threats of impeachment – or actual impeachment in some cases – of incumbents.

The need to change focus

The foregoing profile clearly shows that the political elite in Nigeria lacks the capacity, motivation and drive to provide good leadership, especially one that matches the high expectations elicited by charismatic legitimation. Indeed, the lesson from studies of elites in places like Nigeria and India, regarded as the major flaw of charismatic legitimation, is that emphasis on the innate personal qualities or even proven abilities of individual leaders raises the stakes of leadership and complicates the leadership crisis. First, it encourages the personalisation of power and personality cults that then subordinate the interests of the state to those of the father figure. Nothing destroys or weakens the common good more than this, especially where the state suffers from such fundamental problems as unresolved ownership and legitimacy crises and the political elite lacks the vision, interest and discipline necessary to construct and mobilise national integration. Modernisation theorists who assigned the roles of transforming the new states that gained independence after World War II from artificial entities to nation states to charismatic leaders clearly underestimated the dangers of unrestrained power. With hindsight, it was an error of judgment not only on the part of scholars but citizens, activists, nationalists and civil society constituents as well to hinge the development of the new states so much on the choices, exemplary conduct and innate goodness of so-called great leaders. It is for this reason and the imperatives propelled by the democratic revolution that it has swept across the developing world since the late 1980s and that as Kothari has rightly argued, the problem of leadership should now be approached from the perspective of an institutional crisis rather than a leadership crisis per se (see also Yuki 1999). This paradigm shift is of course not new. Long ago, Burns (1978) had argued that leadership without strong institutions is weak and unsustainable. But it has taken the failures, disappointments and huge costs of charismatic legitimation for the leadership question, including how to accommodate former presidents whose activities endanger democratic consolidation in some countries (Southall and Melber 2006), for the point to be finally appreciated and domesticated. This is the focus of the concluding part of this article to which we now turn.

Goodbye charismatic legitimation, welcome institutional leadership

The democratisation struggles that finally ended military rule in Nigeria in 1999 differed from previous progressive struggles in the country in a very significant way: whereas the success and potential of anti-colonial struggles, military coups and governments depended very much on the heroes that led them, those of democratisation, which involved civil society coalitions as well as opposition and pro-democracy groups moved away from the followership of individual leaders to the installation of effective and durable democratic institutions and processes. Part of the response in the literature was the emphasis on agency, not as the reality creating functions of individual efforts, but as 'part of the production of certain social formations and the dynamics of interaction between people and between societies and their predicaments and the environment' (Van Dijk et al. 2007, 1). The fact that many of the leaders of the various groups had been at the receiving end of the tyranny and excesses of personalised and exclusionary power was helpful in reaching the conclusion that although innate goodness and exceptional qualities were helpful ingredients of leadership, they were not to be worshipped; and the best form of leadership was that restrained by institutional checks. Thus, in contrast to the ingredients of good person-centred leadership profiled by Achebe (1983, 10–45) to include exemplary leadership, mental or intellectual rigour, patriotism, capacity for just rule, ability to treat every group equally, meritocracy and incorruptibility, Aka (2005, 61–2) argues that leadership 'derives its ultimate significance from its capacity for institutionalisation' and lists the imperatives of leadership as follows:

> Nigeria needs leaders able to minimise the political importance of ethnicity and other sectional or particularistic identities; establish procedures for equitable resource allocations; rationalise the government apparatus; promote political participation; augment productive capacities to meet changing demands ... and ... design and implement an effective reconciliation policy when occasion demands.

The paradigm shift and identification of the imperatives of institutionalised leadership do not, however, amount to the fact that a revolution has occurred in Nigeria. To be sure, the political elites as major beneficiaries of the old order have a stake in maintaining the status quo, and have since 1999 resisted the struggles championed by civil society, pro-democracy and opposition groups to tame the elite. The struggles, which enjoy substantial support from donors and the international community, mainly involved reforms in key areas like strengthening legislative oversight, judicial independence, elections and electoral process, anti-corruption, the constitution and constitutionalism. The outcomes have been rather mixed. Legislative autonomy and oversight have been strengthened, anti-corruption agencies have been established and have been fairly effective, due process has been introduced to guide procurement and public sector financial transactions, and attempts have been made at electoral and constitutional reforms to address issues of the immunity of incumbent presidents and governors and the autonomy of the electoral commission, which is believed to be a requirement for free and fair elections. Yet, in spite of these, the electoral process remains fundamentally flawed (the 2003 and 2007 elections are said to be some of the most rigged elections ever witnessed in the country); corruption has increased in prevalence, size and sophistication; godfathers remain very powerful; and most of all, the country remains deeply divided with the crises of ownership and legitimacy still largely unresolved. But even so, civil society has been unrelenting and resilient in engaging the state and making sustained demands were for rights, accountability, participation and consultation. One of the interesting developments in this respect, which is an integral part of the civil society inspired agenda-setting shift in leadership paradigm, is the changed outlook of Pentecostals and other religious leaders whose code of God ordained leadership had the potential of rekindling assumptions of charismatic authority in popular perception. They have increasingly said goodbye to the voluntary choices of goodness and joined civil society coalitions to insist on institutional imperatives and safeguards of responsible and accountable leadership.

References

Achebe, C. 1983. *The trouble with Nigeria.* London: Heinemann.

Adejumobi, S., and A. Momoh, eds., 1995. *The political economy of Nigeria under military rule, 1984–1993.* Harare: Southern Africa Political and Economic Series (SAPES).

Aka, P. 2005. The need for an effective policy of ethnic reconciliation. In *Nigeria in the twenty-first century: strategies for political stability and peaceful coexistence*, ed. E. Udogu. Trenton, NJ: Africa World Press.

Ake, C. 1985. *Political economy of Nigeria.* London: Macmillan.

Ake, C. 1966. Charismatic legitimation and political integration. *Comparative Studies in Society and History* 9, no. 1: 1–13.

Akinrinade, S. 2006. An army of ex-presidents: The military and democratic consolidation in Nigeria. In *Legacies of power: Leadership change and former presidents in African politics*, ed. R. Southall and H. Melber. Uppsala: Nordiska Afrikainstitutet.

Bayart, J. 1991. Finishing with the idea of the third world: The concept of the political trajectory. In *Rethinking third world politics*, ed. J. Manor. London: Longman.

Bayart, J. 1993. *The state in Africa: The politics of the belly.* London: Longman.

Bayart, J., S. Ellis, and B. Hibou. 1999. *Criminalization of the state in Africa.* Oxford: James Currey.

Beyer, J. 1999. Training and promoting charisma to change organization. *Leadership Quarterly* 10, no. 2: 307–30.

Burns, J. 1978. *Leadership.* New York: Harper and Row.

Chabal, P., and J.-P. Daloz. 2005. *Culture troubles: Politics and the interpretation of meaning.* London: C. Hurst.

Cornwall, A., and V. Coelho. 2007. Spaces for change? The politics of participation in new democratic arenas. In *Spaces for change? The politics of citizen participation in new democratic arenas*, ed. A. Cornwall and V. Coelho, 1–29. London: Zed.

Dudley, B. 1982. *An introduction to Nigerian government and politics.* London: Macmillan.

Eisensadt, S. 1968. Introduction: Charisma and institution building: Max Weber and modern society. In *Max Weber, the charisma and institution building*, ed. S. Eisensadt, 1–19. Chicago, IL: University of Chicago Press.

Hoffmann, B. 2009. Charismatic authority and leadership change: Lessons from Cuba's post-Fidel succession. *International Political Science Review* 3, no. 5: 229–48.

Jones, H. 2001. Magic, meaning and leadership: Weber's model and the empirical literature. *Human Relations* 54, no. 6: 753–71.

Kothari, R. 1988. *State against democracy: In search of humane governance.* Delhi: Ajanta.

Nwabueze, B. 1994. *Nigeria '93.* The political crisis and solutions. Ibadan: Spectrum.

Olukoshi, A. 1995. Bourgeois social movements and the struggle for democracy in Nigeria: An inquiry into the 'Kaduna mafia. In *African studies in social movements and democracy*, ed. M. Mamdani and E. Wamba-dia-Wamba, 245–78. Dakar: Council for the Development of Social Science Research in Africa (CODESRIA) Books.

Osaghae, E. 1995. Amoral politics and democratic instability in Africa: A theoretical exploration. *Nordic Journal of African Studies* 4, no. 1: 62–79.

Osaghae, E. 1999. Exiting from the state in Nigeria. *Journal of African Political Science* 4, no. 1: 83–98.

Osaghae, E. 2005. The state of Africa's second liberation. *Interventions: International Journal of Postcolonial Studies* 7, no. 1: 1–21.

Othman, S. 1984. Class, crisis and coup: The demise of Shagari's regime. *African Affairs* 83, no. 333: 441–61.

Parry, G., ed. 2005. *Political Elites*, second edition. Essex: European Consortium for Political Research (ECPR) Press.

Shils, E. 1958. The concentration and dispersion of charisma: Their bearing on economic policy in underdeveloped countries. *World Politics* 11, no. 1: 1–19.

Southall, R. and H. Melber, ed. 2006. *Legacies of power: Leadership change and former presidents in African politics.* Uppsala: Nordiska Afrikainstitutet.

Takaya, B., and S. Tyoden, eds., 1987. *The Kaduna mafia: A study of the rise, development and consolidation of a Nigerian power elite.* Jos: University Press.

Turner, S. 2003. Charisma reconsidered. *Journal of Clinical Sociology* 3: 5–26.
Van Dijk., R., M. de Bruijn, and J-B. Gewald. 2007. Social and historical trajectories of agency in Africa: An introduction. In *Strength beyond structure: Social and historical trajectories of agency in Africa*, ed. M. de Bruijn, et al. Leiden: Brill.
Wallerstein, I. 1961. *Africa: The politics of independence.* New York: Random House.
Yuki, G. 1999. An evaluation of conceptual weaknesses in transformational and charismatic leadership theories. *Leadership Quarterly* 10, no. 2: 285–305.

Between elite protectionism and popular resistance: The political economy of Nigeria's fractured state since juridical independence

Adekunle Amuwo

School of Politics, University of KwaZulu-Natal, South Africa

This piece attempts a new reading of the political economy of the Nigerian state within the context of the epoch-making British colonialism, the spin-off effects of structural imperialism and the stranglehold of an increasingly desperate transnational capital. The principal argument is that whilst these structures do not explain everything – to the extent that the Nigerian ruling elite has played a key agential role in the country's underdevelopment – they tend to create the conditions for the largely amoral and anti-people politics and policy of the fractious ruling elite. Programmed to implode by colonialism with all the booby traps of a lopsided federal system and a mono-cultural economy (that a largely venal and rickety oil economy has all but entrenched) and the scenarios of failure constituted by primordial cleavages, the resultant elite protectionism in its multiple manifestations hides the saliency of class struggle. In addition, the artificial postcolonial state – with no cultural resonance on the ground, but representing, with political power, the primary means of class relations and reproduction – has been cynically exploited by the ruling elite and transnational capital. Popular resistance to the current gridlock will succeed only insofar as the dominated classes radicalise the struggle for popular democracy and for the construction of an autochthonous Nigerian state through class struggle.

> We must remember that the European agreements that had carved up Africa into states paid little attention to cultural and ethnic boundaries and ethnic groups had little opportunity and need to form political alliances or accommodations under repressive colonial rule... Think of countries such as Canada which have been trying for hundreds of years with mixed success to accommodate only two linguistic groups – English and French – and you get an idea of the problems of African states with far greater cultural and linguistic divisions
>
> Richard Robbins (2002)

> Consider the extent to which the Second World War of just six years duration has pervaded the consciousness of our developed world for generations and imagine how four centuries of enslavement might have seized the entire social and cultural ethos of an undeveloped continent
>
> Bob Geldof in Shah, n.d.

> It is undeniable that there has been poor governance, corruption and mismanagement in Africa. However, the briefing reveals the context of the legacy of colonialism, the support of the G8 for repressive regimes in the Cold War, the creation of the debt trap, the massive failure of Structural Adjustment Programmes (SAPs) imposed by the IMF and the World Bank and the deeply unfair rules on international trade. The role of the G8 in creating the conditions for Africa's crisis cannot be denied. Its overriding responsibility must be to put its own house in order, and to end the unjust policies that are inhibiting Africa's development
>
> Summit Action for Southern Africa (2002) in Shah, n.d.

Introduction and the *problèmatique*

Juxtaposed against the tendency of mainstream Nigerian/ist political economy scholarship to analyse Nigeria's postcolonial state in near absolute (negative) terms, the by-no-means monolithic Western capitalist state is not a purveyor of only positive values. Writing on the role of the latter in the contemporary phase of predatory capitalist globalisation, Jacques Gélinas, the Canadian sociologist, argues that 'the state is increasingly perceived (by citizens) as a system that cheats, spends lavishly, mismanages and wastes public funds, in addition to favouring friends, groups and companies close to power'. While the state's putative responsibility is the defence and promotion of the public interest and the citizens' social rights, 'there is a growing gulf separating the political class from the people. As soon as they are elected, politicians forget they are representatives of the people and become their party's servants'. What is more, 'after casting a vote in the ballot box, the voter is left to accept the deeds and misdeeds of his or her elected representatives' (Gélinas 2003, 196–7). If the Western state has become so degenerate, what can be said about the nature and character of the postcolonial state in Nigeria?

The postcolonial state cannot but be *sui generis* on account of the rampant authoritarianism and systemic predation that gravely defined the colonial state and framed colonial politics, power and economy. The Nigerian post-independence ruling elite has had to contend with at least two extremely complex elements of the colonial legacy: (a) Nigeria was programmed by British imperialism and colonialism to implode through the booby traps of a lopsided federal system and the scenarios of failure constituted by primordial cleavages inherent in the political economy; and (b) cleaning up the messy Augean stables bequeathed by British colonialism – and the ruling elite has spent the better part of the first 50 years of independence doing so. If it has all but done a good job of it thus far, it is because of two factors. One, the ruling elite's class interests have prevented it from seeing the bigger picture of a truly emancipated Nigeria. In its bid to use the state as an instrument for resource and power accumulation, the ruling elite has had to deal with salient external and internal forces such as the imperatives of trans-national capitalism; the interests, whims and caprices of the dominant military-political-business complex; and the anti-imperialist and anti-capitalist political struggle of the popular but dominated classes. Two, neo-colonialism in its varying manifestations, breathes down heavily on the neck of the ruling elite, thus denying it the relative autonomy to do the job in relative quietude. The ruling elite has been severely constrained by three factors: the epochal character of colonialism on the country's politics, economy, and society; the logic of structural imperialism and capitalist globalisation; and the objective interests of the ruling elite and transnational capital.

The principal *problèmatique* of this paper is that while external factors do not explain everything – to the extent that the Nigerian ruling elite has played a key agential role in the country's underdevelopment – they tend to create favourable conditions for the amoral and anti-people politics and policy of the fractious ruling elite. In addition, the artificial postcolonial state – with little or no cultural and moral resonance on the ground, but representing, alongside political power, the primary means of class relations and reproduction – has been cynically exploited by the ruling elite and transnational capital. Popular resistance to the current gridlock will succeed only if the dominated classes come to terms with the class-based political economy (disguised as rampant ethnicity) and radicalise the struggle for popular democracy and the construction of an autochthonous Nigerian state. The theoretical framework is constituted by a combination of structure and agency. In responding to the question posed by Stapleton (2009, 490): 'does the person make the times or do the times make the person' our response is both, but with a caveat. In other words, inherited structures in Nigeria have been enduring, but it does not mean that human creativity cannot surmount them. By the latter is meant the totality of a people's 'strength, organisations and institutions in overcoming the confines of structure'.

The context of this article is two-fold. One, in terms of the geo-political and strategic interests of Britain and other powers, Nigeria is too important to be allowed to be the genuinely relatively autonomous actor it had wanted to be in the global political economy at independence (Amuwo 2009b). Two, in the contemporary phase of capitalist globalisation, the nation state is becoming an ever more complex structure and social institution due to a growing unstable juxtaposition between the nation-state/inter-state system and transnational social groups and classes operating through states and related institutions. Thus, Robinson's (2007, 23) argument that 'capitalist imperialism' is considerably more complex than the facile North-South/Centre-Periphery framework. The emphasis, in short, is on new forms of transnational class relations and class cleavages not only globally, but also within countries, regions, cities, and local communities (Amuwo 2009c).

The article is divided into five sections. The first section analyses the epoch-making elements of British colonialism. The second critically interrogates the specificity of the Nigerian postcolonial state, whilst the third traces the transition from economic nationalism to economic globalisation showing how the ruling elite protects its interests. The fourth section discusses resistance politics by the dominated classes; and the fifth, the conclusion, ponders the way forward.

Elements of an epoch-making colonial project

The starting point necessarily has to be the impact of the British colonial design and policy on Nigeria. Three elements of this policy merit attention. One, on account of the anointing of the country's neo-conservative fraction of the emergent ruling elite (with the political North as its hub), the battle line was inexorably drawn between political and class forces bent on protecting the status quo and those nudged onto resistance politics as an instrument of social change. While progressive politics and politicians were muzzled, the colonial authorities pulled all the stops to ensure that political power was won, at all levels of government, by conservative parties and politicians. In relation, for instance, to Mallam Aminu Kano's pro-poor Northern Elements Peoples Union (NEPU), the Northern People's Congress (NPC)'s policy blueprint was adjudged 'more sober and mature' and its politico-ideological orientation reformist and pragmatic enough to be preferred to NEPU which was considered as a threat to the colonial system (Diamond 1988, 35; Soyinka 2006, 61ff). This singular political stroke is a major constitutive element in the malformation and malfunctioning of the Nigerian state: the grossly unjust political economy in place; the rancorous and debilitating political behaviour this has elicited; and the zero-sum nature of the political game.

Two, the creation of an extremely lopsided federal system, which Ejobowah (2005, 183) refers to as 'an egregious imbalance in the size of the constituent regions, as the North more than doubled the combined geographical size of the East and West and actually used its size and population to control the federal government'. The colonial administration saw nothing wrong in the three-region structure 'despite clear warnings and manifest evidence of its flaws' (Diamond 1988, 59, 72), in particular the ultimately dire coincidence, in the regional system, of region, party and ethnicity. There is perhaps no better explanation than the fact that the colonial government calculated that the arrangement would be protective of the long-term economic and geo-strategic interests of Britain. Writing during the country's civil war (May 1967–January 1970), Mckenna (1969, 668) contended that 'the identification of the three regions (later four) with a particular political party and a single predominant ethnic group effected a polarisation of political forces which certainly contributed to the present cataclysm'. Professor Richard Sklar, veteran Nigerianist, concurs and goes as far as arguing that 'this deepening regionalism and the manifest contradictions in the regional system constituted the most damaging legacy of colonial rule'. Invariably, he reasons that 'by preserving Northern Nigeria especially as an area of cultural authenticity and autonomy, with its own strong institutions, Britain inadvertently contributed to the forces which culminated in the Nigerian civil war' (Diamond 1988, 29). As the political contraption that passed for democracy was disintegrating before his very eyes, Dr Nnamidi Azikiwe, the first republic's president, suggested that 'in order to evolve into a near perfect union, the whole of Nigeria should be divided and so demarcated geographically and demographically that no one region would be in a position to dominate the rest' (Azikiwe 1965, 456–7).

A further element is the obfuscation of the class character of the state, society and politics by the glittering light of ethnicity. Since the principal means of primitive accumulation are the state and political power, ethnicity hides the significant class differentiation and struggles that have been the hallmark of Nigerian politics since the colonial period. Since class interests are often falsely conflated with ethnic and group interests and are projected by trans-national capital and its powerful Western media allies as proof that the 'African natives' cannot govern themselves, mainstream Nigerian/ist scholarship has tended to appropriate uncritically the well-worn unruly primordialism of the ruling elite as the driving force of the country's political economy.

To be sure, it can be argued, following Aiyede (2009, 263–4), that the struggle amongst ethno-nationalities for a share of Nigeria's so-called 'national cake' has, over the past 50 years, fuelled ethnic, regional and communal tensions; pitted proponents and opponents of specific modalities of territorial restructuring against one another and stimulated new forms of parochial, divisive and exclusionary identities. But this is no more than on face value. This is because, as Diamond (1988,

8) has correctly observed, ethnicity is a political, not a cultural phenomenon, to the extent that 'ethnic conflict is rooted in competition for resources and power rather than conflict over cultural values'. This explains why ethnic conflicts are principally class conflicts. If the class character of first republic politics was lost to analysts in the maze of spectacular ethnic engineering and primordial manifestations, it was an open sore for subsequent political dispensations. 'The major political conflicts of the second republic', writes Diamond (1988, 72), '(were) generated not by ethnic cleavage but by party, ideological and class interests'.

Class differentiation in Nigeria has also been a function of what Watts and Lubeck (1983, 112) refer to as the aggregate of activities centred on the key oil sector and state intervention in favour of transnational capital and capitalist class. Diamond (1988, 76) adds that while ethnicity continues to enjoy some political saliency, it does appear to have lost its cutting edge: 'it no longer organises, much less polarises national political conflict. It no longer can be manipulated to block change and suppress dissent. It no longer looms as an imminent threat to the democratic future'. In the intervening years between the second republic and the last national elections in 2007, the class divisions were exacerbated by the liberalisation, deregulation and privatisation policies of the economic structural adjustment programme (SAP) implemented by military and civilian governments alike. These reforms also entrenched a large chunk of the oil resources into the hands of a tiny cabal.

The political saliency of ethnicity comes into sharp focus in its use as 'a vote-catching mechanism' (Diamond 1988, 80; Watts and Lubeck 1983, 114) and as an instrument for winning and retaining power and for sharing scarce national resources. If class has progressively trumped ethnicity, analysis of Nigeria's political economy, which places undue premium on ethnicity at the expense of class, misses the deep structural roots of class in the colonial project and borders on the sensational.[1] After all, what the British left behind was an arsenal of artificial state and artificial institutions whose central ethos, mores and values – being a cultural paradigm of British politics – were divorced from the concrete political sociology and social anthropology of the Nigerian peoples and their traditional forms of government and governance. Shorn of the material and economic base of politics and political power in Nigeria, superstructural analysis is often superficial.

Nigeria's class structure was created through the activities of the colonial state and the trading firms – its objective handmaiden (Diamond 1988, 60). As we show below, the post-independence ruling elite followed suit by using both the state and the ruling party, with a mixed record of success vis-à-vis national growth and development. On the primitive accumulation of wealth and capital, the emergent bureaucracy/technocracy, political elite and incipient domestic capitalist class did well for themselves through, amongst others, legal and illegal access of the finances of regional agricultural marketing boards and statutory corporations, the public construction and public works sector, and the fixing of salaries and emoluments by legislators (Diamond 1988, 37, 62–3). On the latter, the practice has not changed, each time, there is no false note whatsoever across party and ideological divides, however rudimentary the latter may appear to be.

On the economic orientation of the British colonial system in Africa in general and in Nigeria in particular, Walter Rodney's 1982 seminal work, *How Europe underdeveloped Africa* has been very illuminating. Four insights from him are particularly apposite here. One, the dialectical relationship between Europe's development and Africa's underdevelopment: 'colonialism was not merely a system of exploitation, but one whose essential purpose was to repatriate the profits to the so-called mother country. From an African viewpoint, that amounted to consistent expatriation of surplus produced by African labour out of African resources. It meant a development of Europe as part of the same dialectical process in which Africa was underdeveloped' (Rodney 1982, 149). Two, the specific Nigerian type: whereas less than a half million Europeans had 12 modern hospitals devoted to their health, 40 million Nigerians could only access 52 hospitals. Also, the Lever Brothers that took over in 1929 from the Niger Company (which operated in the country between 1885 and 1897, as a chartered company with full governmental and police powers) simply continued the practice of the country's ruthless exploitation (Rodney 1982, 211). The third point is that Rodney considers the loss of power by the colonised to the colonisers as the most important variable in relations between the two, suggesting that the former could not defend its national interests against British superior firepower and sheer coercion. Thus for him, 'when one society finds itself forced to relinquish power entirely to another society that in itself is a form of underdevelopment' (224). Finally, the continent's arrested development as the product of the removal of the African people from history, through the pre-mediated colonial policy of non-industrialisation of the continent, is the culmination of the subjection of the African people to colonial brutality (225).

The result is that the inherited economic structures were not properly adapted for competition in the extremely rough and unequal terrain of the global economy (Huxtable 1998, 281). For all the massive positive (and negative) changes wrought by the post-civil war oil economy on the Nigerian polity, the continuities and cumulative impact of inherited structures of governance adumbrated above have, more than anything else, defined the country's economic environment (Forrest 1986, 4026). This explains why, for instance – and as detailed below – the gains of economic indigenisation in the short-lived oil boom years of the 1970s were not harnessed in the 1980s, but, rather, were all but wiped out by subsequent orthodox market reforms. The consequence is that the process of class formation has been intensified even though it has hardly resulted in issues and ideas-based politics. This is so, according to Bienen (1983, 102), partly because 'neither peasant organisations nor trade unions in the industrial sector have been strong organisations pushing for redistribution of income'. Similarly, 'people in the urban informal sector similarly have not constituted a force for effective radical change'. Political power and its attendant resource control is the principal thing and those who control it are placed in a pole position to control virtually everything else. Thus, where the modern formal sector industries more or less monopolise direct state subsidies, joint venture monopolies, and tariff protection and, by so doing, unify the ruling elite around the protection of its privileges, peasants and other informal sector producers are hardly organised as a political force. This explains why, 'they have been largely ineffective in protesting state's relative neglect of their specific needs' (Watts and Lubeck 1983, 138).

The Nigerian postcolonial state

In light of our discussion above, three preliminary remarks are in order. One, there should be no illusion whatsoever about the repercussion of structural imperialism: externally-imposed states of colonial vintage have historically proved more extraverted than introverted (Reno 1998, 107). The Nigerian state was sucked, at independence, into the vortex of unequal relations and false partnership with former colonial (and other Western) powers at the expense of a genuine social compact with the Nigerian people. Two, as an archetypal neo-colony, Nigeria has appeared trapped since independence between two social logics: the imperative of popular democratisation and people-friendly and genuine development on the one hand, and the stranglehold of structural imperialism and neo-colonialism, on the other. Fifty years on, the latter logic remains ascendant.

The third point is about the artificiality of the state and its effects on the other sectors of the Nigerian society. As an institutional framework, the colonial state's principal objective of maintaining law and order by all means possible in order to extort all sorts of legal and illegal taxes is unsuitable for the running of the most elementary form of constitutional democracy, let alone the construction of a democratic developmental state. As Beckman (1982, 45) reminded us long ago, 'law and order is never abstract and classless. It is defined by the class character of the state'. Nigerian nationalists hardly learned any worthwhile lesson about how to run a complex, modern state, except, of course, the use to which the state's hard power could be put to suppress both genuine and imaginary political opponents. On this score, Jackson (1993, 139) is clear. We quote him *in extenso*:

> The territorial governments established during the colonial era were themselves not very substantial or elaborate. In most cases, they were little more than elementary bureaucracies with limited personnel and finances and were more comparable to rural county governments in Europe than to modern independent States. They governed large territories and populations with tiny staffs and finances; probably the most cost-effective governments of modern times. And they usually did not and could not alter fundamentally the underlying political culture of the small-scale traditional African societies in their jurisdiction which continued to shape the understanding and behaviour of most Africans. However, it was these foreign structures Africans would claim and inherit when the time came for independence.

Jackson concluded that:

> The colonial jurisdictions and organisations rather than the traditional political systems became the new States of Sub-Saharan Africa and therein perhaps is the root of the very great difficulty Africans in all parts of the vast continent have had in adjusting to the States system. In short, the modern State in most cases operating on a scale greater than anything that existed hitherto was superimposed upon the continent from outside. It is still in many respects an alien institution. *Africa became an overseas extension of European sovereignty* (emphasis mine).

Oyinbo (1971, 9) sums up the phenomenon as follows: 'neither the British nor the Nigerians fully realised how vital the British presence was to the operation of a system which contained gross imbalance, was rooted in an alien culture and the product of another nation's history'. It is this disconnection and dissonance between the cultures and logics of the contending paradigms that explain democratic impasse, post-independence electoral malfeasance and the perennial transition from authoritarian politics to formal political liberalism. This partly explains why elected post-military governments are often little more than the continuation of military rule by other means. This is something that much of the mainstream literature on the country's post-independence political economy has either completely ignored or been unable to explain satisfactorily.

How to apprehend the nature and character of the specific Nigerian postcolonial state, in particular the specificity of the country's artificial state? The contemporary literature is dominated by two mutually reinforcing perspectives. The first perspective – structuralist in essence – contends that the state is a product of Western colonialism and traces the harsh, arbitrary and predatory predilection of the state to its colonial origins. The second insight – essentially agential – argues that African political elite and governments have been involved in adapting, indigenising, tropicalising, appropriating and re-inventing the postcolonial state and are, to that extent, partly responsible for the state's pathologies and malfeasance. The latter perspective seems to valorise the importance of the relative autonomy of the ruling elite but in a decidedly less sanguine manner such that 'whilst Africans have arguably ended up with the type of state they did not bargain for, it is one whose transformation appears to continually elude them' (Obadare and Adebanwi 2009, 508).

Arguably the most important function of the postcolonial state in a typical developing economy has been that of class formation with the state itself being a critical means of production (Mustapha 1986, 86; Miliband in Ekekwe 1986, 18; Diamond 1988, 50). One way this is done, in view of the state's extreme openness to Western and oriental imperialism and transnational capital, is that the latter and domestic capital deflects popular pressures for popular reforms and radical change. Capital readily gets united against social forces that are opposed to it, suggesting that real power may effectively reside in big business and trans-national capital (Beckman 1982, 39; Beckman 1988). Within this context, the state is defined as a captured category that lacks relative autonomy in relation to both domestic and transnational capital, even though it is more tied and beholden to the latter than to the former. It has been suggested that the Nigerian state has triple character. One, it serves transnational capital, by establishing and enhancing the conditions of capitalist accumulation for both foreign and domestic capital. Two, it is a most useful and much sought-after organ of control, domination and extraction in the hands of the ruling elite. Because political power has been about the most significant – and easiest – route to economic power, the competition for its control routinely pits the different fractions against one another in what are classical political wars of attrition.

Thus, members of the different factions – military-commercial, bureaucratic, political, intellectual, cultural, chiefly estate and so on – smart and lucky enough to access and stay in power for only a couple of years are assured handsome and rounded dividends from the use of the state as a private resource.[2] Having acquired a thick financial muscle, such men – and women – would, thenceforth, always be available to contest coveted political offices in the land, almost always at higher levels. Several analysts (see, for instance, Bienen 1983, 102–3; Diamond 1988, 77–8; Kalu 1996, 236; Momoh 1996, 155–6; Osoba 1978; Falola and Ihonvbere 1985) have underlined the umbilical cord between political power and private accumulation in the Nigerian post-colony. On the emerging Nigerian ruling elite in the 1960s and 1970s, Osoba (1978, 377) made the following observation: 'many of them were perceptive enough to realise that, in view of the general poverty in the country and the scarcity of capital, good connections with government and the parties controlling them were indispensable if their ambition for wealth were not to remain a mere pipe dream'. As the next section shows, since the 1980s, this phenomenon has worsened from the perspective of social change and genuine national development.

But why has it been relatively easy for the Nigerian ruling elite to subvert the public ethos of the state and sabotage its historic role of delivering basic security and welfare services to the mass of the people? How to explain what Kalu (1996, 240) calls 'the invariable lack of respect and indifference to the legitimacy of the state in Nigeria that seems to run along ethnic lines' and the fact that 'individually and collectively, Nigerians have tended not to have allegiance to the state-nation imposed by the British in 1914?' We return to the thesis of the artificial state. Thus, in addition to Kalu's observation, if most Nigerians see the country's ruling elite as 'distant, selfish and lacking in integrity' (Lewis 2003, 131), it is a combination of the structural imperatives of the Nigerian state since the colonial period that drives a wedge between governors and governed; the dissonance between the ethics and praxis of politics such that public venality including the privatisation of the state has virtually become a directive principle of state policy; and the disconnect between the civic public realm and the civic primordial realm. After all, the ruling elite knows no other state aside the one handed over to them by the British colonial system.

Thus, when Nigerian politicians and bureaucrats/technocrats massively defraud the state, what transpires is not so much that the state is thereby weakened and its delivery and performance capacity reduced, as Chabal (2009, 131) has argued, as that this is merely a reflection of the original weakness and alienation of the state. As public sector venality and corruption has deepened over the past decades – with the state constantly in a mutually corrupt relationship with transnational capital (in particular oil multinationals) and big business – and largely goes unpunished, impunity sets in, with all the unsettling consequences for public policy and mass welfare. This is how crony capitalism has developed, the domestic arrow-head being 'a rougish power elite (that) continues to destroy Nigeria's promise' (Uwazurike 2007, 91).

But could the Nigerian ruling elite have behaved differently? This is another way of expressing the role of agency in the context of capitalist stranglehold. Though the logic of capitalism in operation in a classic peripheral context such as Nigeria dictates a subordinate role for the Nigerian state and ruling elite, nothing suggests that the role is or has to be static. Yet, the state continues to be too weak to realise whatever nationalistic intentions it harbours (Beckman 1982, 39, 41; Osoba 1978, 63). If, as suggested by Osoba (1978, 66, 65) it is a ruling elite that has tended to 'acquiesce in the structure of dependence and try to make it work as much as possible in their own interest' rather than to 'create a relatively independent and autonomous domestic capital economy order in Nigeria' it is largely because of the formidable constraints arraigned against it. The ruling elite is ensconced here between self-perception and self-reality: if the ruling elite can achieve the latter as an objective interest, why should it settle for the former – subjective interest – and a system that is anything but sustainable?

For all the artificiality of the state and the shenanigans of the ruling elite, the Nigerian state has, however, not been used systematically for only the wrong reasons. It has also been deployed for the right reasons. Nowhere has this come to sharper focus than in the policy of state creation as a response to popular demands for a less lopsided federal system, a more inclusive political system and a more equitable distribution of national resources. Yet, the exercise – the last of which, in 1996, saw the number of states swell up to 36 – has changed very little; only the form, but not the substance, of federalism has altered. A skewed federal structure and a lucrative oil-driven mono-cultural economy have been used as a relatively effective weapon of political hegemony and mass demobilisation by the ruling elite (Ekwe-Ekwe 1985, 619). The policy of state creation has further accentuated the process of class formation and contributed to the solidification of the ruling elite. This is because of the race to the top and the centralisation of power and resources the process, rather paradoxically, has spawned. To the extent that the majority of the states are small, inefficient, ineffective and ineffectual particularly from the standpoint of economic viability and social provisioning, they have become increasingly marginalised in relation to the powerful central government. The negative impact of state creation on class formation from the prism of the subordinated classes is reinforced by an economy that continues to suffer from insignificant productive capacity. This is because 'the issue of new states falls in the realm of distribution and consumption, not production and meaningful development' (Diamond 1988, 179). We now turn our attention to the major elements of the political economy.

Elite protectionism: From economic nationalism to economic globalisation

The description of Nigeria as a 'mixed economy' mirrors the tension, since the colonial era, between external control of the country's big market and attempts by the ruling elite to regulate key aspects of the economy in both their interest and in the public interest. It would appear that the tension between state-managed capitalism and so-called free market capitalism was hardly informed by any form of progressive ideology of development though it was ideology all the same, contrary to mainstream thinking. Thus, the choice of the former was a pragmatic policy thrust informed by the need not only to keep the dominant class factions in power happy but to also satisfy the loud calls for economic nationalism by progressive elements from within and outside the state. Driven by stupendous earnings from the rather short-lived 'oil boom' period of the early 1970s, statist economic ideologies have tended to decline as dependence on shrinking oil revenues grew. Variants of market reforms by successive post-second republic military regimes (Buhari, Babangida and Abacha) and the post-military restoration governments of Obasanjo (1999–2007) and Yar'Adua/Jonathan (2007 to date) appeared to have sounded the death knell for economic nationalism.

There is some evidence, however, that if the indigenisation policy had to wait till the end of the civil war, it was not for lack of interest by the managers of the first republic. The following lamentation in 1961 by Waziri Ibrahim, federal government's Minister for Economic Development (in the heyday of the Cold War), is perhaps an unmistakable proof of Western powers' determination to defend their privileged turf in Nigeria:

> If we want to really set about improving the economy of our country in a particular way, they say we are communists. They can make our countrymen suspect our every move. If they do not succeed by false propaganda, by calling us all sorts of names, if they fail to make us unpopular in order to win their case, they arrange assassination. They can do it

> by poison or by setting our own people against us. They can go to any extent without discrimination (cited in Ekekwe 1986, 97).

To all appearances, the 1972 economic indigenisation policy, officially designated as the Nigerian Enterprises Promotion Decree (NEPD) and its 1976 successor Act, were meant to benefit, on the one hand, the state and the ruling elite and, on the other, the emergent indigenous capitalist class in a win-win situation (Kraus 2002, 396). The rationale was to make public ownership (or controlling interests in 'strategic' industries for reasons of economic nationalism) a vehicle for accelerated economic development; for increasing substantially the low percentage contribution (less than 10%) of the manufacturing sector to the GNP; and for a better disciplining of transnational capital (Biersteker 1983, 192; Momoh 1996, 155–6). It was also an attempt to become more attentive to – and supportive of – a moderately thriving commercial class (and an emergent organised private sector) which had its humble beginnings in the nineteenth century but whose growth was stunted by colonial economic policy (Kraus 2002, 397; Osaghae 1998, 29, 48). In a nutshell, whereas the first schedule of the decree reserved about 26 mostly small-scale economic activities exclusively to Nigerians, the second required sale of 40% equity to Nigerians through stock sales. The 1976 Act, which impacted on the general economic thrust of the state into the 1980s, gave further vent to the policy preferences of economic nationalism through the agency of its state capitalist and nationalist orientation (Kraus 2002, 409–10). The limitations and possible failure of economic nationalism as well as the probable decrease in Nigerian control of the economy (Biersteker 1983, 202; Akinsanya 1983, 162; Joseph 1978, 224) may have been because state centrality in the economy was hardly accompanied by 'rational strategic planning, less corruption and more political accountability' (Nyang'oro and Shaw 1998, 33) on the part of the ruling elite. Furthermore, except in the critical financial sector, the objective to achieve a greater local control of the economy was hardly realised. Biersteker (1983, 2002) cogently explains the fate that befell indigenisation:

> There (were) no counterincentives for investments in indigenously controlled enterprises, hence the programme undermine(d) the basis of accumulation by a national, capitalist class... Indigenisation (encouraged) a comprador role for local business in a society already plagued by strong comprador tendencies. Accordingly, indigenisation may have contributed to a decrease, rather than an increase, in Nigerian control of the economy.

Centred mainly in the oil sector over which the state, transnational capital (typified by Western oil majors) and the ruling elite hold sway, venality has grown to become an effective brake on the country's development. The centrality of the oil economy (that has made Nigeria no more than a rent-collecting state) where oil money is 'a huge slush fund and politics is about getting control over it' (Lewis 2003, 136), is not only emblematic of the country's economic crisis since the mid-1980s, it is also a veritable crisis situation on its own (Ayadi 2005; Herbst and Olukoshi 1994). Not only did too much dependence on oil lead to the neglect of the non-oil sector in general and agriculture in particular, the latter had, by the mid 1970s, been unable to meet the domestic food needs of Nigerians (Ross 2003, 14; Joseph 1978, 232). Rents from oil that have accounted for between 21 and 48% of GDP since 1974 'has done little to raise incomes and alleviate poverty' (Ross 2003, 2). Hosman (2009, 609–32) has shown that in the interface between developing countries and oil majors, whereas Nigeria successfully negotiated for more control over the latter between 1960 and 1979, the ruling elite would subsequently reverse itself in a dramatic about-turn during which concessions were given back to the transnationals and indigenisation laws were all but repealed. Local participation in the critical oil industry was halted. Attributing this inexplicable anti-nationalistic and pro-capital policy reversal to corruption, Hosman (2009, 610) argued that the net effect was 'the eventual inability of the indigenous populations to develop the monitoring, operating and supervisory skills necessary to reduce dependence on the corporations'.

Successive military regimes in the 1980s and 1990s also pandered to the interest of trans-national capital. The Buhari military junta (1984–1985), in an attempt to transform the moribund agricultural sector, amended the 1972 NEPD to allow non-Nigerians to own up to 80% of large farm projects. While some large-scale absentee farmers close to the junta applauded the policy, this was a major policy blunder because until then, 'Nigeria was one of those few third world countries (considering its size) where foreign capital ownership of land was negligible' (Ekwe-Ekwe 1985, 198, 622, 624). The Babangida regime (1985–1993), on its part, was credited with some important market reforms between 1986 and 1992 in areas such as exchange rate, privatisation, and scrapping of marketing boards (hitherto infamous for crass exploitation of peasant farmers). It was claimed that these reforms eliminated 'some of the most glaring inefficiencies in the Nigeria economy and provided significant incentives to expand the non-oil sector'. The lamentation, however, is that 'there is very little evidence, despite strenuous attempts by the government, that politics in Nigeria was transformed in any significant manner' (Herbst and Olukoshi 1994, 499). The formalism gap between the theory and practice of market reforms is due to several factors, chief amongst these the following: the further retrenchment of the state and its material resources into the hands of foreign capital and its local hireling by liberalisation and privatisation policies; and the exclusion of the popular classes. In addition, a new crop of supporters of the Babangida – as well as the Abacha regime – who had made fortunes from the reforms through an intimate relation among the state, capital and business would become prominent actors in the politics of the fourth republic.

The Obasanjo government's *National Economic Empowerment and Development Strategies* (NEEDS), echoing the Abacha government's *Vision 2020*, was conceptualised as an economic reform programme anchored in the private sector and as the principal engine of growth and development. This neo-liberal policy was, however, characterised by the inability of the state to discipline capital. As in the past, this was evident in the oil industry and in the hegemony of the military-business complex, which was dominated by the country's retired military elite and *Corporate Nigeria* (Amuwo 2009a, 46). The Yar'Adua government, which may be regarded, in economic policy terms, as the continuation of the Obasanjo government by other means, sought to expand the frontiers of its predecessor's market-friendly reforms especially in the rationalisation of the key banking industry. Before his death in May 2010, ill-health appeared to have hindered President Umaru Yar'Adua from being as hands-on in economic reforms as he would probably have liked.

The summary of the foregoing is that the Nigerian state has failed to regulate and discipline transnational capital in the national interest. The harvest – reminiscent of

Argentina's crisis of neo-liberalism and the ensuing popular uprising in December 2001 – has been a development strategy blighted by unequal trade, uncontrolled foreign investment and a bourgeoning external debt (Gélinas 2003, 80). With the oil economy in the hands of a cabal and benefiting the ruling elite and a trifle of the population linked to it, the vast majority of Nigerians have been left out in the cold. In the race to the bottom that the logic of the reforms has imposed, the middle class, labour and the peasantry have been the most victimised. According to Osoba (1978, 74), 'the Nigerian bourgeoisie are the social engineers fuelling and servicing the engines of economic, political and cultural oppression planted in (Nigeria) by the world imperialist powers and their (TNCs)'. Progressive social and political non-state forces – organised labour, academics, journalists, human rights NGOs, labour, lawyers, doctors and other professionals, students and the youth, and women – as well as the peasantry have, collectively and sectorally, resisted state policies considered as pro-capital, anti-people and anti-developmental. These social forces have been driven to challenge the status quo (Huxtable 1998, 281).

Resistance politics

Three preliminary remarks are necessary here. One, for all the popular struggles by the Nigerian Left, workers, students and peasants since 1960, there has been an absence of a systematic linkage between progressive political struggle and progressive political formations/parties, which could have harnessed the gains of the struggle for social change (Momoh 1996). Two, since the early 1990s, the key social forces identified above appeared to have lost the cutting edge of the anti-imperialist struggle of yore. The 1990s coincided with triumphal capitalism (on the altar of the demise of socialist practice in the USSR and elsewhere), the ascendancy of the ideology of 'there is no alternative' (TINA) to free market economy, and attempts at de-politicising progressive social forces globally. Since then, there has been a high-wire political struggle in politics and in the media, as far as political grammar and language is concerned. The struggle has been between *the vanished terms* (state, politics, power, classes, class struggle, social change, alternatives, revolutions and ideologies) and *their insipid replacement*, namely governance, communities, social partners, poverty, consensus, alternation (Amin 2006, 22). Three, notwithstanding Nigeria's highly mediatised primordial cleavages, the battle lines between the Nigerian ruling elite and the leaders of resistance politics are generally drawn along class lines. Even when protests are about the enhancement of sectoral interests, they are generally linked to the national democratic agenda, as the political struggle of university lecturers (under the aegis of the Academic Staff Union of Universities (ASUU) and, to some extent, university students (regrouped under the National Association of Nigerian Students (NANS)) have shown over the past decades (Amuwo 1999; Jega 1995; Shettima 1993).

'Resistance', writes Gélinas (2003, 228) from a global perspective, 'is an expression of free citizens that refuse to be impressed by a destructive system they have not chosen. Resisting with all their strength the savage appropriation of the world by a handful of oligopolies, the privatisation of the human genome, the tinkering with our food, the commodification of our air and the poisoning of our water is today becoming an imperative for every free woman and man'. With an ever present ferment of radical politics waiting to be unlocked and activated, resistance to the Nigerian ruling elite has come from several sources and taken multiple forms. Beckman (1982, 42–4; 1988, 30–44) and Momoh (1996, 157–8) have shown that resistance to the Nigerian state has come, inter alia, from workers and petty commodity producers, as well as from petty bourgeois, small, fringe and marginalised capitalists. The latter comes with a tinge of enlightened self-interest in that their survival is not guaranteed by the state's monopolistic arrangements and politics. At the elite level, resistance is essentially reformist such as when one coup regime supplants another – even though coup regimes have, in the past, been seen by sections of the popular classes as an opportunity for a new beginning. Politics of resistance at the elite level reached its apogee during the civil war. At the popular level, resistance has been spearheaded by majority and minority ethno-nationalities, the Niger Delta debacle being emblematic of the latter (Osaghae 2001; Amuwo 2009b; Ikelegbe 2001). On account of the ruling elite's long-standing neglect of the citizenship and nationalist grievances of the Niger Delta coupled with violent repression of the people's protests in tandem with the oil majors, the resistance has changed, in the past decade or so, from acts of defiance and civil disobedience to unambiguous demands for self-determination and (oil) resource control (Obi 2008; Omeje 2006; Osaghae 2001). Ethnic militias bent on defending and enhancing the interests of the majority ethno-nationalities have equally sprung up since the advent of the fourth republic (Guichaoua 2010).

Resistance to the Nigerian state and the ruling elite has regularly come from organised labour/trade unions that have largely remained evergreen, vibrant and militant since the colonial era, defending workers' rights often at great costs to the unions and their leaders. As in the famous 1945 General Strike in favour of appreciable wage increases within the context of a steep rise in the cost of living (Diamond 1988, 163), notable labour strikes in June 1964, May 1981 and several others since then have centred mainly on workers' wages (Momoh 1996, 163ff; Aiyede 2004). Students, university faculty, women, and the press have been at the forefront of nationwide protests against the negative consequences of market reforms for the country's political economy. The 1968/1969 Agbekoya Peasant Uprising in western Nigeria, led by Tafa Adeoye, against the routine exploitation of poor (but not rich) farmers by the state through higher taxes (a classic exploitation of class contradictions within the peasantry), exaction by corrupt officials, cheating by produce buyers and the marketing board (Ekekwe 1986, 71; Mustapha 1986, 88) perhaps testifies to emergent peasant political consciousness. The same goes for the April 1980 Bakolori peasant revolt at the Sokoto-Rima Basin Development Scheme against their displacement by the state and big capital (Momoh 1996, 161–3; Beckman 1982, 51). The Agbekoya declaration is a reading in defiant politics: 'from now on there shall be no more elections as far as we are concerned. We have all decided not to support any political party any more and we shall not vote for any one party any longer. We have had enough' (Ekekwe 1986, 71). Further, class or popular resistance has been disguised by religious forms and symbols. For instance, the *Yan Tatsine Millenarian Movement* of December 1980 led by Mohammed Marawa has been described as 'an overt critique of the materialism and inequality that has accompanied the petroleum boom in Nigeria' (Watts and Lubeck 1983, 142). Similarly, the emergence of *Boko Haram* fundamentalists (*Boko Haram* translates to 'forbidding everything Western, including Western education') who wreaked havoc in parts of northern Nigeria in July 2009 to drive home their demands for the imposition of Sharia rule across the country and the abolition of Western education on the grounds that it is evil has been explained by the failure of governance in the country (Abati 2009).

It is small wonder, therefore, that resistance politics has had a rich harvest: 'from 1970 to 2005, the Nigerian state witnessed over 150 riots, strikes, demonstrations, mini-civil wars, religious mayhem and organised peasant uprisings alone – much of (it) attributable to the economic insecurities of the dysfunctional state, whether under the military or the men in *agbada*' (Uwazurike 2007, 84). However popular grievances have been articulated and whatever form resistance has taken, it would appear that the ultimate strategic goal has remained how to dislodge the country's neo-conservative political establishment from power and set in motion a great popular revival for political change. The fact that this goal has proved elusive till this date is an eloquent testimony to the limitations of popular resistance as well as the success of the state, ruling elite and transnational capital in undercutting popular pressures for social change. This twin phenomenon can be explained by three mutually reinforcing factors.

The first is that while the various sectoral and ethno-nationalist struggles have increasingly become more political and linked to the national democratic agenda, state and capital have had very little difficulty in using ethnicity to demobilise and depoliticise popular struggles. The initial pan-Nigerian political struggle forged for the recovery of the presidential mandate MKO Abiola won in the June 12, 1993 elections (the country's least ethnicised and most successful election thus far), but that later degenerated into a near solo Yoruba run due to the state's use of inducement and coercion is a major case in point. The second is that since workers' and peasants' alienation and exploitation at the shop-floor level in the formal or wage economy is vitiated – or compensated for – at the informal level by access to the moral and social solidarity inherent in the country's communal life (Uwazurike 2007, 89), means revolutionary pressures do not build up as quickly as expected. Finally, while Nigeria has always been ripe for progressive social change, it is not clear if the anti-military and pro-democracy forces, wearied by the long and bloody struggle against repressive military rule from 1984 to 1999, are still intact. This is because of the increasing depoliticisation of the country's rich array of CSOs and NGOs and their strategic subordination to rampant neo-liberalism. Since 1999, Nigeria – like post-1994 South Africa – has become very safe for super-exploitation by capitalist globalisation, transnational capital and the ruling elite. Popular resistance appears increasingly trumped by the protectionism of the state and capital.

What is to be done?

The summary of this piece is that since 1960 the Nigerian people have had to deal with the crisis of a neo-conservative macro politics, policy and ideology derivative of the constraints imposed by a combination of epochal colonial legacy, structural imperialism, transnational capital, postcolonial state and the ruling elite. In future, Nigerian governments need praxis – that is, 'practice combined with a critical approach' (Gélinas 2003, 187) – akin to *business as unusual* or risk entrenching themselves in the same pit of *business as usual* where promises of political change are not matched by political practice.

But how to proceed? There are two ways of doing so and these are probably not mutually exclusive: pragmatically and radically. That is to say, respectively, through a cumulative reform process and an anti-capitalist/anti-imperialist development trajectory. There is a reformist process in place which, while not fitting the bill of the thrust of this article, is already too radical for the country's structure of class domination (Diamond 1988, 30). This pragmatic approach is anchored in the various struggles adumbrated above as well as in the ameliorative and service provisioning role of CSOs and NGOs at both *treetop* and *grassroots* levels. This would notably include the monitoring and performance evaluation work of governments at all levels that the Nigerian section of Transparency International (TI) is doing. It is an eminently significant political work that cannot be ignored. According to Bilikisu Yusuf (in Maier 2000, 302), a scion of TI, 'we are the majority and the elite who manipulate all these things are a tiny minority, powerful yes, but they cannot compete with us... civil society must hold them to account and refuse to let them get away with it'. Tied to this is the hope that has, since the 1990s, been routinely expressed in 'the resurgent rule-setting and watchdog role of the civil society' as well as constitutionalism 'to check the arbitrariness of state management and to enhance the quality of leadership' (Osaghae 1998, 318).

The pragmatic approach has its limits, however. In the face of the legacy of colonialism and the spin-off effects of structural imperialism and transnational capital, this approach has failed to reduce domestic inequality, a national minimalist development agenda. For Bratton (2008, 631) this consists of 'the attainment of a measure of socio-economic development that reduces existing inequalities between political elites and ordinary citizens'. The approach would find it difficult to cope with a more radical interpretation of the work of civil society as 'the people in the face of power' and an organised citizenry in action. In the words of Gélinas (2003, 194), 'the source of all power lies in the people and its grassroots organisations. Only an organised people aware of its strength can defy the two other great powers: the oligopoly lobby and the state'. One reason for this is that most Nigerians are *stricto sensu,* subjects, not citizens, by virtue of a fractured and artificial postcolonial state with which they have had very little positive relations since independence. To bring the Nigerian people meaningfully back into politics would require an initial deliberate process of politicising (and *politicalising,* that is, bringing them back to the public sphere and space) and conscientising workers and the peasantry. The goal would be to empower them to understand their unique identity in the socio-economic and political relations of power and production; to appreciate class struggle as the 'motor of economic and political development', as well as realise that their objective interests are not coterminous with those of the ruling elite and transnational capital (Ekwekwe 1986, 190).

Only a radical or revolutionary approach can do this. One is here reminded of Albert Einstein's famous dictum that *no problem can be solved with the mindset that created it* (Gélinas 2003, 188). Osoba (1978, 77) sees a revolutionary solution to the crisis in Nigeria's political economy in the creation of a people's revolutionary movement as the product of the combination of the 'rich practical experience of life' of the masses and the intellectuals' theoretical knowledge'. To succeed, all anti-imperialist and anti-capitalist groups are called upon to arm themselves and the people with 'a genuine revolutionary culture and a discipline and invincible revolutionary organisation, unshakable commitment to the principles of social justice and equity, to the liberation of our people from material and cultural deprivations and implacably opposed to all forms of exploitation'. Amin (2006, 14) and Jones (2005) concur by underlining the need for subordinate classes to seek to transcend the logics of capitalism and imperialism in their effort to create a 'social Nigeria' where capitalism is tempered and disciplined by a pan-Nigerian social compass between capital and labour.

Contrary to the make-believe by the ideologues of capitalist globalisation, realistic alternatives are certainly possible. The problem is that not only the masses, but also the country's opportunistic ruling elite have seemingly become convinced that globalisation is 'inevitable and inescapable' and that 'those who oppose it are... unrealistic or idealistic' (Gélinas 2003, 183). Did not President Obasasanjo say, for instance, that globalisation has come to stay, suggesting that Nigerians should imbibe its tenets hook, line and sinker? Because the country's developmental challenges are a function of both domestic and external factors, political economy changes at the internal level without a corresponding fundamental alteration of the external context is not likely to produce the desired result. Similarly, the demand for global justice needs to be anchored in a foundation of domestic justice. A major element of the latter would be the participation of both genders on equal footing. The rationale for this is that the global order cannot be based on the economic exploitation of 4/5th of mankind – any more than a national system cannot be anchored in the socio-political exclusion and economic marginalisation of over half of the citizenry (Gélinas 2003, 238). Going beyond capitalism would also entail weaning Nigeria out of oil, in order to break the stranglehold of capital and the state on the mono-cultural economy that has served them so well and begin the onerous task of diversifying the economy. Unless this is done, massive proven oil and natural gas reserves may go to waste. According to an estimate, oil reserves are between 24 and 31.5 billion barrels (which, at the current production rate of 2 million barrels daily, may last between 32 and 43 years) compared to a staggering 124 trillion cubic feet of natural gas reserves, the ninth largest in the world (Ross 2003, 3).

Finally, while pragmatic reforms may be useful, only by radicalising the struggle for democracy and for the construction of a genuine Nigerian state through class struggle will Nigeria be saved.

Notes

1. Thus, Karl Maier (2000, xx) misses the point when he argues that 'ethnic and religious prejudices have found fertile ground in Nigeria, where there is neither a national consensus nor a binding ideology' and that the vote 'often has little meaning other than the opportunity to promote the champion of one's ethnic group or region'. MKO Abiola's landslide electoral victory (to cite only this example) in the annulled 12 June 1993 national elections (including, notably, in Kano State from where hailed his opponent, Bashir Tofa), is a major rebuttal of the ethnicity paradigm. In this context, it appears sensible to ignore the rather simplistic (and misleading) explanation ascribed to a retired soldier that the Yoruba people did not vote for Obasanjo in 1999 because 'he was [*sic*] a retired former general' (ibid, 295). Further, whereas he rightly concedes that Nigeria is 'a colonial construct' (ibid, xxviii) as well as 'the bastard child of imperialism, its rich mosaic of peoples locked into a nation-state they had no part in designing' (ibid, 7), Maier (2000, xxvii) sensationally announces the *raison d'être* of his book, *this house has fallen* (with the almost apocalyptic sub-title of *Midnight in Nigeria*) as that of portraying 'the most intractable crisis points and the ethnic and regional tensions threatening the survival of

what is perhaps the largest failed state in the third world'. In light of the interrogation of the British colonial legacy attempted in this piece, it can be argued that since there is not yet a Nigeria house, it could not have fallen! It is, in any case, extremely difficult to see how a colonial construct *in toto* could simultaneously be independent Africa's 'show case for democracy' except, of course, if one buys into the self-serving British colonial historiography of the period. With typical foreboding, Maier (2000, 301) concluded his chronicling of the country's *history in a hurry* as follows: 'By early 2000, there appeared to be scant reason for optimism. There were simply too many problems, too much anger, and too little time. *Nigeria seemed to be an approaching tropical firestorm* and there was nothing the new civilian government, however honorable its intentions, could do to stop it' (italics mine). And that was barely six months into the post-military Obasanjo government. The point to emphasise here is that the dominant neo-liberal analytical framework in African/ist scholarship, informed as it is by the theoretical understanding of colonialism as an episodic event in African history, misses the structural/epochal/watershed nature of colonialism. Once the latter is edited out of the analysis, what comes to the fore is a wretched populist analysis that ends up demonising the state *qua* state and praises ordinary Africans' 'extraordinary dynamism and ingenuity such that once the heavy hand of the state had been removed there would be scope for genuine developmental progress' (Chabal 2009, 10).

2. The seeming unbridled and untamed enmeshment of structures, interests and power has resulted in high-level public scandals, bribery and corruption. A most contemporary one is the N27 billion Halliburton bribery scandal in which about 80 Nigerian and foreigners representing the top echelons of the country's political and military establishment and technocrats – including four ex-heads of state, two of their wives, ex-governors and ministers – were indicted in April 2010 by the US law enforcement officials in engaging in a decade-long bribing scheme to secure contracts in Nigeria (Umejei 2010). Further, from the standpoint of our structural/class analysis, it is understandable why, around the same time, the Nigerian senate, in amending the 1999 Constitution, deleted Section 66 (1) (h) which disqualifies a person from standing for election once they had been indicted by a panel of inquiry (*The Guardian* 2010).

References

Abati, R. 2009. Boko Haram and the evil of ignorance. *The Guardian*, 31 July.

Aiyede, E. 2004. United we stand: Labour unions and human rights NGOs in the democratisation process in Nigeria. *Development in Practice* 14, nos. 1–2: 224–33.

Aiyede, E. 2009. The political economy of fiscal federalism and the dilemma of constructing a developmental state in Nigeria. *International Political Science Review* 30, no. 3: 249–79.

Akinsanya, A. 1983. State strategies toward Nigerian and foreign business. In *The political economy of Nigeria*, ed. I. Zartman, 145–84. New York: Praeger.

Amin, S. 2006. *Beyond US hegemony? Assessing the prospects for a multi-polar world.* New York: Zed.

Amuwo, A. 2009a. The political economy of Nigeria's post-military elections, 1999–2007. *Review of African Political Economy (ROAPE)* 39, no. 119: 37–61.

Amuwo, A. 2009b. Towards a new political economy of the Niger Delta question in Nigeria. *Politikon: South African Journal of Political Studies* 36, no. 2: 237–57.

Amuwo, A. 2009c. Capitalist globalisation and the role of the international community in resource conflicts in Africa. *Africa Development* 34, nos. 3–4: 227–67.

Amuwo, A. 1999. *Confronting the crisis of the university in Africa: Nigerian academics and their many struggles.* Harare: African Association of Political Science.

Ayadi, O. 2005. Oil price fluctuations in the Nigerian economy. *OPEC Review* 29, no. 3: 199–217.

Azikiwe, N. 1965. Essentials for Nigerian survival. *Foreign Affairs* April: 447–61.

Beckman, B. 1988. Peasants and democratic struggles in Nigeria. *ROAPE* 15, no. 41: 30–44.

Beckman, B. 1982. Whose state? State and capitalist development in Nigeria. *ROAPE* 23, no. 1: 37–51.

Bienen, H. 1983. Income distribution and politics in Nigeria. In *The political economy of Nigeria*, ed. I. Zartman, 85–104. New York: Praeger.In Zartman.
Biersteker, T. 1983. Indigenization in Nigeria: Renationalization or denationalization? In *The political economy of Nigeria*, ed. I. Zartman, 185–206. New York: Praeger.
Bratton, M. 2008. Vote buying and violence in Nigerian election campaigns. *Electoral Studies* 27: 621–32.
Chabal, P. 2009. *Africa: The politics of suffering and smiling*. London and New York: Zed Books; Pietermaritzburg: UKZN Press.
Diamond, L. 1988. *Class, ethnicity and democracy in Nigeria: The failure of the first republic*. Houndmills: Macmillan.
Ejobowah, J. 2005. The new political economy of federal preservation: Insights from Nigerian federal practice. *Commonwealth & Comparative Politics* 43, no. 2: 178–93.
Ekekwe, E. 1986. *Class and state in Nigeria*. London and Lagos: Longman.
Ekwe-Ekwe, H. 1985. The Nigerian plight: Shagari to Buhari. *Third World Quarterly* 7, no. 3: 610–25.
Falola, T., and J. Ihonvbere. 1985. *The rise and fall of Nigeria's second republic*. London: Zed.
Forrest, T. 1986. The political economy of civil rule and the economic crisis in Nigeria (1979–84). *ROAPE* 35: 4–26.
Gélinas, J. 2003. *Juggernaut politics: Understanding predatory globalization*. London and New York: Zed.
Guichaoua, Y. 2010. How do ethnic militias perpetuate in Nigeria? A micro-level perspective on the Oodua People's Congress. *World Development* (in press).
Herbst, J., and A. Olukoshi. 1994. Nigeria: Economic and political reforms at cross purposes. In *Voting for reform: Democracy, political liberalization and economic adjustment*, ed. S. Haggard and S. Webb, 453–502. Washington, DC: World Bank.
Hosman, L. 2009. Dividing the oils: Dynamic bargaining as policy formation in the Nigerian petroleum industry. *Review of Policy Research* 26, no. 5: 609–32.
Huxtable, P. 1998. The African state toward the 21st century: Legacies of the critical juncture. In *The African state at a critical juncture between disintegration and reconfiguration*, ed. L. Villalon and P. Huxtable, 279–93. Boulder, CO and London: Lynne Rienner.
Ikelegbe, A. 2001. Civil society, oil and conflict in the Niger Delta region of Nigeria: Ramifications of civil society for a regional resource struggle. *The Journal of Modern African Studies* 39, no. 3: 437–69.
Jackson, R. 1993. Sub-Saharan Africa. In *States in a changing world: A contemporary analysis*, ed. R. Jackson and A. James, 136–56. Oxford: Clarendon.
Jega, A. 1995. Nigerian universities and academic staff under military rule. *ROAPE* 64, no. 22: 251–6.
Joseph, R. 1978. Affluence and underdevelopment: The Nigerian experience. *Journal of Modern African Studies* 16, no. 2: 221–39.
Jones, B. 2005. Rethinking African development: What is the social base of Africa's alternatives in the era of neo-liberalism? Paper read at the 11th CODESRIA General Assembly on *Rethinking African development: Beyond impasse, towards alternatives*, Maputo, 6–10 December.
Kalu, K. 1996. Political economy in Nigeria: The military, ethnic politics and development. *International Journal of Politics, Culture and Society* 10, no. 2: 229–47.
Kraus, J. 2002. Capital, power and business associations in the African political economy: A tale of two countries, Ghana and Nigeria. *Journal of Modern African Studies* 40, no. 3: 395–436.
Lewis, P. 2003. Nigeria: Elections in a fragile regime. *Journal of Democracy* 14, no. 3: 131–44.
Maier, K. 2000. *This house has fallen: Midnight in Nigeria*. New York: Public Affairs.
McKenna, J. 1969. Elements of a Nigerian peace. *Foreign Affairs* July: 668–80.
Momoh, A. 1996. Popular struggles in Nigeria, 1960–1982. *African Journal of Political Science* 1, no. 2: 154–75.
Mustapha, A. 1986. The national question and radical politics in Nigeria. *ROAPE* 37, no. 4: 81–96.
Nyang'oro, J., and T. Shaw. 1998. The African state in the global economic context. In *The African state at a critical juncture between disintegration and reconfiguration*, ed. L. Villalon and P. Huxtable, 27–42. Boulder, CO and London: Lynne Rienner.

Obadare, E., and W. Adebanwi. 2009. Transnational resource flows and the paradoxes of belonging: Redirecting the debate on transnationalism, remittances, state and citizenship in Africa. *ROAPE* 36, no. 122: 499–517.
Obi, C. 2008. *Nigeria's Niger Delta: Understanding the complex drivers of conflict.* Joint Swedish Defence Research Agency (FOI)/The Nordic Africa Institute Lecture Series on African Security no. 1.
Omeje, K. 2006. Petro-business and security threats in the Niger Delta, Nigeria. *Current Sociology* 54, no. 3: 477–99.
Osaghae, E. 1998. *Crippled giant: Nigeria since independence.* London: Hurst.
Osaghae, E. 2001. From accommodation to self-determination: Minority nationalism and the restructuring of the Nigerian state. *Nationalism and Ethnic Politics* 7, no. 1: 1–20.
Osoba, S. 1978. The deepening crisis of the Nigerian national bourgeoisie. *ROAPE* 13, no. 3: 63–77.
Oyinbo, I. 1971. *Nigeria: crisis and beyond.* London: Charles Knight.
Robbins, R. 2002. *Global problems and the culture of capitalism.* Boston: Allyn and Bacon.
Reno, W. 1998. Sierra Leone: Weak states and the new sovereignty game. In *The African state at a critical juncture between disintegration and reconfiguration*, ed. L. Villalon and P. Huxtable, 93–108. Boulder, CO and London: Lynne Rienner.
Robinson, W. 2007. Beyond the theory of imperialism: Global capitalism and the transnational state. *Societies Without Borders* 2: 5–26.
Rodney, W. 1982. *How Europe underdeveloped Africa.* Washington, DC: Howard University Press.
Ross, M. 2003. *Nigeria's oil sector and the poor.* UCLA, Department of Political Science, Los Angeles.
Shah, A. n.d. Conflicts in Africa: Introduction. Global issues (Social, Political, Economic and Environmental Issues that Affect USAII). http://www.globalissues.org/article/84/conflicts-in-africa-introduction
Shettima, K. 1993. Structural adjustment and the student movement in Nigeria. *ROAPE* 56, no. 1: 83–91.
Soyinka, W. 2006. *You must set forth at dawn.* Ibadan: Bookcraft.
Stapleton, T. 2009. Review of *Strength beyond structure: Social and historical trajectories of agency in Africa*, eds. M. de Brujin, R. van Djik, and J-B. Gewald. Leiden: Brill, 2007. In *African Affairs* 108, no. 432: 490–1.
The Guardian. 2010. Editorial: Amending the 1999 Constitution. 8 April.
Umejei, E. 2010. N27bn Halliburton scam: IBB, Abdusalami, Diya, 77 others indicted. *Daily Independent*, 15 April.
Uwazurike, C. 2007. Ikenna Nzimiro, anthropolgist, sociologist and iconoclast: On the intellectual legacies of a radical nationalist. *Dialectical Anthropology* 31, nos. 1–3: 73–97.
Watts, M., and P. Lubeck. 1983. The popular classes and the oil boom: A political economic and rural and urban poverty. In *The political economy of Nigeria*, ed. I. Zartman, 105–44. New York: Praeger.

The petroleum industry: A paradox or (sp)oiler of development?

Cyril I. Obi

Senior Researcher, Nordiska Afrikainstitutet, Uppsala, Sweden

This article addresses one of the fundamental questions facing Nigeria at 50, as it relates to the role of the petroleum industry in the nation's development crisis. The relationship between the petroleum industry and Nigeria's development is approached from two levels – the nature of the global political economy of oil and the ways the Nigerian oil industry has served foreign and domestic elite interests. This explains why the transfer of ownership of the petroleum industry in the 1970s did not result in the transfer of control, nor address the structural deficiencies in the industry. Petroleum has been 'instrumentalised' in the high-stake politics and struggles involving transnational and local social forces, contributing to multiple crises. However, it is noted that the prospects of an oil-driven national developmental project cannot be entirely foreclosed, but it would require a new equitable social contract, a visionary leadership and a democratic developmental state.

After over five decades of oil production and exports, earning the country hundreds of billions of dollars, Nigeria, Africa's most populous country, has some of the world's worst human development indicators, indicating a paradox between its immense oil wealth and the poverty of most of its citizens. This article explores the linkages between the 'politics' and 'economics' of the petroleum industry in Nigeria, particularly its impact on the country's development. Being highly dependent on oil revenues and profits that dominate state revenues and foreign earnings since the end of the civil war in 1970s, Nigeria could be described as a 'petro-state'. One of the fundamental questions facing Nigeria at 50 is whether oil is entirely to blame for the crisis of development that the country is immersed in. Most discourses about Nigeria's immense, but unfulfilled development potential appear to be hinged upon the view that 'oil has been a disappointment' (General Buhari (retired), quoted by Thompson 2007). As an editorial in the *Guardian* (2009) lamented, '... it has been to our eternal shame that, unlike most other oil-producing countries, we have neither taken firm control of the industry nor have we reaped bountifully from the proceeds. That is why Nigeria is an unflattering example of the oil curse'.

Two issues are relevant here, Nigeria's lack of control, in spite of state ownership of the oil industry, and the wide gap between oil wealth and development, a trend symbolically represented by the paradoxical reality that Nigeria exports crude oil, but imports refined petroleum products despite having four (operating below capacity) refineries. Is the 'oil curse' responsible for 'spoiling' Nigeria's chances for development? This is a question that must be addressed given the nexus between resource endowment, governance and economic growth. Added to this are the highly volatile struggles over access to, and control over, oil by competing elite factions, and militias tapping into deep-seated grievances against prolonged oil extraction backed by state repression that alienates and impoverishes local inhabitants, and oil pollution that destroys local livelihoods in the oil-rich Niger Delta region. The latter attack state security forces, oil company pipelines, assets and personnel, disrupt oil production and threaten national stability. At stake are the interests of the world's largest oil multinationals: Shell, Chevron Texaco, Exxon Mobil, Total and Eni-Agip that produce over 80% of Nigeria's oil; and the dependence of the US, EU, China and India (in varying degrees) on oil imports from Nigeria (Obi 2009a), feeding into the increased securitisation of Nigeria's oil and the Niger Delta in the strategic energy calculations of the world's established and emerging powers. The stable supply of (cheap) oil from Nigeria has been prioritised within the context of US national security (Obi 2006, 2009a; Klare and Volman 2004, 226–7; AOPIG 2002; Krueger 2002).

The relationship between the oil industry and Nigeria's development is best approached from two levels: the nature of the global political economy of oil and the way the Nigerian oil industry has been integrated into it to serve foreign and domestic elite interests. In this regard, state dependence on oil multinational companies (MNCs), and the complex and volatile nature of Nigerian oil politics defines exclusive power over oil rents as the ultimate prize of political contestations. Also, as the case of the Niger Delta shows, the stakes in controlling oil (power) are very high and are underpinned by violent transnational and state-backed oil extraction, pollution and dispossession, local resistance and conflict (Obi 2010). It is hardly surprising that since Nigeria became a petro-state in the late 1960s, power has remained largely in the hands of surviving leading actors in the various military regimes or their approved civilian successors. Together, they have consistently demonstrated a complete intolerance for political opposition and lack of accountability to the Nigerian people. By the same logic, the state has been bound to, and remained protective of oil multinationals based on their common interests in oil extraction and the maximisation of profits.

This article is divided into five. The introduction outlines the centrality of oil to development and politics in Nigeria, and its connections to globalised oil capital and energy security. This is followed by a conceptual discussion of the oil-development nexus, and its local-national-global linkages. The third section examines the history of the oil industry in Nigeria over five decades and proffers explanations for its structural deficiencies. Fourth, the complex politics and ramifications of the insurgent resistance and conflict in the Niger Delta are analysed both in terms of their impact on development in the context of increased and global securitisation of the energy resources in the region. The fifth and concluding section explores the prospects for Nigeria's petroleum industry and national development.

Conceptual issues: Does oil 'curse' development?

The issue of an 'oil curse' is fundamental for addressing the view expressed in some quarters that Nigeria would have fared better if it did not have oil. Notions of an 'oil boom' followed by an 'oil doom' have informed a particular reading of Nigeria's postcolonial developmental trajectory in which the role of oil has been constructed in largely negative terms. This view is partly reinforced by the discourse on an 'oil curse', based on 'a correlation between the abundance of natural resources – especially oil – on the one hand, and a set of negative economic, political and social outcomes, on the other' (UNRISD 2007, 11). These negative consequences include, 'rent-seeking or corruption, the Dutch-disease, and conflict' (Fearon 2005; Herbst 2000; De Soysa and Neumeyer 2007, 202; Collier and Hoeffler 2004). Also of note is the view that natural resources like oil fuel the 'rentier effect or mentality', in which ruling elites are steeped in unproductive activities, lack of accountability and wasteful spending of public resources, with negative consequences for politics, governance and development (Yates 1996, 22; Oliveira 2007).

Taking the argument of a correlation between resource endowment and negative developmental outcomes a step further, it has been observed that 'oil wealth often wreaks havoc on a country's economy and politics, makes it easier for insurgents to fund rebellions and aggravates ethnic grievances' (Ross 2008, 2). It could also lead to 'astonishingly successful strategies of political survival amidst decay, on the other hand' (Oliveira 2007, 62). At the core of the oil curse is the economic concern with demonstrating the 'paradox of plenty', and the likely negative outcome(s) of oil endowment in developing countries. However, the pathologies of an oil curse thrive on a determinate relationship between oil and negative outcomes, a position that simplifies what is in reality a far more complex relationship, which is neither inevitable nor natural.

On face value, Nigeria shows all the classic characteristics of an oil-cursed political economy and can be said to be an example of a country where the oil paradox has 'spoiled' development. But this is only part of the story, as the curse is really a political and economic construct – a product of a particular constellation of social forces, histories and hegemonic power relations built around the commoditisation of particular resources in the global market. In this sense, oil is not the curse, rather it is the cursed – by the world's most powerful corporate and strategic actors for whom hydrocarbons are the driving force of globalised industrial capital and power. It is these forces and their local elite partners which have systematically subordinated third world oil producers to the demands of a globally integrated energy market system that contributes towards creating and nurturing those same conditions that work against development in many petro-states. In this regard, some authors have pointed to the shortcomings of the oil curse perspective (Watts 2004, 2007; Obi 2009c), showing that it is a combination of particular roles played by global, national, state and local actors that eventually define the developmental outcomes of each case. Developmental outcomes in oil-rich countries are the result of structural, historical and social factors, and can be either negative – curse, or positive – blessing.

The global political economy of oil

Petroleum or 'oil' is the most viable source of energy in the world, and a strategic commodity. It lies at the heart of industrial production, modern transportation, energy and military power. At a more fundamental level, oil is the energy source around which modern capitalism revolves. At the core of the global political economy of the oil industry lie the oil MNCs that control the complex integrated operations of the industry on a global scale. They are collectively the world's wealthiest and most powerful corporations. Oil MNCs are much richer than the individual petro-states with which they do business. Such states are not accountable to their citizens as they live off external oil rents, while the companies are not accountable to the citizens of the countries that they do business with. As such it is often easy for the transnational partners to collude and unleash violence when their interests in oil extraction are threatened.

Another explanation for the global might of oil MNCs lies in the strong influence they wield over their home governments. As the sole guarantors of steady supplies of cheap energy, employment for their citizens, profits for shareholders/investors and revenue for their home-governments, these companies are strategic to the energy security, wealth and global influence of the Western powers, particularly the United States. The intimacy between oil multinationals and their home governments is exemplified by the way both are connected to each other.

Oil MNCs contribute funds to the major political parties in the West. In the United States, Exxon Mobil and Chevron Texaco have contributed to the campaign war chests of both the Republican and Democratic Parties. Also these companies spend large amounts on lobbying Congress (Hamilton et al. 2004, 19). This revolving door relationship between oil and public office is replicated in Nigeria (Rowell, Marriot and Stockman 2005, 87).

The result of the entanglement of oil MNCs and the political class in their home countries is not limited to the accumulation of power, but the projection of economic, strategic and energy security interests abroad. Thus both actors mutually support each other in the quest to defend, expand access to, and control their share of the world's oil. What is involved is a strategic alliance to pursue their corporate interests in the context of their countries oil foreign policies. For countries that are global industrial and military powers, or aspire to become such powers, uninterrupted global access to oil is the imperative of these times. This has become more urgent in the emerging context of a new global energy security paradigm hinged on four elements 'supply sources, demand centres, geopolitics and market structures' (WEF/CERA 2006, 4; Yergin 2006).

The global political economy of oil is hinged upon the immense power and wealth that oil as a commodity commands and the 'securitisation' of its supply, demand and market stability by the worlds powers. Through the commoditisation of oil, the oil MNCs exercise immense leverage over the oil markets, and sources of supply, including the integration of petro-states and local petro-elites into geo-strategic political/security arrangements. In spite of the recent entry of oil firms from China, India, Korea, Brazil and other countries into the Nigerian oil scene, the fundamental moorings of its petroleum industry remains globally anchored and consigns Nigeria in the face of a low-level indigenous oil capital and state's 'petro-dependency', to the position of a subordinated supplier of cheap oil to the world market, a condition that negates the 'oiling' of national development.

The evolution of the oil industry in Nigeria

The oil industry in Nigeria has gone through three phases: the oil concession, state participation, and deregulation eras. The earliest era had its roots in the first oil exploration work by the German Bitumen Company based on a 1914 colonial minerals oil ordinance granting the monopoly of oil concessions in Nigeria to

'British or British-allied capital' (cited in Obi 1997, 140). Under this law, Shell D'Arcy (later Shell-BP) was granted an oil concession covering the entire Nigerian mainland in 1938, and eventually struck oil in a commercial quantity in 1956 in Oloibiri (in present-day Bayelsa state) in the Niger Delta, with oil exports commencing in 1958. This set the stage for the entry of other oil MNCs (Mobil, Texaco, Esso, Agip and Safrap) to take up the oil acreages given up by Shell in 1958. The early era of the oil industry was characterised by foreign control and non-participation by the state that simply collected rents and taxes (Soremekun and Obi 1993).

This trend changed by the 1970s, largely as a result of the increased contribution of oil to national revenues, the 'OPEC revolution' that led to the quadrupling of international oil prices, and the economic nationalism of the Nigerian post-civil-war military government that embarked on the indigenisation the oil industry. Specifically, Decree No. 51 of 1969 transferred 'the entire ownership and control of all petroleum in, under or upon any lands on Nigeria', to the federal military government. The government took up equity participation in all oil marketing MNCs, and merged the Ministry of Petroleum Resources with the Nigerian National Oil Corporation (NNOC) to form the Nigerian National Petroleum Corporation (NNPC), a state oil corporation. The NNPC represented the state's interest in the oil industry, including its equity interest based on a 60:40 ratio in the downstream sector of the oil industry. The state also built three new oil refineries: Warri (1978), Port Harcourt II (1989), and Kaduna (1980), apart from the one it had taken over earlier, Port Harcourt I (built by Shell-BP in 1963), to ensure secure supplies of refined products for the rapidly growing domestic market and provide revenue for government. Another aspect of the state's foray into the downstream sector was the commissioning of petrochemical plants at Ekpan (near Warri), at Eleme (Port Harcourt II), and the Kaduna refinery. These were expected to use the feedstock from the refineries to produce raw materials for the manufacturing sector.

In the upstream sector, the NNPC also had a 60:40 cost and profit sharing ratio with the oil MNCs. In the case of Shell Petroleum Development Company (SPDC), after the BP component was nationalised in 1979, the formula used was as follows: NNPC 55%, Shell 30%, Elf (now Total) 10%, and Agip (ENI) 5%. The indigenisation policy of government basically led to state incorporation into the transnational operations of the oil industry. However, in spite of the state's ownership of oil, and having a greater share of oil profits (and costs), it still had a structurally unequal relationship with its partners – oil MNCs that are much wealthier and have control over oil technology and the management of the companies.

The sudden downturn in global oil prices in 1977 and 1981 had disastrous consequences for Nigeria. The oil-dependent Nigerian economy went into recession as oil exports and revenues shrank, and by 1982 the country had entered discussions with the International Monetary Fund (IMF). Many companies were closed and workers were retrenched. The resort of the government to repression to stem the rising tide of opposition and protest compounded the economic crisis. The widespread manipulation of the 1983 general elections by the ruling National Party of Nigeria (NPN) and its loyalists in the security agencies followed this.

The oil industry and the structural adjustment programme (SAP)

The lack of legitimacy of the NPN government, dubiously 're-elected' in fraudulent elections earlier in the year (Hart 1993, 397–418), created the conditions for a faction of military generals to overthrow the civilian government on 31 December 1983 (Ibrahim 2007, 3). However, the new military regime led by Generals Buhari and Idiagbon was itself overthrown within two years in a palace coup that brought General Ibrahim Babangida to power in August 1985. In 1986, Babangida announced the adoption of a 'home grown' Structural Adjustment Programme (SAP) approved by the IMF and the World Bank as well as the country's creditors. It was within the rubric of the SAP that a deregulation programme aimed at rolling back state participation in the economy began with the deregulation of the oil sector.

This started with the so-called removal of domestic petroleum product price(s) subsidies, which in reality was the aligning of domestic prices to international prices for petroleum products. Using the rhetoric of *appropriate pricing*, the government deregulated the price of petroleum products, allowing it to rise upwards as a way of raising revenue, curtailing domestic demand and freeing more oil for export. This was also directed at opening up the domestic oil sector to foreign investors. Thus, in January 1986, domestic prices of petroleum products were increased by 80% at once, under the pretext that savings made from the new prices would provide the government with revenue to revamp social infrastructure and aid economic recovery, and also provide a price disincentive (based on exchange rate differentials between the Naira and CFA Franc) against the smuggling of petroleum products from Nigeria to neighbouring Francophone countries.

Within the SAP framework, the government embarked on a new phase of a 'de-indigenisation' of the oil industry, where the emphasis was on rolling back state participation, and opening up the oil sector to foreign and local private investors. It sold off its equity participation in some of the downstream oil marketing companies, and commercialised the NNPC. The state also sought to promote more investments in the upstream sector by the oil MNCs through a package of incentives and placing new oil blocs in the deep offshore and onshore on offer. These were directed at increasing oil production and exports, with a view to producing revenues for external debt management and economic recovery programmes.

Some Nigerian companies also got licences to explore for, and produce oil, but most of them, due to the huge costs or capital requirements involved, remained marginal players. Oil MNCs consolidated their hold over the industry in this 'de-indigenisation' phase, concentrating on the upstream sector, but also dominating the downstream marketing sector – where some Nigerian 'independent marketers', were becoming increasingly visible and accounted for 30% of the domestic market. During this period, the effort made to commercialise Nigeria's four (state-owned) refineries did not succeed, partly for political reasons, and because of the poor state they were in. The situation worsened under the General Sani Abacha-led military regime. This had succeeded that of Babangida, after the latter had fomented political crises by annulling presidential elections in June 1993, and foisted an unelected Interim National Government (ING) on the country. The ING lasted barely six months before it collapsed with General Abacha the ING's Defence minister, seizing power on 17 November 1993. Under Abacha as head of the ruling military Provisional Ruling Council (PRC), the refineries suffered more serious neglect and constantly broke down paving the way for the importation of refined petroleum products and providing further justification for more price hikes. However, Abacha's death on 8 June 1998 and the coming to power of the General Abdulsalami Abubakar-led regime, paved the way for a return to democratic rule on 29 May 1999.

The oil industry since 1999

The coming to power of a new democratic government under retired General Olusegun Obasanjo (who had been Nigeria's military Head of State between 1976 and 1979) in 1999 provided a new boost for the deregulation of the oil industry in Nigeria. From 1999, all existing 'price subsidies' in petroleum products were 'removed' after about eight price increases, in what was really a process of closing the gap between domestic and global prices of refined petroleum products. It also represented a form of sales tax on refined petroleum products leading to a substantial rise in domestic fuel prices with its attendant multiplier effects – a rise in the price of local goods and services, and a decline in the living standards of most Nigerians.

Apart from the ideological justification provided by the economic tsars, the Obasanjo years hinged on a commitment to market-based reforms as the basis of economic efficiency and growth. However, the hard reality was that state-owned refineries were beset by technical problems and operated well below their installed capacities. This problem persisted in spite of the fact that between 1999 and 2003, about US$250 million was spent on the repair and maintenance of oil depots, pipelines and other oil infrastructure. The paradox of Nigeria being Africa's largest, and the world's sixth largest, oil producer and exporter of crude oil, and a net importer of significant amounts of refined petroleum products strengthened the case for the privatisation of its state-owned refineries; after several failed attempts the refineries are yet to be privatised. A possible explanation is that some powerful political and business interests built on the highly lucrative importation of refined products stand to lose out if the refineries are restored to full operability.

Government divestment from the oil marketing companies, such as the National Oil and Chemical Marketing Plc (NOLCHEM, now Conoil), African Petroleum Plc (AP) and Unipetrol Plc (now Oando) led to their privatisation between 2000 and 2002. It also announced plans to privatise the NNPC's marketing arm – the Pipelines and Products Marketing Company (PPMC), and invited bids from investors seeking to establish private refineries. Such new investments were expected to expand private domestic participation in the downstream sector, while making up for the shortfall in domestic products' supplies as a result of the near-collapse of Nigeria's four refineries with a combined installed capacity of about 450,000 barrels per day (bpd). In this connection, 18 companies were given approval in 2002 to build refineries (Alexander's Gas and Oil Connections, Company News 2002). By January 2006, the head of the NNPC, announced that government and five oil companies, Shell, Chevron Texaco, Exxon Mobil, Total and Agip (ENI), had concluded plans to build refineries with a combined installed capacity of 1 million bpd in the country (Oduniyi 2006). Up till 2010, however, none of these refinery projects had taken off. Another aspect of the oil policy related to the consolidation of the equally strategic Nigeria Liquefied

National Gas (NLNG) Project (NNPC – 49%, Shell – 25.6%, Elf – 15%, and Agip (ENI) – 10.4%) expected to be another huge money-spinner for the country.

Various governments have also sought to expand investments in the upstream sector of the oil industry with the aim of doubling daily oil production from the present 2.5 million barrels per day (mbd) to 5 mbd by 2010. Although the EIA Country Analysis Briefs on Nigeria (2005) optimistically reported that 'Shell in 2004, announced plans to invest $9 billion in Nigerian oil and gas projects, Chevron Texaco announced that it would invest $2.5 billion in the Agbami oil field, while Exxon Mobil would spend $2.6 billion on the Erha oil field', the escalation in insurgent militancy and the government's late or non-payment of its joint venture commitments to its oil MNC partners led to the decline in oil investments from 2005. The situation was further compounded by Obasanjo's policy of opening the door to oil investors from all parts of the world under rather non-transparent conditions. The new entrants into the upstream sector included, China National Offshore Oil Company (CNOOC), China Petrochemical Corporation (SINOPEC), China National Petroleum Corporation (CNPC), Korean National Oil Corporation (KNPC), Oil and Natural Gas Corporation (ONGC)-Videsh of India, Statoil of Norway and Petrobras of Brazil.

The granting of oil licenses between 2005 and 2007 underscored the increased opening up of the upstream sector to national oil companies from Asia and South America, to the discomfort of oil MNCs. A second factor was the state's promotion of Nigerian participation in the oil industry by its insisting on local content in all joint venture oil contracts, and that 10% of each Oil Exploration Licence (OEL) granted to investors should go to Nigerian-owned oil companies. Thus, rather than a complete surrender to foreign oil companies, the Nigerian state and petro-elite sought greater incorporation using the 'nationalist' platform to claim a certain percentage of participation in oil investments and oil contracts for Nigerian oil companies. This provided the Nigerian petro-state with some leverage in the context of increased international competition for its oil, the quest to obtain more benefits, part of which fed into the political patronage calculations of the ruling elite (*Africa Confidential* 2006, 1–2).

However, the efforts at greater indigenous participation in the oil industry have largely failed. The NNPC still produces (excluding oil produced under Joint Venture Agreements (JVAs)) less than 100,000 barrels of oil, out of Nigeria's daily output capacity of almost 2.5 million barrels, most of which is produced by the oil MNCs, leaving a few Nigerian indigenous oil companies to produce a little oil from marginal or small fields, or struggling for concessionary oil blocs. The regulatory arm of the oil industry, the Department of Petroleum Resources (DPR), though autonomous, faces severe limitations. These are related to problems of limited funding, weak institutional capacity, and inadequate equipment to monitor effectively the sophisticated operations of the oil industry.

Although the Nigerian state has continued to assert its ownership and access roles, actual control still resides externally in the hands of the international oil companies: Shell, Chevron Texaco, Exxon Mobil, Total and Eni. Thus, while the Nigerian petro-state owns the oil, and asserts control over access to it in the context of the globalisation of the oil industry, it does not control 'its' oil at its most critical level, production. In the current phase of globalised oil production, the 'four sisters' depend more on contracting the tasks of 'construction, installation', 'searching for and wining oil' to transnational oil service companies (such as Willbros and Halliburton, that also hire contract oil workers) in which they also have substantial interests (Rowell et al. 2005, 103; Menotti 2006, 3).

In this context, the oil MNCs largely 'administer multiple contracts with oil service providers' (Menotti 2006, 3), whose costs the Nigerian State bears (a larger share), without any real net gain (except oil rents) in terms of the transfer of technology or skills. What we are left with after over 50 years of oil production is yet another effort at indigenous participation in the oil industry in 2010, through the signing of a Nigerian Oil and Gas Industry Content Development law by President Goodluck Jonathan in April 2010, and the non-signing of the Petroleum Industry Bill (since 2008) aimed at reforming the oil industry (for greater diversification, international competiveness, efficiency, and local participation), but being resisted by oil MNCs.

Thus the Nigerian oil industry has remained largely hobbled by structural constraints, but more important is its extraversion, which serves the demands of the global oil market and the interests of the transnational petro-elite. Its politics expressed both with regard to the leverage of oil MNCs over the state, and state ownership of oil, have meant that the capture of state power remains the ultimate price of the contestations between competing factions of the ruling petro-elite, while huge oil revenues reinforce the repressive capacity and impunity of the state in ways that undermine the democratisation of society. Nowhere is this as acute as in the complex struggles for resource control in the Niger Delta.

The struggle for resource control in the Niger Delta: Local and global dimensions

The Nigerian government formally took over the ownership of oil by executive fiat through military decrees nos. 51 of 1969, and 9, 15, and 38 of 1971 that transferred all power over all oil revenues, from both onshore and offshore sources, to the federal military government and its appointees. Later, the Land Use Decree of 1978 (later the Land Use Act of 1979) gave the state power over all lands that it could appropriate in the public interest.

By using the fiscal instrument to centralise political and oil power, the federal government effectively subordinated the constituent units/regions or states to its post-war hegemonic national unity project. Oil ownership overdeveloped the allocative capacities of the federal government in relation to other tiers, in a context where the capacity to allocate was divorced from the control over oil production (Obi 1998, 266). This fed into fractional struggles for the control of power over federal power. Indeed, the sharing of oil revenues has remained a source of political instability.

From 1970, federal ownership of oil led to the progressive reduction of derivation as a revenue allocation principle and to its replacement by the Distributive Pool Account (DPA) or Federation Account that emphasised population size and equality of states as principles of revenue allocation. As a result the derivation principle was reduced from 50% in 1970, 5, 1.5, and then 3% by the mid-1980s (Ikein and Briggs-Anigbo 1998), and then increased in 1999 with the return of democratic rule to 13%.

Although the ethnic minorities of the Niger Delta gained some measure of self-determination as a result of the states creation exercise(s), and the national unity project gave some Niger Delta elite some access to lucrative state and federal appointments and patronage, the people felt short-changed by the fact that in spite of their support for the federal side during the war, they remained marginalised from the ownership and control of the oil produced from their region. The sense of grievance was worsened by federal neglect, widespread impoverishment and increased oil-related environmental degradation of the Niger Delta. It was also believed that a 'distant' federal government dominated by elite from the majority ethnic groups and foreign oil multinationals had no regard for the rights and welfare of the ethnic minorities of the Niger Delta.

The struggle for resource control is directed at a return to 'the principles of true federalism' which demands a re-negotiation of the structure of the Nigerian federation in ways that transfers power over the oil to the oil-producing states of the Niger Delta. Following the well-known Ogoni resistance in the early 1990s (Obi 2001; Obi 2009a, 474–6) led by the Movement for the Survival of Ogoni People (MOSOP), the largest of the Niger Delta oil minorities, the Ijaw mounted a new struggle for the control of oil. In December, Ijaw youth from six states of the Niger Delta, organised under the Ijaw Youth Council (IYC), met in Kaiama, the birthplace of Ijaw martyr Isaac Adaka Boro.

There, on 11 December 1998, the IYC drew up the Kaiama Declaration (KD 1998). This asserted that, 'all land and natural resources (including mineral resources) within the Ijaw territory belong to the Ijaw communities and are the basis for our survival'. The IYC refused to recognise 'all undemocratic decrees that robbed the Ijaw of the right of ownership and control of our lives and resources, which were enacted without our participation and consent'. On this basis, they demanded 'self-government and resource control by the Ijaw people', and gave all oil multinationals an ultimatum to quit the Niger Delta by 30 December, 'until issues related to the ownership and control of Ijawland and oil were resolved'.

In response, the federal government declared a state of emergency in the Niger Delta, and flooded the region with armed troops. Ijaw protesters were arrested, and anti-riot police shot some during demonstrations in support of the Kaiama Declaration (Ukeje 2001, 29). The Ijaw local resistance was repressed, but as in the case of the Ogoni, it survived, and re-generated itself particularly after the return to democratic rule in 1999. Across the Niger Delta other radical groups organised around the demands for the control of local autonomy, and self-determination for the control of oil appeared. These groups included the Movement for the Payment of Reparations to Ogbia, which set forth an Ogbia Charter of Demands; from the Egi people came the Aklaka Declaration; from the Oron National Forum, the Oron Bill of Rights; and there was also an Ikwerre Charter of Demands.

The widespread feeling that the only language the state-oil alliance understood was that of violence gained ground. It further sharpened the quest of the militia groups to seize power over oil. Their struggles found expression along four poles: against the state-oil alliance; against local traditional rulers, chiefs and elite who were reportedly colluding with the state-oil alliance to betray their people in exchange for pay-offs, contracts and lucrative appointments; factional fighting within the same communities for power, or over the spoils of oil; and inter-community or inter-ethnic conflicts over the control of oil territory. In spite of their rhetoric, the militias had an ambiguous relationship with the Niger Delta elites, opposing and collaborating with them based on exigent calculations.

Two logics are at play in the complex oil politics and conflicts in the Niger Delta. The first relates to the intensification of the factional struggles over the control of oil revenues, constructed as the campaign for resource control by the oil producing (South-South) states of the Niger Delta, demanding a derivation-based redress in Nigeria's fiscal federalism that would translate into their ownership of at least half of the oil revenues realised from their 'territory'. An explosive spin-off from this campaign was the 'militantisation' of the quest for resource control from 2006 (Obi 2009b, 121–3).

The emergence of militia groups as opposed to the non-violent campaign of the 1990s was partly the result of the militarisation of the region. The best known militia alliance, the Movement for the Emancipation of the Niger Delta (MEND), engaged in kidnapping and holding hostage expatriate oil workers, blowing up oil installations and attacking security personnel in the Niger Delta as part of its local and global campaign for resource control. MEND and other Niger Delta militias provided alienated, unemployed and marginalised youth, some of them university and high school graduates, with a platform to challenge the federal hegemony over oil and to tap into anger against the state and the oil MNCs to draw attention to their cause and to benefit as individuals from their capacity to unleash violence capable of disrupting a critical transnational energy resource flow. It is germane to point out that militias are propelled by a set of motives that are not only economic but straddle a range of grievances and fluid opportunistic acts, which may or may not be criminal in intent.

The second point relates to the post-9/11 securitisation of the oil in the Niger Delta by the West (led by the US), in the face of increased militant activity in the region capable of undermining their interests in the oil-rich region. What lies at stake is the security of global oil investments in Nigeria's Niger Delta and Nigeria. In this regard, the energy import-dependent United States perceives Nigeria as a regional strategic partner (Obi 2006, 171–3). This is because Nigeria provides about 12–15% of US oil imports, hosts billions of dollars worth of investments by oil MNCs, and is poised to become a major international exporter of Liquefied Natural Gas (LNG).

For this reason, Western and US policy-makers, oil interests and strategic analysts are increasingly concerned by the threats posed to the MNCs, expatriate oil company staff, and the steady flow of oil exports by protesting oil communities and militia groups. Furthermore, some concerns relate to the possibility of terrorist strikes against Western oil interests in the Niger Delta and the Gulf of Guinea. These have contributed to the forging of closer military co-operation ties at the bilateral and multilateral levels, and the increased presence of the US Navy and AFRICOM in the Gulf of Guinea (Yacoob 2004; Krueger 2002; Greenberg and Cain 2005; Volman 2009). This has fed into international military assistance programmes to strengthen the capacity of the Nigeria state to rein in the militants, curb the activities of transnational criminal networks (trading in stolen crude), and protect Western energy interests in the Niger Delta.

The struggle for resource control has fed factional struggles within the Delta and at national and global levels. As a result, the Nigerian petro-state is consumed by struggles over power and the capacity to retain power over oil and guarantee the internal order necessary for transnational oil business. Thus, the ruling elite battles to maintain its power and the conditions for the reproduction of its hegemony and continued legitimacy as the (enriched) custodians of vast oil and gas deposits in a highly competitive and globalised world.

Conclusion: Prospects for Nigeria's development under a globalised oil industry

In spite of over two decades of adjustment and post-adjustment, Nigeria has remained a petrolised political economy. Earnings from oil dominate the economy (despite attempts at its diversification) and are central to political life, making politics and economics different faces of 'oil' in Nigeria. The most recent policies of the Jonathan presidency raise the question of whether Nigeria's current increased oil profile would, unlike the past, translate into the country's development. Apart from the formidable challenges facing the Nigerian oil industry, the issue of corruption is an important factor in explaining how Nigeria, believed to have earned about US$600 billion in oil revenues since 1960, with fully 70% of its population living below the poverty line (Wurthmann 2006), can now efficiently use its oil wealth as the basis for rapid development.

This suggests the limited impact of agencies like the Economic and Financial Crimes Commission (EFCC) that successfully prosecuted several high profile cases, and Nigeria's (voluntarily) signing up to the Extractive Industries Transparency Initiative (EITI), directed at promoting transparency in revenues paid to resource-exporting countries. However, the impact of the EITI on the transparency of oil revenues remains limited and riddled with discrepancies. Also oil projects have been tainted by corruption as the recent scandal involving bribes paid to top Nigerian officials by the US company oil services company, Halliburton, shows. There have also been incidences of opaque withdrawals from the nation's excess crude account (Pindiga 2006), and the persistent lack of development in Niger Delta states that have received increased revenue allocations since 2000.

However, some qualified success has been achieved in terms of the opening up of the telecommunication sector, debt forgiveness, financial sector reform, and the privatisation of government enterprises. However, domestic manufacturing has remained poor. The influx of cheap(er) imports, policy inconsistencies and the poor state of basic infrastructure, particularly electricity supply and the frequent increases in the domestic prices of fuel leading to cost-driven inflation and low consumer purchasing power, has contributed to poor socio-economic performance. The situation has been further compounded by political crises, including communal unrest, and poor governance at all levels of government. What the evidence also suggests is that the current market-led reforms have benefited a few 'powerful' Nigerians (and their foreign partners), while the majority of Nigerians have experienced a marked decline in their quality of life.

The foregoing poses several challenges. The more obvious one is that the prospects of Nigeria's development will, for the foreseeable future, remain inextricably tied to the fluctuating fortunes of the global oil market, and a transnationally-oriented Nigerian oil industry. The second is that the possibilities for economic re-distribution and social transformation in Nigeria lie both in the hands of the ability of a highly fractious political elite torn apart both by the struggles over oil power as well as competing narrow personal interests to reach a consensus on how to resolve their differences harmoniously, and respect the rules of political competition.

The inherently unstable character of the Nigerian state, marked by its immersion into the class struggles within Nigeria, and a globally integrated world poses another critical challenge. The reality of the limited autonomy of the state is manifested in the narrow social base of political power, corruption, the relative weakness and instability of public institutions, and the external anchorage (state dependence on oil MNCs) of the fiscal basis of the state–oil nexus. This feeds into the 'over-politicisation' of social life, as politics defined as an organised struggle for the capture of state power overshadows all else, undermining democracy and the emergence of a 'developmental ethos' that is so critical to Nigeria's socio-economic transformation.

Thus, the pervasive influence of 'politicised oil' is expressed in the contradictions and inequities spawned at the levels of production and distribution. It has continued to undermine the prospects for democratic politics and sustainable development that are so critical to Nigeria's transformation. But it should be noted that it is not oil (in itself) that defines the structure of the Nigerian state, rather it is the character of the state that has led to the instrumentalisation of oil by hegemonic domestic and transnational social forces intent on fostering the continued integration of the country into the global capitalist system on the basis of clearly disadvantageous terms. For this dominant class, oil is a blessing, and the basis of the reproduction of 'development as an imperial project' (Cheru 2009, 275–8). This class inflicts a developmental paralysis 'underlined by poor political governance, elite predation and lack of accountability' on the people for whom oil endowment becomes a 'curse'.

Although the prospects for transformation in Nigeria may be difficult, they cannot be entirely foreclosed. A lot would depend on the emergence of a visionary and committed ruling elite and leadership capable of forging a new equitable social contract between the Nigerian state and its citizens, within a popular-democratic and an equitable participatory framework. This can then serve a firm basis for social transformation that would necessarily involve a re-negotiation of the power relations in the global oil industry by a developmental Nigeria state and a socio-industrial project intent on anchoring its oil and gas resource(s) to the welfare, social emancipation and development of its peoples.

References

Africa Confidential. 2006. West Africa: Oil and oligarchs. *Africa Confidential* 47, no. 1: 1–2.

African Oil Policy Initiative Group (AOPIG). 2002. *African oil: A priority for US national security and African development*. Washington, DC: AOPIG.

Alexander's Gas and Oil Connections. 2002. Company news: Africa 7, no. 12, June 13. www.gasandoil.com.

Cheru, F. 2009. Development in Africa: The imperial project versus the national project and the need for policy space. *Review of African Political Economy* 36, no. 120: 275–8.

Collier, P., and A. Hoeffler. 2004. Greed and grievance in civil wars. *Oxford Economic Papers* 56: 663–95.

De Soysa, I., and E. Neumayer. 2007. Resource wealth and the risk of civil war onset: Results from a new dataset of natural resource rents. *Conflict Management and Peace Review* 24, no. 3, 201–18.

Fearon, J. 2005. Primary commodities exports and civil war. *Journal of Conflict Resolution* 49, no. 4: 483–507.

Foreign Policy in Focus: PetroPolitics Special Report. 2004. January, www.fpif.org/papers/03petropol/index_body.html.

Greenberg, B., and D. Cain. 2005. US-Africa partnership are key to waging war on terrorism. US Department of State, International Information Programs, http://usinfo.state.gov/af/Archive/2005/Mar/15.

Guardian. 2009. Editorial, petroleum industry bill: Need for caution. *Guardian*, October 22.
Hamilton, J., L. Stockman, M. Brown, G. Marshall, G. Muttitt, and N. Rau. 2004. *Beyond oil: The oil curse and solutions for an oil-free future*. Oxford and London: Rising Tide, Platform and Friends of the Earth. www.noneoil.org.
Hart, C. 1993. The Nigerian elections of 1983. *Africa* 63, 3: 397–418.
Herbst, J. 2000. Economic incentives, natural resources and conflict in Africa. *Journal of African Economies* 9, no. 3: 270–94.
Ibrahim, J. 2007. Nigeria's 2007 elections: The fitful path to democratic citizenship, *Special Report* 182. United States Institute of Peace, January.
Ikein, A., and C. Briggs-Anigbo. 1998. *Oil and fiscal federalism in Nigeria: The political economy of resource allocation in a developing country*. Aldershot: Ashgate.
Kaiama Declaration. 1998. www.ijawcenter.com/kaiama_declaration.html
Klare, M., and D. Volman. 2004. Africa's oil and American national interest. *Current History*, May.
Krueger, J. 2002. Oil stakes in West Africa. *Africa notes* no. 11, December. Washington, DC: Africa Programme, Centre for Strategic and International Studies.
Menotti, V. 2006. The other oil war: Halliburton's agenda at WTO: A policy brief on the energy services negotiations in the World Trade Organization (WTO). California: International Forum on Globalization. www.ifg.org/reports/WTO-energy-services.
Obi, C. 1997. Globalisation and local resistance: The case of the Ogoni versus Shell. *New Political Economy* 2, no. 1: 137–48.
Obi, C. 1998. The impact of oil on Nigeria's revenue allocation system: Problems and prospects for national reconstruction. In *Federalism and political restructuring in Nigeria*, eds. K. Amuwo, A. Agbaje, R. Suberu and G. Herault. Ibadan: Spectrum Books and IFRAA.
Obi, C. 2001. Global, state and local intersections: Power, authority and conflict in the Niger Delta oil communities. In *Intervention and transnationalism in Africa: Global-local networks*, eds. T. Callaghy, R. Kassimir and R. Latham. Cambridge: Cambridge University Press.
Obi, C. 2006. Foreign interests and environmental degradation. In *Africa-US relations: Strategic encounters*, eds. D. Rothchild and E. Keller. Boulder, CO: Lynne Rienner.
Obi, C. 2009a. Structuring transnational spaces of identity, rights and power in the Niger Delta of Niger. *Globalizations* 6, no. 4: 467–81.
Obi, C. 2009b. Scrambling for oil in West Africa. In *A new scramble for Africa?*, ed. R. Southall and H. Melber. Scottville: University of KwaZuluNatal Press.
Obi, C. 2009c. Nigeria's Niger Delta: Understanding the complex drivers of violent oil-related conflict. *Africa Development* XXXIV, no. 2: 103–28.
Obi, C. 2010. Oil extraction, dispossession, resistance, and conflict in the Niger Delta. *Canadian Journal of Development Studies* XXX, nos. 1–2: 219–36.
Oduniyi, M. 2006. FG, oil majors to build 1m BPD refinery. *This Day* (Lagos), January 18.
Oliveira, R. 2007. *Oil and politics in the Gulf of Guinea*. London: Hurst.
Pindiga, H. 2006. Crude account: FG withdrew $13 bn, says Tukur. *Daily Trust* (Abuja), June 16. www.dailytrust.com/news.
Ross, M. 2008. Blood barrels: Why oil fuels conflict. *Foreign Affairs* 87, no. 3: 2–9.
Rowell, A., J. Marriot, and L. Stockman. 2005. *The next Gulf: London, Washington and oil conflict in Nigeria*. London: Constable.
Soremekun, K., and C. Obi. 1993. The changing pattern of private foreign investments in the Nigerian oil industry. *Africa Development* XVIII, no. 3.
Thompson, C. 2007. 'Curse of oil' sees corruption soar in Nigeria. *Independent*, January 31. http://www.independent.co.uk/news/world/africa/curse-of-oil-sees-corruption-soar-in-nigeria-434405.html.
Ukeje, C. 2001. Oil communities and political violence: The case of ethnic Ijaws in Nigeria's Niger Delta. *Terrorism and Violence* 13, no. 4: 15–36.
United Nations Research Institute for Development Research (UNRISD). 2007. Report of the UNRISD International Workshop, 1–2 March, UNRISD Conference News.
Volman, M. 2009. China, India, Russia and the United States: The scramble for African oil and the militarization of the continent. *Current African Issues* 43.
Watts, M. 2004. Resource curse? Governmentability, oil and power in the Niger Delta, Nigeria. *Geopolitics* 9, no. 1: 50–80.

Watts, M. 2007. Petro-insurgency or criminal syndicate? Conflict and violence in the Niger Delta. *Review of African Political Economy* 24, no. 114: 637–60.
World Economic Forum (WEF)/Cambridge Energy Research Associates (CERA). 2006. *The new energy security paradigm*. WEF: Geneva.
Wurthmann, G. 2006. Ways of using the Africa oil boom for sustainable development, Africa Development Bank. *Economic Research Working Paper Series*, no. 84.
Yacoob, H. 2004. US forces coming to oil-rich Gulf of Guinea – USAF Commander. *Vanguard*, August 10. www.vanguardngr.com/articles/2002.
Yates, D. 1996. *The rentier state in Africa: Oil rent dependency and neocolonialism in the Republic of Gabon*. Trenton and Asmara: Africa World Press.
Yergin, D. 2006. Ensuring energy security. *Foreign Affairs*, March/April: 69–82.

The Nigerian federal system: Performance, problems and prospects

Rotimi Suberu

Department of Politics and International Relations, Bennington College, Vermont, USA

The transformation and centralisation of the Nigerian federation by 'soldiers and oil' has produced contentious and contradictory outcomes. Many influential commentators describe the current centralised system of federalism as a veritable source of, rather than a credible solvent for, the country's multifaceted crises of unity, democracy, and development. A more balanced perspective would distinguish between the system's remarkable achievements in alleviating inter-group political inequality and insecurity, and its conspicuous failures to advance good democratic and economic governance. Ultimately, focused reforms, especially electoral and anti-corruption reforms, will be required to consolidate Nigeria's real successes in mitigating potentially disintegrative ethno-political conflicts and to assuage current agitations for the wholesale restructuring or dismantling of the federal system.

Contemporary debates about Nigeria's political and socio-economic failures have routinely implicated the presumed pathologies, incongruities and liabilities of the country's federalism. Despite (and often because of) the massive transformation and reorganisations it has witnessed in 50 years of national independence, the Nigerian system of federalism is often denounced as a veritable source of, rather than a viable solvent for, the country's multifaceted crises of poor governance, ethno-political conflict and socio-economic underdevelopment. Three recent major interventions in Nigeria's federal debate are particularly instructive.

First, in a paper written to coincide with 50 years of Nigerian federalism (1954–2004) and published in the prestigious *Publius: The Journal of Federalism*, Ladipo Adamolekun, the eminent Nigerian public administration scholar, chronicled and bemoaned the 'bastardisation' or hyper-centralisation of Nigerian federalism since the collapse of the First Nigerian Republic in 1966, concluding that 'the Nigerian federation is at a crossroads and has two options: devolution or death' (Adamolekun 2005, 383). Second, in a 2006 report entitled 'Nigeria's faltering federal experiment', the International Crisis Group highlighted multiple, overlapping, flashpoints and fault-lines in the country's federalism, including lethal indigene-settler conflicts in Jos (in Plateau State) and other ethno-religiously mixed cities, the insurgency in the oil-rich Niger Delta region, and the nationwide proliferation of ethno-separatist and chauvinistic religious movements and agendas. According to the report, 'Nigeria's federal system and politics are deeply flawed, contributing to rising violence that threatens to destabilize one of Africa's leading countries' (International Crisis Group 2006, 2).

Third, following reports in the international media about yet another bout of ethno-religious bloodletting in Jos during early 2010, Libyan Leader Muammar Gaddafi, questioned the viability or sustainability of the very idea of Nigeria, 'which was made and imposed by the British in spite of the people's resistance to it' (British Broadcasting Corporation News, 16 March 2010, http://news.bbc.co.uk/2/hi/africa/8570350.stm). Instead, he called initially for the bifurcation of the federation into separate Muslim and Christian states, but subsequently revised his position into a proposal for the dissolution of Nigeria into several independent ethnic entities. According to Gaddafi, 'The model that fits Nigeria is the Yugoslav model ... which included several peoples, like Nigeria, and then these peoples gained independence and the Yugoslav union was ended in peace' (*Next*, 29 March 2010).

This essay reassesses the evolution, performance, problems and prospects of Nigerian federalism with a view to promoting a more balanced federalist debate in and on Nigeria. The Nigerian federal system, this analysis contends, represents a reasonably viable and successful mechanism for managing inter-group conflict and preventing ethno-political disintegration. However, Nigerian politics have largely neglected or de-prioritised federalism's other potential roles in promoting democratic and economic development. The contemporary crisis of the Nigerian federal system, therefore, represents a tragedy of incomplete reform in which the democratic and developmental deficiencies of the federal framework have gravely undermined the system's otherwise remarkable achievements in enhancing inter-group security and unity. Consequently, the challenge of federal reform is not to fundamentally reconfigure or restructure current institutional structures of ethnic conflict management. Rather, robust institutions of democratic and economic development, including electoral and anti-corruption reforms, are needed to reinforce and enhance current federal processes for cauterising ethnic instability.

The following pages will chronicle the major phases of Nigerian federal development, discuss the significant achievements (as well as shortcomings) of the federal system in ethnic conflict management, analyse the system's woeful failures in the domains of democratic and economic governance, and outline an agenda for the reform of Nigerian federalism.

Evolution and transformation of Nigerian federalism

The development of Nigerian federalism can be demarcated into the following six phases coinciding with key historical benchmarks in the country's broader political evolution: the late British colonial period (1954–1960); the First Republic (1960–1966); the first phase of military rule, including the civil war (1966–1979); the Second Republic (1979–1983); the second phase of military rule, including the abortion of an elaborate transition to the Third Republic (1984–1999); and the Fourth Republic (1999 to date). To elaborate, the Nigerian federation was first instituted, under British colonial rule in 1954, to hold together Nigeria's fissiparous society, including two historic colonial administrative regions (North and South), three major ethnic groups (Hausa-Fulani, Yoruba, and Ibo), hundreds of ethnic minorities, and almost equal number of Muslims and Christians. The federation consisted of three regions, namely, the Hausa-Fulani-dominated Northern Region (comprising more than half of the country's population and approximately two-thirds of the federation's territory), the Yoruba-based Western Region, and the Ibo-dominated Eastern Region.

The post-independence First Nigerian Republic (1960–1966) combined a Westminster-style parliamentary system with the colonially inherited federal structure of three (a fourth region, the Mid-West, was added in 1963) large, but unequal, regions, each of which was dominated by a major ethnic group and controlled by a party based on that group. This was succeeded by military rule from 1966 to 1979, during which the soldiers broke the four regions into 12 and later 19 smaller states in a largely successful bid to undermine the Ibo-led Eastern Region's war of secession and to consolidate Nigeria's post-civil-war unity. Civilian rule was restored in the Second Republic (1979–1983), which incorporated the basic features of the military's integrationist political engineering, including the 19-state federal structure, the replacement of the parliamentary system with a strong executive presidential system, the formal prohibition of sectional parties, the centralisation or unification of the local government and police systems, and the massive shift of fiscal and legislative powers from the states to the central government.

The military re-imposed their rule from 1984 to 1999, and during that period the number of states grew from 19 to 36, while the soldiers sabotaged an elaborate programme of political transition to a Third Nigerian Republic and created a climate of repression leading to an escalation of centrifugal ethno-regional and religious agitations. Finally, since 1999, the country has seen the political disengagement of the military and witnessed the longest era of uninterrupted civilian rule in the federation's history. Under the political dominance of the People's Democratic Party (PDP), this period has seen both a historic inter-civilian transition from the presidency of Olusegun Obasanjo to that of Umaru Yar'Adua as well as the implementation of modest socio-economic reforms and the reassertion of state rights in reaction to years of predation and over-centralisation under military rule. Yet, this civilian dispensation is vexed by numerous challenges to its stability, including massive political and electoral corruption, an insurgency in the oil-rich Niger Delta, a southern-based clamour for fundamental constitutional restructuring of the federation and the decentralisation of natural resource control, and a regionally divisive, political succession and power sharing crisis precipitated by Yar'Adua's chronic ill health and eventual death in May 2010.

The major turning points in this trajectory involved the intervention of the military, the outbreak of civil war, and the creation of the 12-state framework that, along with the phenomenal expansion in oil production and revenues, produced fundamental, centralising, changes in the structural configuration and institutional architecture of the Nigerian federation during the late sixties and early seventies. Yet, debates persist in Nigeria regarding the value and viability of these centralising changes.

One perspective, which was most recently articulated in the Adamolekun essay and is quite popular among the leaderships of southern regional organisations, celebrates the pre-military era of Nigerian federalism as the 'golden age' of federal development in the country. The extensive decentralisation of this period, Adamolekun contends, 'allowed each of the two orders of government (federal and regional) to make choices in both the political and economic spheres', thereby generating a healthy, but informal, competition among the regional governments for the delivery of public goods as well as incentives for the mobilisation of 'own' economic resources. The period since the onset of centralising military rule in 1966 destroyed these elements of 'choice, incentive, and competition', with dismal consequences for the political and socio-economic performance of successive military administrations as well as post-military civilian governments (Adamolekun 2005, 384–5; Akande 2003). While highlighting the failures of Nigeria's current post-military framework in fostering ethno-religious conflict as well as poor economic governance, however, Adamolekun is surprisingly silent on the widely acknowledged ethnic asymmetries and insecurities engendered by the pre-1966 federal framework.

A second perspective is represented in the writings both of noted Nigerian federal scholars like Isawa Elaigwu and Egite Oyovbaire, and of distinguished external observers of Nigerian politics like Larry Diamond, Donald Horowitz, Arend Lijphart, Richard Sklar and Crawford Young (Diamond 1988; Elaigwu 2005; Horowitz 1985; Lijphart 1977; Oyovbaire 1985; Sklar 1999; Young 1976). This perspective sees the pre-1966 federal system, with its flagrant inequalities in the populations of regional governments, as a 'bizarre version of federalism', which appeared to have been 'designed in such a way as to virtually guarantee its failure' (Diamond 1988, 155; Lijphart 1977, 163). Indeed, far from producing a 'golden age', the pre-1966 federal system distorted Nigeria's complex ethnic balance, fuelled ethnic and regional polarisation, destabilised a fledgling democratic republic, and set the stage for ethno-military infighting and secessionist warfare. Furthermore, while the old regions were certainly more economically competitive than the current states, the 'three- or four-region system' was not 'sufficiently decentralised for meaningful economic and social development. ... Hence, the addition of states was, in this respect, a positive development' (Osayimwese and Iyare 1991, 101). Indeed, while it has fostered centralism and produced local-level tensions, the military's dissolution of the old powerful regions into demographically smaller and constitutionally weaker states has helped to crosscut major ethic identities, foster inter-regional integration, promote inter-group political equilibrium, and prevent a recurrence of large-scale ethno-secessionist warfare.

Federalism and conflict management

In his seminal 1985 work, *Ethnic groups in conflict*, as well as in a more recent article on 'The many uses of federalism,' Horowitz cites Nigeria as a model of constructive federalist ethnic conflict-management (Horowitz 1985; 2007). Indeed, as Horowitz demonstrates and the analysis in this section will try to corroborate, Nigerian federal institutions have contributed to the cauterisation of conflict in multiple interrelated ways.

First, by establishing separate constituent units for the country's minority non-Hausa-Fulani, non-Yoruba, and non-Ibo communities, which account collectively for approximately a third of the Nigerian population, Nigeria's current federal structure operates to protect the nation's smaller ethnicities from the unrestrained political hegemony of the biggest three groups. Whereas the 1954–1966 federal system had denied the minorities the security of their own states or regions, the current 36-state structure includes some 14 states that are populated mainly by minority populations. Although it has not been possible to give each minority group a state of its own (and strident agitations for new states have persisted in many of the more ethnically heterogeneous minority-populated states) the multi-state federal system has enabled 'a variety of ethnic minority states to play an increasingly active role in a more fluid and decentralized polity' (Rothchild 1991, 39). Not surprisingly, despite the insurgency among the southern ethnic minority communities of the Niger Delta, anti-secessionist sentiment and support for Nigeria's continued existence has been relatively strong among Nigeria's ethnic minority communities since the 1967 state-creation exercise (Suberu 2004).

Second, by establishing the states as relatively autonomous arenas of political authority and resource competition, Nigerian federalism has served to devolve ethnic conflict away from the federal government or a few regional centres to the various state capitals. This devolution, in turn, has helped to localise ethnic conflicts in individual states and to lessen the possibility that such conflicts will engulf other constituent units or overwhelm the national political system. Although it has generated inter-religious violence especially in Kaduna, the implementation of Sharia law is illustrative of the remarkable capacity of the Nigerian federal system to devolve, diffuse and defuse potentially disintegrative sectional conflicts. Essentially, Nigeria's current federal institutions have enabled states in the Muslim north to institute fairly elaborate systems of Islamic courts in response to the demands of their predominantly Muslim populations without threatening the cultural autonomy or security of non-Muslim populations in other states or violating the basic secularity or religious neutrality of the common federal arena. More important, divergent perspectives, strategies, and practices regarding Sharia implementation have developed from state to state in the Muslim north, thereby helping to quarantine the Sharia issue at the level of each state, while also potentially promoting the roles of the states as innovative laboratories of sub-national governance.

Third, Nigerian federalism has mitigated conflict by providing asymmetry-like arrangements for areas with distinctive needs or identities. Nigeria is, of course, not a formally asymmetrical federation in which constituent states enjoy different constitutional prerogatives or competences. Rather, all Nigerian states have equal legal and constitutional prerogatives, and the principle of inter-state equality is widely invoked in several policy domains, including the allocation of revenues, the distribution of federal developmental undertakings, and the creation of new states. However, the Nigerian constitution has incorporated provisions that have created de facto, as distinct from de jure, asymmetries. Thus, the constitutional provisions permitting any states to establish Islamic and/or customary courts have enabled the northern Muslim states to maintain fairly elaborate systems of Islamic courts and laws that are absent elsewhere in the federation. Additionally, the constitution implicitly promotes forms of economic asymmetry. Section 162 (2) of the constitution, for instance, provides for the reallocation, on the basis of the derivation or constituent-unit-of-origin principle, of 'not less than thirteen percent of the revenue accruing to the federation ... directly from any natural resources'. This rule has led to the payment of billions of dollars in oil revenues exclusively to the oil-rich states in response to the militant agitations for resource control in the Niger Delta region, although the non-transparent management of the derivation revenues has left the Niger Delta insurgency unresolved.

Fourth, Nigerian federalism has functioned to fragment and crosscut the identities of each of the three major ethnic formations of Hausa-Fulani, Yoruba and Igbo. Whereas the old regional system had institutionalised the demographic and political dominance of these groups in the relatively oversized Northern, Western, and Eastern Regions, respectively, the current 36-state structure distributes the core population of each majority ethnicity among at least five states. As Henry Hale has shown, such administrative subdivision of numerically dominant ethnicities can help to avoid excessive disparities in the sizes and political influence of constituent units, thereby containing the dual power situations, ethnic minority insecurities, and dominant community imaginings that have been at the heart of state collapse or civil war in many ethnic federations with core or super-dominant constituent units, including First Republic Nigeria, Yugoslavia, the Soviet Union (USSR), and Pakistan (Hale 2004). Indeed, the administrative subdivision of each of Nigeria's three major ethnicities into multiple constituent units has helped to alleviate ethno-centrifugal challenges to federal authority, contain fears of inter-group domination, and expose important historical, territorial, or sub-ethnic cleavages within each of the major ethnic groups. Although the major ethnic groups continue to demonstrate considerable internal cohesion as they compete with each other in bidding for supremacy in national politics, this ethnic solidarity is significantly less incendiary than the aggressive ethnic sub-nationalisms that had expressed themselves through the old regional system, provoked ethnic minority paranoia, fuelled secessionist tendencies, and brought the country to the brink of disintegration.

Fifth, the subdivision of each major group into several states has combined with the creation of several minority-controlled heterogeneous states to promote constituent unit identities as a cleavage that is independent of, and even competitive with, raw ethnic identities. This is because the division of a country into multiple subunits, especially when they are not strictly isomorphic with ethnic boundaries, 'can create incentives for political actors to see at least some issues in terms of competition among those units, rather than among ethnic groups' (Horowitz 2007, 107). For instance, the intergovernmental legal conflict in 2004 over the 'Allocation of Revenue (Abolition of Dichotomy in the Application of the Principle of Derivation) Act' pitted 22 non-littoral/non-oil producing states, including all 19 states in the north and three south-western states, against the federal government and 14 mainly oil-bearing and/or littoral states. Each of the two opposing sides involved a coalition of states that cut across Nigeria's ethnic, tri-regional and religious fault-lines. More significantly, conflicts between the federal government and the states over issues like revenue sharing, macro-economic stabilisation, anti-corruption reform, the management of local governments, decentralisation of governmental functions, and other states rights issues, have highlighted non-sectarian, functional and jurisdictional policy cleavages, thereby diluting the traditional crystallisation or polarisation of Nigerian government and politics around ethnic, regional or religious fault-lines.

Sixth, Nigeria's multiplicity of ethnically heterogeneous states can provide sites 'at which politicians of various groups can encounter each other, become familiar with each other, engage in bargaining, and learn about the needs and aspirations of groups other than their own before they rise to the national level, where more complex and delicate issues of national policy may need to be resolved' (Horowitz 2007, 107). A good example is the crafting of a compromise formula in 2000 for Sharia implementation in Kaduna state under the leadership of Governor

Mohammed Makarfi in response to the ethno-religious crisis in the state over the issue. Based on the recommendations of consultative committees, on which Muslims and Christians were equally represented, the compromise formula involved the establishment of new customary courts and chiefdoms for minority non-Muslim southern Kaduna tribes, the delegation of the authority to make religion-based by-laws to local councils, the exemption of religiously mixed parts of the state (including several sections of Kaduna city, the administrative capital) from the application of any parochial laws as a way of preserving the 'cosmopolitan and heterogeneous complexity' of these areas, and the prohibition of the notoriously abusive religious vigilante groups (Suberu 2004, 338). Partly because of his exemplary leadership in moderating Kaduna's Christian-Muslim fault-line, Makarfi's candidacy for the Nigerian presidency was widely promoted in 2006. And, although the PDP's presidential nomination in 2007 eventually went to the governor of neighbouring Katsina, Makarfi and several other governors subsequently assumed important political roles at the national level as senators or members of the federal cabinet. This political socialisation role of federalism in conflict management is one that is likely to become more significant as Nigeria's fledgling democracy endures over several electoral cycles.

Seventh, Nigerian federalism has functioned as an effective form of electoral reform. In the First Republic, the disproportionate size of the Hausa-Fulani-dominated Northern Region allowed the Hausa-Fulani (who constituted only about 30% of the Nigerian population, but about 60% of the northern population) to use their region as 'a springboard to national power' to the chagrin of other groups. But the dissolution of the regions into multiple states 'changed the arenas that groups and parties could dominate', and promoted greater proportionality in the relationship between ethnic group size and electoral strength. In essence, the Hausa-Fulani could no longer 'dominate Nigerian politics from their disproportionately large Northern base' and, therefore, had 'to seek genuine coalitions with other groups' (Horowitz 2007, 962).

Eighth, as underscored by the aforementioned effect of state creation on Hausa-Fulani coalition behaviour, Nigerian federalism has helped to 'provide a stimulus for interethnic alignments and coalitions' (ibid). This is because the proliferation of groups and sub-groups through state reorganisations has made it much more difficult 'for one group to aspire to control the whole government through the democratic process', thereby enhancing incentives to form inter-ethnic coalitions. Such coalitions, in turn, 'are much more likely to attend to the interests of multiple groups, thereby reducing conflict, especially if the coalitions are formed before elections' (ibid).

Ninth, Nigerian federalism has served as an instrument for the more or less equitable representation of groups and units in the institutions of the central government. This objective is most effectively institutionalised through the federal character principle, which mandates the equal representation of the states in several federal institutions. Thus, not only do three members represent each state in the powerful, popularly elected senate (the upper house of the bicameral federal chamber), but also the federal cabinet must include at least an 'indigene' of each state. What is more, to be elected president, a candidate must win not only a plurality of votes nationally, but also at least 25% of votes in two-thirds of the states and in the federal capital territory. Indeed, the federal character principle has spawned a vast repertoire of more or less informal consociational practices that are designed to distribute, balance and rotate key political offices among the country's states, ethnicities, religious groups, regions and other cultural or geographical constituencies, including the six quasi-official geo-political zones (northwest, northeast, and middle-belt in the north, and southwest, southeast, and Niger delta or south-south in the south).

Tenth, and finally, particularly since the seventies, Nigerian federalism has functioned as a distributive mechanism for the devolution of centrally-controlled oil revenues, and related economic opportunities, to the constituent states and localities of the federation. This is achieved primarily through an elaborate revenue-sharing scheme, which provides for the centralised collection, and then the vertical (federal-state-local) and horizontal (inter-state and inter-local) distribution, of the country's major revenue sources. While revenue redistribution has produced massive and multiple contradictions in the Nigerian setting (discussed below), Nigerian and comparative experiences suggest that such intergovernmental financial transfers, when properly calibrated, can serve as a veritable mechanism not only for the mitigation of inter-regional economic disparities but also for the fiscal appeasement of separatist units or regions. For instance, one of the major inducements promoting moderation in the behaviour of Sharia-implementing states in Nigeria has been the overwhelming dependence of the northern Muslim constituent units on centrally redistributed oil revenues.

Its multiple conflict-management roles notwithstanding, contemporary Nigerian federalism has entailed enormous costs and contradictions. Three of these have been particularly conspicuous and contentious. The first involves the perpetration by states and local governments of discriminatory practices that exclude so-called non-indigenes (Nigerians resident in a constituent state that does not incorporate their presumed historic ancestral or indigenous communities) from opportunities (educational admissions, bureaucratic placement, political offices, land and other economic resources, federal projects) available in such states. This has engendered a monumental crisis of internal citizenship in Nigeria, including convulsive violence between indigenes and long-settled non-indigenes in states such as Plateau, Taraba and Benue.

A second contradiction is the persistent political and legal contention between the federal government and the states over the reorganisation, funding, and elections of local government areas or councils. This conflict derives from the hyper-centralising legacy of military rule in promoting a uniform system of local government in Nigeria, the struggles of Nigeria's post-military constituent state administrations to reassert state control over, or curb federal government interventions in local government administration, and the ambiguous provisions of the 1999 constitution regarding the status of localities.

A third contradiction of the current federal framework in Nigeria is the massive political corruption that takes place at federal and particularly state and local levels, producing a syndrome of decentralised corruption, which is significantly generated and reinforced by the federal revenue distribution system. It is to this last pathology that we now turn.

The economic and democratic underdevelopment of Nigerian federalism

Since the expansion of oil revenue receipts in the seventies, the country's federal governance has consciously de-prioritised or politicised issues of intergovernmental fiscal responsibility, accountability, viability and sustainability. Indeed, the 1975 Ayo Irikefe Panel on State Creation explicitly rejected the principle of economic viability as a basis for federal reform in Nigeria. Instead, the Panel defended a purely centrist and re-distributive approach to intergovernmental fiscal relations. In the words of the Panel, 'each state [in the federation] was not, and should not, be required to function as a ... self-sufficient unit ...' Rather, the 'country as a whole constitutes a single economic system and so long as this system is viable, the viability of the component units can be assured through the redistributive actions of the Federal Government' (FRN 1976, 13).

The centrist or unitary nature of Nigeria's fiscal federalism is underscored by the fact that the federation currently derives about 90% of its public revenues and foreign exchange earnings from the oil wealth of the southern Niger Delta region, thereby making the country the most oil-dependent federation in the world. The 1999 constitution formally upholds the principle of distributive federalism by providing for the centralised collection and redistribution of the oil revenues through the Federation Account, which is the repository for all major, centrally collected revenues, including mineral, import and company taxes. The Account is then shared, according to a law of the National Assembly, based on proposals submitted to the Assembly by the president on the advice of the Revenue Mobilisation Allocation and Fiscal Commission (RMAFC), vertically between the centre, the states and the localities, and horizontally among the sub-federal tiers.

Currently, revenues in the Federation Account are distributed vertically in the proportions of 48.50%, 26.72%, 20.60% and 4.18% to the federal government, states, localities, and centrally controlled special funds, respectively. Horizontally, the Federation Account revenues devolved to the sub-federal governments are respectively shared among the states and among the localities on the basis of the following indices and percentage weights: Equality (equal shares to each state or locality designated in the federal constitution) 40%; Population 30%; Social Development Needs 10%; Land Mass and Terrain 10%; and Internal Revenue Generation Effort 10%.

Federally collected revenues constitutionally exempted from this general vertical/horizontal distributive scheme include: the 13% minimum revenues from natural resources to be paid exclusively to the states of derivation; the net proceeds of centrally collected taxes on capital gains and stamp duties to be paid also to the states of derivation; the income tax of diplomatic, military and police functionaries and residents of Abuja, regarded as independent revenues of the Federal Government; and the value-added tax (VAT), which replaced the state-based sales tax in 1994 and is shared according to a distinct allocation rule, vertically and horizontally. In addition, the states administer and retain personal income tax, collected under a uniform national income tax law, while the localities are constitutionally empowered to assess private 'houses or tenements for the purpose of levying such rates as may be prescribed by the House of Assembly of a State' (FRN 1999, Fourth Schedule). Their control of potentially lucrative personal income and property taxes notwithstanding, the Nigerian states and localities, in aggregate, depend on federal revenue transfers for 90% of their finances (World Bank 2003, 51).

The Nigerian system of centralised intergovernmental fiscal transfers and revenue distribution has impeded, rather than advanced, the goals of 'promoting development, maintaining economic equilibrium, stimulating significant additional revenues, diversifying revenue sources, and enhancing fiscal efficiency' (Phillips 1991, 110). Several reasons account for the dysfunctional nature of Nigeria's fiscal federalism.

First, Nigeria's fiscal federalism is hyper-centralised, promoting the economic hegemony of the central government and the financial subordination and complacency of the sub-national authorities. It, therefore, lacks the type of competitive economic decentralisation, including economically self-governing sub-national jurisdictions, associated with a system of 'market-preserving' or prosperity-promoting federalism (Aiyede 2009). Rather the growth in centralised federal power in Nigeria has been characterised by the large-scale misallocation of resources and the subordination of economic development imperatives to political considerations (Phillips 1991; Osayimwese and Iyare 1991).

Second, the absence of current, accurate and/or broadly acceptable population and socio-economic data casts serious doubts about the reliability of the revenue allocation indices designed to promote redistribution in Nigeria. Third, in so far as it has been impossible to make all the states or the localities nearly exactly equal in population, the substantial weight assigned to the horizontal principle of inter-unit equality produces significant per capita disparities in the access of the sub-federal governments to federal revenues, while unleashing strong pressures for the proliferation of new sub-national state and local administrations. As claimed by Phillips (1991, 110), 'the continuing significant use of population and equality as the factors for determining resource allocation is largely without an objective basis and constitutes a major obstacle to making Nigeria's [revenue allocation system] a dynamic and effective instrument for development'.

Fourth, partly as a result of the scheme's focus on a politicised allocation formula, rather than on actual needs and the overall consequences of the federal fiscal regime or the effectiveness and quality of public and fiscal policy, human development indicators and regional socio-economic disparities in Nigeria remain among the worst in the world. Thus, basic social indicators like life expectancy, maternal mortality, access to primary healthcare, nutritional health, school enrollment, literacy rates, industrial employment, volume of bank savings and deposits, energy availability and consumption, access to potable water, communication facilities, gender equity, and non-religious associational life, are worse for the northern Nigerian states than for the southern states. More specifically, there are significantly higher disease and epidemic burdens in the north than the south, where an estimated 80% of hospital beds are located. In essence, for all its formal emphasis on fiscal redistribution and solidarity, the Nigerian revenue allocation system has failed woefully to promote genuine inter-regional socio-economic equity. Rather, the revenue allocation system has been more successful in promoting accumulation among an ethnically and regionally diversified elite group, than in ensuring mass-based social equity across the regions of the federation.

Fifth, while it automatically and unconditionally devolves a considerable amount of centrally collected revenues to the sub-national authorities, the revenue allocation system lacks a mechanism to ensure the effective utilisation of these revenues by the states and localities, which suffer from very weak budget formulation, accounting, recording, and reporting systems. In addition, the system lacks a mechanism for promoting the effective contribution of sub-national administrations to national macro-economic management. As things stand, the poor quality of public financial management at the sub-national level, where approximately half of national public spending takes place, represents a huge macro-economic challenge in Nigeria (IMF 2009).

Sixth, and most importantly, the constitutionally and statutorily mandated (and, hence, more or less politically automatic) access of governments to centrally collected and redistributed oil revenues that are not generated from the taxation of the population has promoted grand corruption and patronage politics, including the theft of 'more than $380 billion in public funds ... by those in government between 1960 and 1999' (Human Rights Watch 2007, 16). The oil-based funding of constituent states and local governments by legally guaranteed central financial transfers has been a particularly powerful inducement to corruption at the sub-national level. This is because these governments are neither responsible to the centre nor accountable to their constituents for the use of the transfers. Rather, despite their overwhelming dependence on central, oil-based, financial transfers, the state governments regard such transfers as an unconditional, constitutional entitlement that is not subject to central government discretion or oversight under Nigeria's federal practice. Between 1999 and 2007, 31 governors were indicted or brought under investigation by Nigeria's anti-corruption bodies for various breaches of the public trust, including embezzlement, money laundering, false declaration of assets, maintaining foreign bank accounts in contravention of the statutory code of conduct for Nigerian public officers, and the fraudulent acquisition of properties abroad.

Corruption has been equally rampant at the local government level. Thus, a 2007 report on local government corruption in oil-rich Rivers State highlights several examples of embezzlement that included, for example, the illegal allocation to the chair of Khana's local government in 2005 of salary and allowances worth $376,000, which were 'nearly half the total amount allocated for the wages and allowances of Khana's 325 health-sector workers'; the allocation in 2006 to the chair of Tai's local government of a security vote of $300,000, which exceeded the council's total capital budgets for either health or education; and the illegal awarding during 2005–2006 by the chairman of Opobo Nkoro's local government of $91,000 worth of construction contracts to himself (Human Rights Watch 2007, 32, 36, 56).

The large-scale economic corruption in the Nigerian federal system has been closely intertwined with massive electoral corruption, which has been the most basic source of federal democratic instability in Nigeria. Monumental electoral shenanigans were a primary element in the collapse of federal democracy in the First and Second Nigerian Republics, and the proximate factor in the abortion of the Third Republic. Although the Fourth Republic has endured longer than any of its predecessors, elections held under the Republic (in 1999, 2003, and 2009) have been 'successively less fair, less efficient, and less credible' (Joseph 2008, 96). Electoral corruption, which is enormously facilitated by the overwhelming presidential and gubernatorial control over the appointments and funding of the so-called Independent National Electoral Commission (INEC) and the 36 State Independent Electoral Commissions (SIEC), has distorted and degraded Nigerian federalism in the following, interrelated, ways.

Electoral corruption has undermined the incentives for inter-ethnic coalition and accommodation inherent in the 'federal character' electoral rules that require presidential and gubernatorial candidates to obtain broad geographical support. Instead of generating and mobilising genuine support across the nation's ethnic, regional and religious fault-lines, candidates have been able to use force and fraud to manufacture seemingly broad-based, but actually farcical, electoral mandates. For instance, although his policies on the Niger Delta during the 1999–2003 period were extremely unpopular in the region, President Obasanjo was still credited with landslide victories in the Niger Delta states in the 2003 elections. In essence, as long as parties and candidates can simply concoct election results they will have very little incentive to cultivate or exhibit the ethnically conciliatory or moderate behaviour necessary to achieve the broad geographical support mandated by formal electoral rules.

Similarly, electoral corruption in Nigeria has impeded the development of the robust, nationally integrated party systems considered to be crucial for the stability and development of federations in general, and multi-ethnic federal systems, in particular. Without the competitive discipline of a credible electoral system that rewards partisan coalitions with power on the basis of the voters' verdict, Nigeria's parties will continue to be weak, faction-ridden, personality-driven institutions lacking internal democracy, viable organisations, coherent policy platforms, vibrant social bases, effective representation for women and other marginalised social groups, and genuine cross-regional, inter-religious, and/or trans-ethnic appeals. Even the PDP, which proclaims itself to be Africa's largest party and is in fact impressively multi-regional, remains a fractious and ideologically inarticulate conglomerate of politicians, whose great common enterprise is the doling out of patronage along ethno-geographical lines.

Electoral corruption has promoted political over-centralisation, and retarded decentralisation, in the Nigerian federation. A promise of Nigeria's three-tier federalism is that the existence of multiple state governments and local administrations, with significant policy autonomy and access to resources, can disperse the stakes of political competition, making struggles for control over the centre less intense and helping political pluralism and policy innovations to gain footholds in different states and localities governed by various parties. But the malign hand of electoral manipulation has suppressed this federalist genius, producing an artificial condition of single-party domination of central, state and local governments (Suberu 2007). Thus, in the First, Second and current Fourth Republics, the ruling parties at the national level used their control of key electoral and security institutions to dislodge opposition parties at the regional or state level, thereby foisting an oppressive, ethnically provocative, single-party hegemony on the entire federation. Regional and state governments have similarly used their control of the institutions for local electoral administration to undermine opposition control, and thus political devolution and diversity, at the local level.

At the same time as it has fostered an artificial near-monolithic party system in the Nigerian federation, electoral manipulation has obstructed the development of the robust intergovernmental co-partisanship associated with genuinely integrated party systems. Such co-partisanship promotes the sustainability of federal programmes and policies through the support of those agendas by state governments that share the same party label and electoral interests with the federal government.

However, because it is largely the byproduct of electoral manipulation and corruption, inter-governmental co-partisanship in Nigeria often fails to yield genuine political or policy consensus between levels of government. During Obasanjo's civilian presidency, for instance, the PDP federal government orchestrated the impeachment or political subversion of several PDP state governments (including Anambra, Bayelsa, Oyo, and Plateau states), while many PDP state governments similarly challenged the federal government's positions on major policy issues like Sharia implementation, anti-corruption reform, and the savings of windfall oil revenues.

Finally, electoral manipulation has directly contributed to ethno-regional conflict and communal violence in Nigeria's multi-ethnic federation. The control of federal, state, and local administrations by corruptly imposed and politically unaccountable governments has obstructed the alleviation of the inter-regional inequalities and mass poverty that fuel violent ethno-regional militancy and religious extremism. In the Niger Delta, for instance, the mismanagement of derivation revenues by fraudulently elected, and thus politically unaccountable, state and local governments has fuelled militant uprisings against the region's ecological neglect, economic underdevelopment, social inequalities, and abysmal governance. Similarly, in Jos the rigging of local government elections by the state government in 2008 directly provoked convulsive ethno-religious violence.

An agenda for federal reform

Reflecting the profound and pervasive dissatisfaction with the performance of Nigerian federalism, the country's contemporary political discourse is significantly dominated by the theme of federal reform. Yet the quest for constitutional reform in general and federal restructuring, in particular, has proven to be deeply conflicted, unproductive, abortive and unpromising. Standing in the way of constitutional change is the absence of the broad political consensus and commitment necessary to surmount the relatively onerous constitutional amendment formula, which requires the approval of any change by a two-thirds majority of the total membership of each house of the National Assembly (or a four-fifths majority if the change pertains to certain entrenched clauses) supported by the resolution of the Houses of Assembly of two-thirds of the states. Rather, three different constituencies, with distinct perspectives and approaches, have dominated the movement for federal constitutional reform in Nigeria.

The first group involves a largely southern-based agglomeration of ethnic associations calling for a sovereign conference of ethnic nationalities that would restructure Nigeria into a 'true federalism'. Major components of these groups, which congregated in 2005–2006 under the banner of a Pro-National Conference (PRONACO) coalition, include the Yoruba-based Afenifere, the Ohanaeze Ndi Igbo, Union of the Niger Delta, Ijaw National Congress, Movement for the Survival of Ogoni People (MOSOP), Itsekiri Leaders of Thought, Movement for National Reformation, and the Patriots. Some of their most radical proposals for restructuring Nigerian federalism include the abandonment of the centrist executive presidential system and the return to parliamentary rule, the promotion of effective political decentralisation via the consolidation of the 36 Nigerian states into fewer (6–18) and bigger federating units, the decentralisation of the current unitary police force, the entrenchment of a constitutional right to ethnic self-determination and secession, and the transfer of control over natural resources from the center to sub-national regions, states or communities (PRONACO 2007).

A second group consists of a coalition of more than 100 civic (rather than ethnic) associations that have rallied under the banner of The Citizens Forum for Constitutional Reform (CFCR). The CFCR is distinguished less by its commitment to any distinct agenda of federal restructuring than by its advocacy of a bottom-up, process-led, people-driven, and participatory approach to constitutional reform that would enshrine such principles of contemporary democratic constitutionalism as inclusiveness, diversity, participation, transparency, autonomy (from governmental manipulation), accountability, accessibility and legitimacy. Nonetheless, the CFCR's 2002 *Model constitution of the federal republic of Nigeria* incorporates major proposals for federal reform including sub-national control of natural resources, a discrete list of state legislative powers (as distinct from the amorphous residual powers granted to the states under the 1999 constitution), full sub-national control of state and local government electoral processes, independent state police units, and separate state constitutions. At the same time, the model constitution embraces strong elements of centrist, national socio-economic democracy, including provisions for the unilateral amendment of the federal constitution by the federal government, central government powers of taxation over devolved natural resources, and strong guarantees of federation-wide social (education, health care and housing) and residency rights.

Lastly, in response to the broad clamour for constitutional change from Nigeria's ethno-regional and civic associations, the federal government launched its own constitutional review programme in 1999. The programme has, however, morphed into a largely opportunistic, corrupt, circuitous, conflicted, and ultimately abortive process of constitutional reform. The major protagonists in this official process of constitutional reform include the tri-partisan Presidential Committee on the Review of the Constitution (PCRC), the 394-member National Political Reform Conference (NPRC), and successive panels of the National Assembly's Joint Committee on Constitutional Review (JCCR). What these bodies have in common is their sponsorship by the federal government, their endorsement of the constitutional amendment formula enshrined in the 1999 constitution (as distinct from the more participatory and popular constitutional review processes envisaged by Nigeria's civic and ethnic groups), and their commitment to multiple but relatively modest, rather than fundamental, changes to the current federal system. These include alterations to the current maximum two four-year terms for political executives at national and state levels (in order to facilitate or regulate ethno-political alternations in power), adjustments to the intergovernmental distributions of legislative and judicial competencies, the restructuring of state-local government relations, a review or greater formalisation of the political status of local traditional rulers, and an expansion in the percentage of centrally collected revenues transferred to the oil-bearing states on a derivation basis (NPRC 2005).

However, despite sharing a broad consensus on the appropriate methodology and scope of political change, the official constitutional reform agencies have exhibited significant disagreements within and between their members regarding specific amendment proposals, especially with respect to the status of local government and the length of terms for political chief executives. Indeed, the official constitutional reform strategy suffered a major setback in 2006 when President Obasanjo and the governors sought to remove the two-term limits on their tenures. Yet, so unpopular was this 'third term agenda' that it was not only resoundingly defeated on the floor of the senate in 2006, but also caused the wholesale rejection by the senators of over 100 other amendments embodied in the JCCR's 2006 Constitutional Amendment Bill.

Since 2007, the official strategy of constitutional review has focused on a narrower range of constitutional reform issues, especially electoral reform. However, the lack of genuine commitment to basic democratic constitutional change by the federal executive and bickering between the senate and House of Representatives' members of the JCCR, among other factors, has stymied the official constitutional reform process. This is in spite of the eventual endorsement by the National Assembly and a majority of State Assemblies in July 2010 of a modest package of constitutional amendments, including guarantees of financial autonomy for the national electoral commission and federal and state legislatures, alterations to the national and state electoral calendars, and the formalisation of the acting powers of the vice-president and deputy governors. These changes were broadly condemned in Nigeria as mere constitutional tinkering that trivialised the popular demands for significant political reforms in the country.

Nonetheless, Nigeria's experience with constitutional politics since 1999 casts doubts about the desirability and viability of a strategy of comprehensive, mega-constitutional, change. Rather, the most realistic options for federal reform in Nigeria would involve a strategy of focused constitutional and non-constitutional (statutory) change in five specific areas, namely, electoral administration, local government structure, non-indigene citizenship and residency rights, revenue sharing, and fiscal accountability and transparency.

The massive and systematic corruption of electoral processes at federal, state and local levels constitutes the most immediate and fundamental impediment to robust federalism and national integration as well as democratic consolidation and good economic governance in Nigeria. Consequently, as recommended by the Electoral Reform Committee (ERC), which was established by the Yar'Adua administration in the wake of domestic and international criticisms of the flagrant manipulation and mismanagement of the 2007 elections, the '1999 constitution should be amended to ensure that the INEC becomes truly independent, non-partisan, impartial, professional, transparent, and reliable as an institution and in the performance of its constitutional functions' (ERC 2008, 25). The ERC makes several specific recommendations for improving the quality and credibility of Nigerian elections, including the creation of new electoral oversight bodies, the adoption of a mixed Proportional Representation-Plurality electoral system, and the streamlining of the processes for the resolution of electoral petitions. However, its most important recommendation, which deserves to be prioritised over other electoral and broader constitutional reform ideas, is the proposal for the open solicitation and screening of nominees for the Board of INEC by the independent National Judicial Council (NJC) before the appointment and confirmation of the Board by the National Council of State and the senate, respectively. This would put an end to the egregious manipulation of appointments into INEC by the presidency.

The ERC also proposed the assimilation of the current severely discredited SIEC into a reformed INEC in order to guarantee the credibility of local government elections. This recommendation is consistent with the positions of the NPRC and the

2003–2007 JCCR, both of which proposed a more direct role for the federal government in the reorganisation, funding and electoral administration of local governments in order to constrain the political manipulation and financial exploitation of the localities by the state governments. While it apparently enjoys the broad support of political and bureaucratic functionaries at the local government level, such centralisation or nationalisation of the local government system is not only very unpopular among the state governments and the nation's ethnic and civic constitutional reform movements, but it was also rejected by the PCRC and 1999–2003 JCCR, both of which supported a less nationally integrated local government system. Yet, the creation of non-partisan federation-wide oversight agencies, like the NJC and the proposed new INEC, is not necessarily synonymous with federal government domination or inconsistent with the exercise of a significant degree of state initiative and autonomy. Rather, such national agencies of restraint can help to advance the goals of good, rule-based, democratic governance at federal, state and local levels. At the same time, care must be taken to avoid the degeneration of national oversight and regulation into crude hyper-centralisation. Thus, the constitutional entrenchment of the current 774 local government areas should be altered to make it possible for states either to reorganise their local government structures without ratification by the National Assembly and/or federal constitutional amendment, or to create politically effective and legally viable tiers of local governance and administration (community development councils, areas or districts) below the uniform national tier of local government.

Both the value of credible national agencies of restraint and the dangers of unbridled state autonomy are underscored by the phenomenon of violent discrimination against non-indigenes at the sub-national level. Although legitimised by the constitutional principle of federal character, indigene-based discriminatory policies, which effectively relegate millions of Nigerians into second-class status in their own country, violate constitutional guarantees of non-discrimination and equal citizenship rights across the federation. An independent, constitutionally-entrenched National Human Rights Commission can perhaps play an important role in promoting and enforcing the citizenship rights of so-called non-indigenes in the states. Yet, it should be noted that discrimination against non-indigenes has attracted routine or rhetorical denunciations from successive Nigerian presidents as well as more concrete proposals by some state governments (for example, in Abia and Niger), constitutional review bodies, and legislators in the National Assembly for a national policy that would replace indigene-ship with residency in the states (over a specified number of years) as the basis for obtaining full legal membership and socio-economic entitlements in Nigeria's constituent units. However, given the entrenched local interests (at elite and mass levels) benefiting from indigene-based socio-economic discrimination, these attempts to address Nigeria's crisis of internal citizenship have proved completely ineffective. Ultimately, an effective, long-term solution to the indigene-ship issue, and to divisive sectional competition for public resources in Nigeria more generally, would require economic development, which would expand socio-economic opportunities to individuals and groups in the private sector outside of the ethno-politically fraught government sector.

One way to promote such national economic development and mitigate inter-group discrimination and inequality is to transform the current revenue sharing system from a mechanism for dividing the spoils of national oil wealth among federal, state and local elites into an instrument for efficient and equitable economic governance. Essentially, this would involve the distribution of substantial proportions of the current federation account not as politically automatic disbursements on the basis of such unreliable and simplistic criteria as population and inter-unit equality, but in the form of conditional grants to fund expenditure obligations of the states and localities in areas such as education, health, and rural infrastructures, and to reward the transparent, efficient, and effective use of both federal revenue transfers and internal revenue sources. Putting such a system in place would require the establishment of an independent Fiscal Commission that is much more politically independent and technocratic, yet socially accountable and responsible, than the current RMAFC.

A final and related challenge of federalism in Nigeria involves containing the entrenched culture of political corruption through laws and programmes to encourage fiscal responsibility and efficiency among all levels of government. To be sure, the period since the restoration of civilian rule in 1999 has witnessed major initiatives designed to enthrone a culture of fiscal prudence, integrity, transparency and accountability in the management of oil revenues. The measures include the establishments of the Independent Corrupt Practices Commission (ICPC), Economic and Financial Crimes Commission (EFCC), Nigeria Extractive Industry Transparency Initiative (NEIT – designed to promote the reporting and disclosure of all revenues paid or payable to government by oil companies), Excess Crude Oil Account (into which was saved windfall oil revenues above a predetermined budgetary benchmark), Fiscal Responsibility Act (designed to promote budgetary discipline), and Public Procurement Act. Yet, these measures have been largely limited to the federal level, have been resisted or trivialised by the state governments, and have lacked adequate political insulation, making them vulnerable to emasculation or manipulation by the very political class whose excesses they are designed to curb. Like the proposed new INEC, these mechanisms need to be removed from the direct control of the executive and brought under the purview of a politically insulated agency such as the NJC.

Conclusion

Contemporary political and scholarly debates about Nigerian federalism often overlook both the flagrant shortcomings of the country's pre-1967 regional federalism and the significant achievements of the current, more centralised, federal framework. Whereas the pre-1967 federalism had fuelled ethno-regional conflict, inequality, insecurity and secessionism, the current 36-state system has functioned quite successfully to crosscut major ethnic identities, foster inter-regional integration, promote inter-group equilibrium, and generally contain major destabilising challenges to Nigeria's continuity as a single political community.

Indeed, Nigeria's current federal architecture exhibits several features that many students of comparative federalism and ethnic conflict-management would consider judicious, although there is no widespread consensus on an optimal federal design (Suberu 2009). These features include the constitutional devolution of significant policy-making competences (in education and health, for instance) to constituent states, the fragmentation of numerically dominant ethnic and religious communities into multiple sub-national jurisdictions, demarcation of the federation into relatively plentiful and symmetrically sized jurisdictions, electoral incentives for the formation of federation-wide political parties, formal and informal ethnic power sharing arrangements, the effective representation of constituent states in the federal government through the establishment of a robust upper legislative chamber, and the creation of a relatively sturdy central government with sufficient powers and resources potentially to secure national unity and development.

Yet, while they have been effective in preventing a recurrence of ethno-secessionist warfare, Nigeria's current federal institutions have failed to promote the country's democratic and economic development, thereby undermining the integrative achievements of those institutions. These shortcomings reflect a fundamental defect in the country's constitutional framework. This has failed to establish and entrench strong, non-partisan, and truly independent electoral, anti-corruption, fiscal, and related institutions of vertical and horizontal restraints that can secure federal democracy and good economic governance by constraining the abuse of power by political office-holders at federal, state, and local levels. Until this fundamental institutional challenge is overcome, Nigeria's prospects as a multi-ethnic federal democracy will remain precarious.

References

Adamolekun, L. 2005. The Nigerian federation at the crossroads: The way forward. *Publius: The Journal of Federalism* 35, no. 3: 383–405.

Aiyede, E. 2009. The political economy of fiscal federalism and the dilemma of constructing a developmental state in Nigeria. *International Political Science Review* 30, no. 3: 249–69.

Akande, B. 2003. *Restructuring: Nigeria's approach to true federalism*. Osogbo: Osun State Government.

Diamond, L. 1988. *Class, ethnicity and democracy in Nigeria: The failure of the first republic*. London: Macmillan.

Elaigwu, I. 2005. *The politics of federalism in Nigeria*. Jos: Aha Publishing House.

Electoral Reform Committee (ERC). 2008. *Report of the electoral reform committee: Volume 1, main report*. Abuja: ERC.

Federal Republic of Nigeria (FRN). 1976. *Federal military government's views on the report of the panel on creation of states*. Lagos: FRN.

Federal Republic of Nigeria (FRN). 1999. *Constitution of the federal republic of Nigeria 1999*. Abuja: FRN.

Hale, H. 2004. Divided we stand: Institutional sources of ethnofederal state survival and collapse. *World Politics* 56, no. 2: 165–93.

Horowitz, D. 1985. *Ethnic groups in conflict*. Berkeley, CA: University of California Press.

Horowitz, D. 2007. The many uses of federalism. *Drake Law Review* 55: 953–66.

Human Rights Watch, (HRW). 2007. *Chop fine: The human rights impact of local government corruption and mismanagement in Rivers State, Nigeria*. New York: HRW.

International Crisis Group (ICG). 2006. *Nigeria's faltering federal experiment*. Africa Report 119, October 25.

International Monetary Fund (IMF). 2009. Nigeria country report, no. 09/315, November.

Joseph, R. 2008. Challenges of a frontier region. *Journal of Democracy* 19, no. 2: 94–107.

Lijphart, A. 1977. *Democracy in plural societies: A comparative exploration*. New Haven, CT: Yale University Press.

National Political Reform Conference (NPRC). 2005. *Main report of the conference*. Abuja: NPRC.

Osayimwese, I., and S. Iyare. 1991. The economics of Nigerian federalism: Selected issues in economic management. *Publius: The Journal of Federalism* 21, no. 4: 89–101.

Oyovbaire, S. 1985. *Federalism in Nigeria: A study in the development of the Nigerian state*. London: Macmillan.

Phillips, A. 1991. Managing fiscal federalism: Revenue allocation issues. *Publius: The Journal of Federalism* 21, no. 4: 103–11.

Pro-National Conference (PRONACO). 2007. *Draft of the peoples national conference proposed constitution for the federal republic of Nigeria*. Lagos: PRONACO.

Rothchild, D. 1991. An interactive model for state-ethnic relations. In *Conflict resolution in Africa*, ed. F. Deng and I. Zartman. Washington. DC: Brookings Institution.
Sklar, R. 1999. Foundations of federal government in Nigeria. Paper for the 42nd Annual Meeting of the African Studies Association (ASA), Philadelphia, Pennsylvania, November 12.
Suberu, R. 2004. Nigeria: Dilemmas of federalism. In *Federalism and territorial cleavages*, ed. U. Amoretti and N. Bermeo. Baltimore. MD: Johns Hopkins University Press.
Suberu, R. 2007. Nigeria's muddled elections. *Journal of Democracy* 18, no. 4: 95–110.
Suberu, R. 2009. Federalism in Africa: The Nigerian experience in comparative perspective. *Ethnopolitics* 8, no. 1: 67–86.
World Bank, 2003. *Nigeria states finance study.* Washington, DC: World Bank
Young, C. 1976. *The politics of cultural pluralism.* Madison, WI: University of Wisconsin Press.

How God became a Nigerian: Religious impulse and the unfolding of a nation

Afe Adogame

Centre for the Study of World Christianity, University of Edinburgh, UK

Nigeria, the most populous country in sub-Saharan Africa with a population of some 150 million people, is an embodiment of historical, cultural, ethnic, religious, social, and linguistic affinities and diversities. Its religious landscape is highly complex and dynamic, comprising a multiplicity of religious traditions, including the indigenous religions, the various strands of Christianity and Islam, as well as newer Spiritual Science movements. These religious traditions have mutually enhanced and transformed each other in a highly competitive context. They serve as significant sources through which many Nigerians seek understanding of their complex reality and existence; they are instrumental in maintaining peace and cohesion but also sometimes in fostering religious violence and conflict. This contribution explores the religious impulse in the unfolding of Nigeria as a nation through the prism of religious history and its interconnectedness with politics; the contestation of ritual and social space and power in Nigeria's religious economy; and also through its negotiation and self-insertion into the global religious marketplace.

The historiography of Nigeria's religions is as complex as its political, cultural and economic tapestry with its rich, vast cultural and religious diversities, 250 ethnicities, and over 400 languages. The religious landscape of this geopolitical entity is complex, fluid, and dynamic. It is characterised by a multiplicity of religious traditions, inclusive of local ethnic-based religions and world views, and various strands of Christianity and Islam, as well as newer spiritual science movements. Another recent phenomenon within Nigeria's multifaith scenario is what has been described elsewhere as civil religion (Olupona 2003).

Accurate statistics for each tradition are difficult to come by and are largely a matter of conjecture. However, it is evident that the major religious traditions in Nigeria are Christianity and Islam, both influenced by indigenous religious traditions. In the past, the politicisation of the census on religious and ethnic grounds resulted in unreliable religio-ethnic demographic data in Nigeria, as population statistics were (and still are) often manipulated for political, economic, and religious ends, not least because such figures constitute one basis for the sharing of national revenue and other resources. That partly explains why religious indices were excluded from the recent national census.

The politics of religious statistics has become even more controversial with the enduring debate about whether Nigeria is a secular or religious state. Whatever the case may be, religious ideas and world views continue to shape the ways that Nigerians explain, predict, and control the events and life circumstances that surround them. Religion or spirituality has served as a significant source through which many Nigerians seek understanding of their complex reality and existence, and it serves as a panacea for their various existential problems of day-to-day living. At the same time, the increasing visibility and mobility, contestation, and instrumentalisation of religion has engendered ambivalences of peace and violence, cohesion and conflict, functionality and dysfunctionality – to the extent that commentators query whether religion is more of a bane than a boon to Nigeria's corporate existence.

Religious competition and conflict emerges not only from increased diversity and resurgence, but also involves internal dynamics of conflict within specific religious groupings. Religious identification, contention, and competition take on new configurations and tackle alternative loyalties in ways that further precipitate interfaith dialogue and mutual collaboration on the one hand; but religious polarity, conflict and violence on the other. Yet the interconnectedness between religion, politics, economy, ethnicity, migration, violence, and conflict do not occur in a historical vacuum. To gauge the religious impulse in the unfolding of the Nigerian nation, we shall undertake a concise periodisation of her religious history in order to locate the contours and prisms of religion's interface with the politico-economy; the contestation of ritual and social space and power in Nigeria's religious economy; and also its negotiation with and self-insertion into global religious landscapes.

The anatomy and taxonomy of a multi-religious heritage

Nigeria's religious tapestry is remarkably robust and complex, and can be periodised under phases that are in themselves not mutually exclusive.

Indigenous religions

Local, ethnic-based religions are apparently the oldest genre. Examples of such indigenous religious forms are delineated in academic circles by the name of the respective linguistic/cultural groupings such as: the Yoruba, Igbo, Edo, Kalabari, Hausa and Tiv religions. This categorisation does not presuppose uniformity of beliefs and rituals among them. Indigenous religions are more or less localised; some beliefs may be more widespread while others may vary from one ethnic group to another. What the categorisation suggests is an aggregation of shared, similar, and related but sometimes quite different belief and ritual systems, often shaped by particular ethnic and social groups, power structures, and even the characteristics of natural phenomenon in each locality. The indigenous religions do not lay claim to any specific historical origins but are believed to be transmitted cross-generationally.

In spite of wide-ranging differences, the varied indigenous religions of Nigerian societies share common affinities in their ideas, rituals, and world views, thus constituting a distinctively indigenous pattern of religious thought and action. The emergence and expansion of Islam, Christianity, Eastern and Western-related spiritualities saw the introduction of new religious ideas and practices into indigenous religions. The encounter transformed indigenous religious thought and practice but did not supplant it; indigenous religions preserved some of their beliefs and ritual practices but also adjusted to the new socio-cultural milieu. Owing to social changes, aspects of indigenous beliefs and rituals were either abandoned, transformed or reinvented due to the impingement of European, Arab and Asian cultures, religions and spiritualities. The change also led to the revival of other aspects of indigenous religious cultures. In many cases, Islam and Christianity became adapted to Nigerian soil. The contact produced new religions, with some appropriating indigenous symbols and giving them a new twist (Adogame 2007, 536).

The historical and cultural significance of indigenous religious traditions is partly discerned in their plurality and multivocality both in Nigeria and the Nigerian diaspora. These indigenous religions encountered other religious forms and responded by revitalising themselves through synthesis, reinvention, and change. Their dynamism is exemplified by their tendency toward growth and innovation, a development that has given birth to what is now described as neotraditional movements. A case in point is Ijo Orunmila, a movement founded in the 1930s by Yoruba Christians seeking to re-establish links with their traditional religious heritage. In 1963 the Arousa Cult (Edo National Church), which developed from Bini indigenous religion, fused with another neotraditional movement, the National Church of Nigeria, to form Godianism. The Bori cult, a neotraditional movement prominent among Hausa women, draws partly on Islamic beliefs and practices. Also significant here are the various transformations of the Nigerian-derived religions in the diaspora, including Santeria, Candomblé, and the numerous Orisa and Ifa-derived religiosities (Olupona 2001; Hackett 1987; Clarke 2004; Adogame 2009b).

Modernising social change has resulted in the decline of some indigenous practices and modes of thought even as it has brought about a revitalisation and modification of others. Thus any claim that Christianity and Islam have totally outweighed indigenous religion is problematic. The indigenous religious world view, or aspects of it, still largely pervade, consciously or unconsciously, in the outlook and vision of many Nigerians, regardless of new religious convictions. The pertinence of indigenous religions for many is evident in the resilient belief in supernatural forces, the reality of ancestors, and the growing popularity of pantheons of divinities such as Ogun, Osun, Emenala, and Olokun. Kingship rituals such as the Igue Festival in Benin City, secret societies such as the Ogboni Society in Western Nigeria, masquerades such as Egungun and Eyo among the Yoruba, divination, healing, and oracle systems such as Arockukwu among the Igbo and Ifa among the Yoruba, and the prevalent belief in the reality of witchcraft and sorcery are instances of avenues through which indigenous religions manifest resilience in the face of a complex, multireligious, and rapidly changing society (Olupona 2001; Adogame 2009b).

Islam

The historiography of new religions in contemporary Nigeria spans the incursion of Islam in the eleventh century, the introduction of mission Christianity from the fifteenth and nineteenth centuries, through to the colonial era from the early twentieth century to the contemporary period. Islam penetrated sub-Saharan Africa long before the advent of European Christianity. Islam penetrated the continent's interior across the West African savannahs and the Sahara Desert to the north. It spread through North Africa by conquest, but the situation differed considerably in sub-Saharan Africa where it took on the insignia of trade and commerce. Islam vigorously pursued a conversion policy that became highly successful in areas now spanning several sub-Saharan countries over the centuries. Its spread to sub-Saharan Africa, including Northern Nigeria, revealed its commercial and sometimes military outlook. The old caravan routes carried Muslim merchants, teachers, and mystics who settled among the African peoples and states. Until about 1450, Islam provided the major external contact between sub-Saharan Africa and the world.

The Islamisation process also served to link sub-Saharan Africa more closely internally through trade, religion, and politics. West Africa, for example, experienced both the cultural influence of Islam and its own internal dynamic of state building and developments. The formation of the powerful empires, such as the Kanem Bornu, Fulani and Hausa States, depended more on military power and dynastic alliances than on ethnic or cultural unity. Prior to the introduction of Islam, there existed many flourishing cultures and dealing with those cultures made significant changes in Islam. It is often claimed that West Africa has a brand of Islam that is 'very African'. One distinctive feature of this Africanised Islam is the manner in which it was integrated into local cultural life. New religious, economic, and political patterns developed in relation to the Islamic surge, but great diversity remained.

Before the sixteenth century, Islam in northern Nigeria was highly synthesised with Hausa indigenous religion. The earliest attempts at propagating Islam produced what remained essentially a religion of the merchants, of the towns, the *Ulama* (learned men), and the ruling class. Islam was also introduced through the influence of Wangarawa-Dyula traders in the city kingdoms of Hausaland. Soon, Islam started to expand among other segments of the population. By 1700, Islam of the Sunni Malikite school had generated immense support among all levels of Hausa society. Through the incursion of Hausa traders in the late seventeenth century, the influence of Islam was reckoned in parts of southwest Nigeria.

By this time the Oyo Kingdom had already been in contact with Hausa Muslims through trade. In 1817 the revolt by the pastoral Fulani, Hausa slaves, and Muslim Yoruba converts in Ilorin dealt a death blow to the Oyo Kingdom, followed by a series of internecine wars around Yorubaland. By the twentieth century, Islam had spread to northern Yorubaland with an emirate in Ilorin, from where it moved on to other Yoruba towns such as Osogbo, Ibadan, Oyo, and Iwo. The evangelisation of the southwest by Hausa traders and preachers was largely carried out through peaceful means. Some Yoruba towns had a predominantly Islamic population, even at the face of competition with Christianity, which was already well established in Yorubaland prior to the advent of Islam. The integration of Islam into Yoruba indigenous cultures gave it a distinct character and flavour that makes it different from Islam in northern Nigeria.

During the nineteenth century, a number of reform movements aimed at purifying Islam and more or less characterised by militancy were launched throughout West Africa. Another motivation of these reform movements was to create theocratic states based on *Sharia*, the Islamic law. The successful *jihad* under the leadership of Uthman Dan Fodio in 1804 turned Islam into a religion of the masses and further resulted in the evolution of a theocratic state, the Sokoto Caliphate. In this state there was extensive autonomy for emirates that recognised the spiritual authority of the caliph (sultan). Over 30 emirates were created during the course of the nineteenth century. The successful execution of the *jihad* also enhanced the spread of Islam within and beyond the north. Through military conquest, the caliphate expanded south into the Middle Belt region, thus leading to the forceful incorporation of other ethnic groups and non-Muslims into the emirates of the Islamic polity.

The diversity and complexity of Islamic movements in Nigeria is partly exemplified by the Sufi orders or brotherhoods. Two major movements involved in the Islamisation process in Nigeria were the Qadiriyya and Tijaniyya. The former is much older and has spread widely in northern Nigeria since the nineteenth century. The Qadiriyya emphasises intellectual pursuits more than the Tijaniyya (which was introduced in the same century). Both brotherhoods have witnessed tension and rivalry for several decades of their existence. Other Islamic organisations oppose these brotherhoods on the basis of doctrine. Thus Yoruba Muslims have formed various societies whose task is to provide Muslims with a modern education that does not conflict with Islamic values. The Ahmadiyya Muslim Movement has made significant impact in the southwest, where it is very popular. In 1923 a group broke away and formed the Ansar-ud-Deen Society. Both movements have enhanced the development of secular education, particularly in Southwest Nigeria. The Ansar-ud-Deen was probably the most popular of these Muslim educational organisations. By 1960 it already ran numerous primary and secondary schools and training colleges.

The Izala (Jamaatu Izalat al-Bida) emerged in 1978, enjoining its members to reject innovation and instead to work for the preservation of the Sunna. The leading representative of Izala until his death in 1992 was Abubakar Gumi, whose most important concern was to try to unite Muslims politically. However, between 1978 and 1985, many northern Nigerian towns and cities were shaken by the armed insurrections led by Mohammed Marwa Maitatsine and his Yan Tatsine movement. Maitatsine had a long history of fomenting Islamic unrest in northern Nigeria. The source of his inspiration was the belief, especially in Sufi Islam, that a *mujaddid* (reformer) will arise each century to purify and revitalise Islam. Maitatsine's brand of Islam seemed largely to combine traditional Muslim conceptions with local indigenous elements.

Islam has also witnessed the emergence of new movements like the Nasru-Lahil-Fatih Society of Nigeria (NASFAT), founded in Lagos in 1995 by Alhaji Abdul-Latif Olasupo to cater to the spiritual and practical needs of young, educated, and upwardly mobile Muslims, and to grapple with contemporary developments while sustaining Islamic goals. NASFAT, like other Islamic societies such as Ansarud-Din, Ansarul-Islam, Anwarul-Islam, Ahmadiyyah Movement, Islahud-Din, Istijabah Group of Muslims, and the Qareeb Society, now has branches in various parts of Nigeria and abroad.

One of the very visible effects of Islam in Nigeria has been the demand and subsequent declaration of Sharia in most northern states of the federation, a development that has produced protests and huge criticisms from the Christian population. The incessant religious riots in northern Nigeria have been given an added impetus with this recent development. The relationship between Islam and Christianity has led to a growing culture of religious violence, particularly in northern Nigeria. Since the 1980s, there have been many violent clashes between Muslims and Christians, especially in the northern cities of Kano, Kaduna, Kafanchan, and Zaria, recently extending to Jos and its environs. Although there are three major religions, religious and political issues and conflicts have revolved largely around the activities of and the interrelationships between Islam and

Christianity. Their involvement in regional and national politics is aptly illustrated by their activities in post-independence politics in Nigeria (Olupona and Falola 1991; Brenner 1991; Rosander and Westerlund 1997; Adogame 2004). We shall return to this point in the next section.

Christianity

Christianity spread along the West African coast, via the Atlantic Ocean, to southern Nigeria. The earliest missionary effort was in the sixteenth century when the Spanish Capuchin Fathers arrived in Warri in 1515, and the Portuguese Augustinian Monks from Sao Tome, entered Benin City in 1570. This early attempt at sowing the seed of Christianity left very scanty footprints in these areas as these missionaries placed political and economic considerations over and above religious interests, leading to the dismal failure of this first attempt at evangelisation.

A more profound attempt at Christianisation was made in the nineteenth century, following the abolition of slavery. This phase of missionary enterprise in Nigeria began with the foundation of mission boards and societies. Pioneered by Methodist and Anglican mission bodies, others such as Baptists and Roman Catholics soon joined to carve out their own spheres of influence. Anglicanism in Nigeria was initiated and nurtured by the Church Missionary Society (CMS) missionaries from 1842, enjoying some success along the coastal towns of Lagos, Badagry, and Abeokuta, where local people were attracted to Christianity and the accompanying Western education. This impact spread to the Niger Delta and eastern Nigeria. With the intensification of mission work into the hinterland in the early twentieth century, Christianity expanded throughout the southwest and the central areas of Nigeria.

The British administration, via indirect rule, and the emirates, deliberately prohibited Christian evangelisation in Muslim areas. As a result, Western education developed very slowly in northern Nigeria compared to in the southwest. It was only in the latter part of the twentieth century that Christianity started to make inroads in the north, already the stronghold of Islam. The missionary enterprise to northern Nigeria was carried out partly by the Sudan Interior Mission (SIM). The SIM, an independent sending agency, devoted its energies to spreading the Christian gospel in northern Nigeria via church planting, literature development and dissemination, general education, and medical work. The SIM gave birth to a number of churches that together adopted the name, the Evangelical Church of West Africa (ECWA).

Just as the western, coastal regions were the first home and indigenous breeding ground for the mission churches in the nineteenth century, so they fulfilled the same function for the indigenous African churches in the twentieth century. Three phases of religious independence can be discerned in Nigeria. The earliest phase refers to churches that broke away from mission churches owing to a number of irreconcilable issues including rigid White (European) missionary control and domination, discrimination against local African leadership, disputes over resources, and a general feeling of marginalisation among educated Nigerians. These include the United Native African Church (1891) and African Church (Bethel) (1901) from the Anglicans, and the United African Methodist Church (1917) from the Methodist Church. Yet in spite of the transformation of church leadership, they were still tied to the mission churches in their liturgical and hierarchical structures. Indeed, some of them still depended largely on the parent churches for financial resources (Kalu 2005; Isichei 1995).

The 1920s and 1930s witnessed the second wave of indigenous Christianity, including the Aladura churches in Nigeria (Adogame 2005). Also referred to as 'prophetic' and 'healing' churches, they share certain basic characteristics in their world view that helped to create a peculiarly Nigerian brand of Christianity. These basic features include the centrality of the Bible, prayers, healing, prophecy, visions and dreams, elaborate rituals, flexible modes of worship, far less stereotyped liturgy, and a charismatic leader (that is, a prophet or prophetess). Though they utterly condemn and reject traditional religion as 'fetish' and 'demonic', their belief systems and ritual structure have affinities with traditional cosmologies. Even so, despite the affinities that abound among them, each has its own religious dynamic. There are differences in specific doctrines and in the details of ritual acts and performance, just as in their histories of emergence.

Their pattern of emergence is two-fold: those that had their nucleus as 'prayer bands' within a mission church, but that later broke away. In Nigeria, the Garrick Braide movement was the earliest in this category, breaking away from the Niger Delta Pastorate Church as early as 1916. Other churches in this category include the Cherubim and Seraphim (1925), the Church of the Lord, Aladura (1930), and the Christ Apostolic Church (1930). The second category is founded through the visionary experience of a charismatic figure and independently of any existing mission church. A typical example is the Celestial Church of Christ, founded by Samuel Bilewu Oschoffa (1947).

The most recent development within Nigerian Christianity is the emergence of Pentecostal/charismatic churches, particularly from the 1950s onwards (Kalu 2008). A huge proliferation of new Pentecostal churches was witnessed in the last two decades of the twentieth century in Nigeria. At least two waves of Pentecostal movements can be discerned. First there are the indigenous Pentecostal groups such as the Redeemed Christian Church of God, the Deeper Christian Life Bible Church, and the Mountain of Fire and Miracles Church. Then there are Pentecostal groups and organisations that have established branches in Nigeria but have their headquarters situated in the West or elsewhere outside Nigeria. These include the Foursquare Gospel Church, the Full Gospel Businessmen Fellowship International, Youth with a Mission, and Christ for all Nations. The former are largely independent and hardly rely on any external financial assistance, with some even embarking on mission activities in Europe, North America, and other parts of the world. Many groups in the latter category rely heavily on their mission headquarters for funds, literature, and sometimes personnel.

Spiritual science movements

Besides the earlier religious trajectories, there are also Spiritual Science movements, extremely heterogeneous groupings distinguished by their quest for spiritual knowledge and power, higher states of consciousness and direct religious experience, as well as the use of procedures, techniques, and practices that draw upon hidden or concealed forces in order to manipulate the course of events (Hackett 1987). Some are eclectic in nature, drawing upon Western esotericism, Eastern spirituality, and indigenous traditions. Groups primarily drawing on Western esoteric traditions are the Ancient Mystical Order Rosae Crucis (AMORC), the Aetherius Society, the Institute of Religious Science, and the Superet Light Mission. AMORC was particularly popular in Nigeria three decades ago, with headquarters in Lagos and branches in parts of the country. The eastern-related movements include the Eckankar, the International Society of Krishna Consciousness, the Unification Church, the Subud Brotherhood, the Grail Movement, the Baha'i Faith, and Soka Gakkai International. The Eckankar Society of Nigeria, with headquarters in Lagos, began in 1973 in Benin City. In 1981 it began an extensive campaign to launch the movement in the country. It now has over 70 branches scattered all over Nigeria (Hackett 1987).

A typical example of an indigenous Spiritual Science movement in Nigeria is the Sat Guru Maharaj (the 'Perfect Master'), a group which combines Sat Mat and Hinduism with elements of Christianity and Islam. Their headquarters is situated at the Ibadan end of the Lagos-Ibadan motorway. Members are easily identified by their red, flowing gowns and a distinct haircut. Although the presence and activities of the various Spiritual Science movements does not rival Christian and Islamic movements, the religious map of Nigeria would be incomplete without taking notice of their presence.

Historicising religious politics

We have provided a concise historical overview of religious politics elsewhere (Adogame 2004, 2009a). Space constraints prevent repetition here, but suffice it to mention that the first three republics in Nigeria were all infused with religious politics. Socio-economic and political imperatives cater to both the politicisation of religion and the religionisation of politics in Nigeria. The scramble for political power has occurred within the framework of religion in ways that magnify ethnic and regional antagonisms and exacerbate misunderstandings between Islam and Christianity. For instance, the political crisis of Nigeria's first republic (1960–1978) under Tafawa Balewa can be, in part, explained by on religious factors.

As soon as Nigeria achieved political independence in 1960, the premier of Northern region, Sir Ahmadu Bello and then, the Sarduana of Sokoto, embarked on a religious 'crusade' that became the foundation stone for religious politics in the nascent nation. The ruling Northern elite were accused of indirectly pushing Islam to enlarge the Sokoto Caliphate (Kukah 1993). From the First Republic till the most recent experiments in democratic rule, intra- and inter-religious violence has loomed large, with numerous incidents of religious conflicts unleashed on an unsuspecting public. The surge of increasingly religious-influenced politics leads constant rounds of fear, attacks, reprisals and marginalisation. It is against this backdrop that the resurgence of Sharia law and the 'Shariasation' of many Northern States can be seen to have political rather than religious undertones.

Ethnic politics is almost being supplanted by religious politics. Islam perceives state power as quintessential in the advancement and propagation of religion. The perceived domination of power by Muslims and the inequitable distribution of national resources have led to a scramble for public space by Christians. The mutual suspicion, distrust engendered by religious functionaries, and the evolution of religious and ethnic bigotry affects the overall security, for the interplay of religion and politics is intricately linked to the virulent competition for national resources.

Almost every action of government and of religious groups undergo public scrutiny and debriefing. It is within this purview that the Christian Association of Nigeria (CAN) emerged to checkmate the activities of the Supreme Council for Islamic Affairs (SCIA) and the Jama'atu Nasril Islamiyya (JNI).

The history of religious politics in Nigeria is characterised by controversial issues of a wide-ranging nature. As we indicated earlier, past census data have been deeply politicised on religious grounds – that is in terms of which religious tradition is numerically and geographically the largest. A closely related theme that has enhanced the polarisation of religious cleavages in Nigerian politics is the inherent tensions that emerge from the desire of the Muslim population to shape and define Nigeria as a religious state and the Christian counterpoise that defines Nigeria as secular. This tendency, which resonates between theocracy and secularism, foregrounds the volatility and polemic that characterise issues such as Sharia and Nigeria's membership of the Organisation of Islamic Countries (OIC).

Another issue of contention concerns religious representation in governance and the modalities for sharing political office. Ethno-religious grievances over the distribution of power and privileges remain one basic theme in the agenda of religious politics. The manipulation of religion to secure political office and the established convention of allocating important political and administrative positions on the basis of religious persuasion have become firmly ingrained in the Nigerian polity. A further strand of controversy hinges on the control of the Nigerian educational system. This has often taken two dimensions with Christians in the North accusing Northern state governments of taking over Christian mission schools and enforcing the Islamisation of the educational system. On the other hand, Muslims in the south-west have opposed the ownership and control of schools by Christian missionaries since independence. With the recognition that education remains a potent tool for religious proselytisation, both Christians and Muslims have established crèches, Bible or Koranic schools and colleges, and more recently, universities, in order to further their religious agendas. Thus, the recent proliferation of religiously-sponsored universities may be interpreted as an integral feature of the ongoing politics of mutual checkmating, as is the politics of space-time allocation to Muslims and Christians in both federal and state-owned electronic media. The use of the media as an engine of religious agitprop not only heightens already existing tensions between Christians and Muslims, but it also promotes 'the geography of religious expression in Nigeria' (Kalu 2003).

Other contested aspects of public space are the role of government in sponsoring pilgrimages and foreign policy on issues that have religious bearing. The impact of religion in such areas as the definition of national interests, the preference of the North for Islamic countries, the role of foreign missionaries and relations with the West and Israel, have often generated inter-religious conflict and outcry. Similarly, visible government participation in and sponsorship of Islamic pilgrimages to Mecca, and the setting up of the Pilgrims' Board, spurred Christians to ask for their own Board and gave birth to state-sponsored Christian pilgrimages to Jerusalem and Rome (Falola 1998, 173–4).

It is apparent, also, that both civilian and military political leaders have often ridden on the crest of religion both to attain power as well as legitimise their positions. The consequences are reflected in the religious violence which has characterised relations between Muslims and Christians. It is also reflected in the increasing appearance of political figures at public religious functions as a form of self-identification.

I have briefly sketched the history and evolution of religious politics in Nigeria. Ethnicity and religion are tools used to galvanise support for violent conflicts between groups. The tendency to use religion to form cohesiveness within groups and rancour between them is common in Nigeria. The motivation is usually not only religious but ethnical, political, economic and nationalistic. Conflict is not a problem in itself when it is properly managed. When management fails, violence can ensue. Institutional mechanisms for conflict management include rule of law, treaties, negotiations, voting, and authority figures; institutions which constitute the broadest level of social capital, facilitating civic engagement, and minimising risks. This leads to the need to explore the politics of religious violence through the prism of boundary formation and negotiation against the backdrop of Nigeria's complex politico-economy, historical, and religio-ethnic specificities.

Fighting for God: Fanning the embers of violence and conflict

Religion often assumes a matter of political significance and unprecedented tension in Nigeria owing to its pluriformity and inherent ambivalences. Religious tension and violence in Nigeria has a clear connection with the proliferation of uncompromising Muslim and Christian activism, a relationship that has led to a growing culture of religious violence particularly in northern Nigeria.

Any treatment of religious violence and conflict in Nigeria should necessarily commence with caveats. First, we must take cognisance of our definitional specificity of religion and its ambiguous role in terms of its simultaneous functionality and dysfunctionality (Adogame 2009a). The double perspective exemplifies its ambiguity in that depending on how this meaning and function is interpreted and conveyed, who conveys it (agency) and for what purposes, being sometimes manipulated by religious or political entrepreneurs for ulterior ends, religious trends may either lean towards brokering peace and/or engineering conflict and violence.

No religion, whether living or extinct, promotes violence in its central tenets, theology and praxis. All religions seem to advocate peace, forcing us to ponder how to comprehend the violent currents which seem to attend religious identification and competition. This raises the crucial question of religious agency, religion as a social agency, and the intricacies of boundary negotiations, a point to which I shall return.

Second, it is expedient to delineate religious violence and contextualise the relationships between religion and violence. John Hall (2003) teases out two strings on which general theories of violence hinge. First, he remarks that some religious violence may be explicable in the same terms as non-religious violence. He maintains, on the other hand, that religion can amplify violent processes that have their central causes elsewhere. In this sense, a distinction is made between religious violence in a specific sense and violence that may have religious dimensions, but can be also explained in other terms. Thus in Nigeria, we can highlight the religious dimension of most violent conflicts including ethnic conflicts, intercommunal violence, and environmentally related conflicts such as the Niger Delta oil crisis.

Most discourses about violence usually revolve around the use of physical force to cause injury, pain to persons, and sometimes, damage to lives and property. The exercise of force may not always be violent. Certain intentional practices that do not involve the use of force may result in physical injury, although some would hesitate to classify them as violent. Force is not an intrinsic feature of violence, and physical injuries are not its only consequences.

Third, what we deem to be specifically religious violence or violence that may have religious dimensions rarely operates in a social vacuum. It is highly improbable that we can grasp the complexity of religious violence in Nigeria without a historical backdrop and understanding of the socio-political, religious, economic and cultural context(s) in question and in turn relating it to external factors that may impinge on such developments. 'Religious violence is embedded in moments of history and structures of culture' (Hall 2003, 365). Contemporary events, and in history, attest to the fact that religion and violence are often interwoven in the tapestry of human history. Violence will take different forms, shapes and sizes according to the circumstances of its experience and expression.

These caveats serve as fillers for comprehending the history and politics of religious violence in contemporary Nigeria through the prism of boundary making and negotiation. Three broad phases of religious conflict can be discerned: the precolonial, colonial, and postcolonial era (Adogame 2009a). The precolonial era was the least competitive on the platform of religion, one in which indigenous religions co-existed and interacted most peacefully. The extent of their reception, negotiation and accommodation of other forms of external religions is exemplified by how they encountered Islam and Christianity, but also how they remained the least aggressive and confrontational in the religious competition and rivalry that ensued. The emergence of religious conflict and violence can partly be understood in terms of the legacy of colonial conquest and occupation, neocolonialism, and the introduction of Arab Islam and European Christianity. Although Islam and Christianity were introduced to various parts of Nigeria much earlier, it was from the colonial historical phase that there emerged a renewed religious encounter, interaction and competition.

Religious boundary formation, reconstruction, and maintenance

Increasing religious mobility, diversity and incessant religious violence and conflict raise crucial issues regarding the shaping, (re-)construction and (re-)negotiation of boundaries between and within religious groups in Nigeria. Gary Bouma (2007) aptly indicates that the facts of religious resurgence, increased religious diversity and increasing religious conflict raise issues about the nature, construction and negotiation of the boundaries between and within religious groups. Appleby (2000) urges the realistic assessment of interreligious relations and a renewed exploration of the nature and transformation of religious boundaries.

There is remarkable evidence of religious expansion and resurgence in Nigeria within Christianity and Islam, but also in forms of indigenous and exogenous religions. As Bouma (2007, 188) notes, this increasing wave of religious mobility and resurgence can be linked to a number of causal factors including reaction against the failure of secularised, liberal and formally organised forms of religion to meet believers' religious needs. A second source of religious resurgence is found in continued failures of justice, the inability to achieve a fair distribution of goods and services, including food and health. It is also a reaction against the failure of the secularist humanist paradigm to deliver peace and prosperity with justice, and to provide satisfactory explanations for evil, inequality, and pain.

Migration moves religions and religious ideas alongside people around the globe. Migration has increased the religious diversity of many societies and as a result has increased interreligious contact. These factors apply to the Nigerian situation to a large extent. Forms of religious resurgence found in Christianity and Islam in Nigeria, spurred by migration, include increased intensity of commitment (social/ religious capital), increased salience of religious identity, the rise of puritanical extremes and a return to political engagement to apply faith such as in the establishment of Sharia law to deal with criminal cases, and the radicalisation of Pentecostalism particularly in Northern Nigeria and the Middle Belt.

Contestation intensifies religious self-definitions that in turn thicken and escalate conflict. A direct result of increased religious commitment and practice is an increase in religious competition and conflict. The formation and maintenance of identities is a crucial factor contributing to conflict and violence. Religious conflict seeks to overcome, eliminate, or convert the 'other' to extinction. Religious imagery employed by leaders and adherents could be offensive, demonising, and thus lead to violence. Conflicts between Christian and Muslim groups in Nigeria are partly over the implementation of their religious ethics in social policy and the religious tone of the nation.

Bouma (2007, 192) remarks that resurgent religion and the attendant increase in religious competition and conflict raises issues of boundaries. Conflict presupposes the existence or declaration of boundaries. The definition of boundaries is also connected with power dynamics. Boundaries are both defined within and outside the group, including by the state, as well as by social, political, and economic stakeholders. Competition and conflict both require the drawing of lines, taking offence at someone or something, and declaring the 'other' to be wrong, normally inferior, or theologically in error. The 'imagined other' is constructed as rhetoric for defining boundaries, in this case religious boundaries.

The role of imagination in boundary creation and maintenance is apparent in conflicts, especially with the use of media such as posters and slogans. The creation of the imagined other is often used to fuel mistrust and hostility. It is commonplace that religions in Nigeria, particularly Islam and Christianity, construct rhetoric of otherness and engage in mutual demonisation. When such religious sentiments are whipped beyond tolerance levels, then the obvious result is violence and conflict. The trajectories of events of conflicts and violence in Northern Nigeria are indicative of this trend.

We can also highlight the ambiguity of social/religious capital either in the sense in which shared values and norms can reduce or reinforce the level of violence and conflict; and in some cases how violence can impair social/religious capital. In the context of violence and conflict in Nigeria, there is an intricate relationship between religious commitment, participation and volunteerism. These resources, generated within the religious groups as social and religious capital, produce viable reservoirs for mobilising members either to facilitate or prevent violence and conflict. Depending on how these resources are understood and interpreted by religious adherents, when adverse situations arise, it leads them either to choose to fight for God or to fight in God's name. Religious and political entrepreneurs have often hijacked these resources and mobilised particularly the vulnerable towards achieving selfish ends. Contestation of power, boundaries and space continue to generate an atmosphere of mutual distrust and suspicion, thus hampering meaningful inter-faith dialogue and coexistence. When religious politics are geared towards universal meaningful and sustainable development rather than sectional ends, this may pave the way towards the attainment of a virile, civil society.

Religion in Nigeria's public square

The Nigerian religious environment reveals a manifold, complex interplay of religion, economy and society. It is important to interrogate the public role of religion, how religion provides space for socio-economic (dis)empowerment, but also as an impetus for social, political and cultural mobilisation. Religion is in continual reciprocal, interactive relationship with the polity, economy, the class system, the family, law and so on. Religion both influences them and is in turn influenced by them, it acts and reacts, is both an independent and dependent variable, both cause and effect.

Religion forms an integral part of the economic system in the Nigerian society. One obvious economic role it plays is as an employer (Adogame 1999, 23). It goes a long way in providing the economic livelihood for religious professionals, their families, and dependants. Furthermore, religious institutions are significant owners of properties and facilities. Mainline churches in Nigeria are proprietors of printing presses and bookshops such as the Church and School Supplies (CSS), CMS, Baptist, Methodist, Ahmadiyya, Da'wah Bookshop, Islamic Publications Bureau, and al-Tawheed Book Centre located in various parts of the country. Pentecostal churches such as the Redeemed Christian Church of God, Deeper Christian Life Church, Living Faith Ministries – Winners Chapel, and Christ Embassy have also established their respective printing presses and bookshops. Through these channels, which provide employment for many, religious organisations produce and disseminate literature and other commodities. These religious organisations acquire and utilise old and new media technologies such as print and electronic media including books, magazines, audio-visual technologies, and internet websites for the transmission of their religious messages as well as the commodification of religious paraphernalia. The procurement of media space and time involves huge financial investments.

Hospitals, clinics and maternities have been built and owned by various religious bodies in ways that their services supplement and challenge the inadequacies of government health care schemes. Examples are the Baptist Hospital at Ogbomoso, the Wesley Guild Hospital, the Sacred Heart Hospital of the Society of African Missions in Abeokuta, the CMS Iyi-Enu Hospital near Onitsha, the Seventh-Day Adventist Hospital at Ile-Ife, the Saint Luke medical centre in Ibadan, the Islamic Hospital at Shaki, the Ahmadiyya Hospital in Ojokoro, and the Ansarudeen Clinic in Surulere-Lagos. African Independent Churches (AICs) and Pentecostal churches have also set up clinics and maternity homes within their sacred spaces.

Religious organisations also run schools, colleges, libraries and universities to compete with and complement existing government-owned and private institutions of learning. These range from earlier mission-owned schools and colleges such as the Baptist Academy, the CMS Grammar School, the Methodist Girls High School, and St. Gregory College to the AICs founded Christ Apostolic Church (CAC) Grammar School and Apostolic Church colleges. New Christian churches have also founded model primary and secondary schools in addition to universities such as the Living Faith Ministries' Covenant University, Redeemed Christian Church of God (RCCG's) Redeemers University, CAC's Apostle Babalola University, and the Seventh Day Adventist's Babcock University. Islamic organisations such as the Ahmadiyya, Jama'atul Islamiyya, Ansaru'd-din Society of Nigeria, NASFAT and the Nawairu-deen Society have also established and funded Koranic schools, Islamic colleges and universities. The Al-Hikmah University in Ilorin and the Islamic University in Kano are cases in point. Religious bodies have invested huge financial and material resources in establishing, maintaining and sustaining the facilities, infrastructures and manpower that these projects and institutions engender.

Beyond a consideration of the religious impact in the national educational and health sectors, religious bodies are visible stakeholders in banking, insurance and other sectors of the Nigerian economy. For instance, the ownership of the Haggai Bank and the New Life Zion Community Bank are linked to the RCCG. Zenith Bank is allegedly owned by Prophet Otubu, the Spiritual Head of the Eternal Sacred Order of the Cherubim and Seraphim. The Golden Insurance Company was the brainchild of the Cherubim and Seraphim (Ayo Ni O). The Church of Nigeria, Anglican Communion, also owns an insurance company in Lagos (Adogame 1999, 26). These religious-owned businesses provide employment just as they are profit-oriented. In vital ways, they contribute to national economy as both economic players and stakeholders.

Several Christian, Muslim and other religious groups are creating religious empires and mega-churches particularly with the invention and proliferation of sacred cities and prayer camps as in the Living Faith Ministries – Winners Chapel's 'Canaan Land', the RCCG's 'Redemption City', the Mountain of Fire and Miracles' 'Prayer City', the Celestial Church of Christ's 'Celestial City', the Church of the Lord-Aladura, 'Mount Taborah', Ogere Camp, and the Sat Guru Maharaji sacred city near Ibadan. Religious structures dominate the appearance and character of many areas, and serve as valuable indicators of religious and cultural changes through space-time. The (re)production and negotiation of ritual spaces evident in the sacralising of the Lagos–Ibadan motorway is a case in point. Such religious emplacement and competition evince ecological, spatial, demographic, aesthetic, cultural and economic impacts on local Nigerian, but also global religious landscapes. Apart from providing employment for many, the value of property, infrastructure, and other endowments in these invented religious spaces is monumental.

Sport arenas and football stadiums with capacity for many thousands are often used for religious events and festivals; several magnificent auditoriums, religious arenas and prayer camps now host singular programmes such as the RCCG's 'Holy Ghost Festival/Congress', the Winners Chapel's 'Shiloh', and Mountain of Fire and Miracles (MFM's) 'Power Must Change Hands'. Such events that attract vast masses of people, sometimes estimated in their hundreds of thousands, cannot be ignored, not least because they cause massive disruptions for local publics and commuters. On the other hand, such events can be a major boost for local economies if we consider the activities of commercial transport owners, gas stations, food, photo and media vendors, soft drinks/bottled water companies, beggars/poor/needy, thieves, security-related agencies, and religious entrepreneurs, etc.

Indeed, politicians and policy-makers cannot afford to take such mass religious arenas for granted as they pose as potential constituencies and clandestine campaign grounds to curry electoral votes. It is no wonder that the RCCG Redemption City hosts a 'Presidential Villa', an infrastructure located on the premises for dignitaries such as presidents, ministers, governors and captains of political, social and economic industry. The Boko Haram, an Islamic group in Northern Nigeria, opposed to any forms of Western education, and seeking the full implementation of the Sharia, which caused a crisis in 2009, is indicative of how social and religious capital engineering can lead to a dysfunctional group mobilisation that unleashes mayhem on an unsuspecting public (Adogame 2009a, 174). Thus, these invented religious avenues can serve as arenas for political mobilisation, economic empowerment, civic engineering, and social/cultural/religious capital formation as well as for subversive political action, and as breeding grounds for religious extremism and charlatanism.

Religious institutions play a distinctive role within the specific local contexts of Nigeria because those constituencies such as governments, trade unions, blue-collar workplaces, cultural associations and families that previously generated trust and sustained broad social networks have deteriorated. It is within this context that we can interrogate how and to what extent religious groups in Nigeria generate religious and social capital (Bourdieu 1986; Putnam 1995) while in the midst of social and cultural flux, and to help us understand the outcomes of religious influence on other parts of life, for instance in areas of voluntarism, economic development, and civic engagement. Attendance at religious events is associated with increased volunteering, and religious beliefs can influence the meaning of volunteering in people's lives. Churches, mosques and other religious organisations act as communication networks that foster religious and civic volunteerism. People are more likely to give money and time, even to secular efforts, if they are church members or members of the mosque (Adogame 2009a, 189).

Religious celebrities and charlatanism

Nigerian religions produce leaders of various hues, different 'folks and strokes'. The history of religious independence in Nigeria is replete with charismatic founders, prophets, leaders, but also sometimes perceived charlatans. The AICs produced religious icons and prophetic figures including Moses Orinmolade of the Cherubim and Seraphim Church, Ayo Babalola of the Christ Apostolic Church, Josiah Ositelu of the Church of the Lord – Aladura, Samuel Oschoffa of the Celestial Church of Christ, and Theophilus Olabayo of the Evangelical Church of Yahweh. Some of these earlier church leaders received hardly any Western-style education but were revered and believed by followers to be well imbued with spiritual power and charismatic gifts.

The founders of several Pentecostal churches were in most cases university graduates and had worked in nonreligious professions. For instance, William Kumuyi, who founded the Deeper Life Bible Church in 1973, was a lecturer in mathematics at the University of Lagos. Chris Okotie, who founded the Household of God Fellowship in 1987, was a lawyer/pop musician. David Oyedepo, the founder and bishop of the Winners Chapel (1983), was originally an architect by profession. The Christ Chapel Church was founded in 1980 by a medical doctor, Tunde Joda. These founders have abandoned their erstwhile professions to undertake full-time church ministry. These churches are very appealing to youths, graduates, and professionals.

The legion of religious entrepreneurs are sometimes identified by their individual peculiarities. Olubunmi Okojie (former Catholic Archbishop of Nigeria), Emmanuel Gbonigi (former Bishop of Akure Diocese of the Church of Nigeria, Anglican Communion), and Tunde Bakare (General Overseer of the Latter Rain Assembly) are outstanding examples of politically engaged leaders particularly in their sustained critique of various governments and politics of the day on wide ranging socio-economic anomalies, political malfunctionality, and on other issues of public interest. On the global front, Peter Jasper Akinola, the former Anglican Primate of the Church of Nigeria, stands out in his mobilisation of leaders of the Global South within the Anglican Communion to oppose same-sex blessings, the ordination of non-celibate homosexuals or, indeed, any homosexual practice; a development that has perceptibly shaken the very foundation and unity of global Anglicanism.

There are religious captains of industry perceived as spiritually powerful, endowed with overarching supernatural, charismatic gifts; exhibiting modest, exemplary life, and unflamboyant lifestyles but commanding a symbolic father-figure role as 'Daddy' or 'Papa'. Enoch Adeboye (General Overseer of the Redeemed Christian Church of God) and David Oyedepo (General Overseer, Winners Chapel) are prominent examplars of this genre. Others are identified as exhibiting and preaching religious piety, modesty and austere spiritual lifestyles (an example being William Kumuyi, Deeper Christian Life Church); or as Pentecostal preachers with flamboyant lifestyles, and with a vivid emphasis on prosperity teaching and ostentatious lifestyles such as the 'funky-preacher' Chris Okotie of the Household of God Church or Chris Oyakhilome of Christ Embassy. Then there are those such as Paul Adefarasin of the House on the Rock Ministry who display a mimicry of African-American evangelists (that is, Bishop T.D. Jakes) in their oratorical rendition and gestures.

The Synagogue, Church of All Nations founded by Temitope Joshua, has come under intense public criticism and vicious demonisation from even the Christian constituency, with the leader often described as a 'fake prophet' and 'Antichrist'. In spite of these criticisms, the church with its international headquarters in Ikotun-Egbe, a suburb of Lagos, has continued to gain worldwide membership and popularity. Although Joshua claims his organisation to be a Pentecostal-type church, he has been largely rejected by the umbrella Pentecostal body in Nigeria, the Pentecostal Fellowship of Nigeria. Meanwhile, the General Overseer of the Christ Praying Assembly (CPA) in Lagos, Kingsley Chukwuemeka Ezeugo, otherwise known as the Reverend King, remains one of the most controversial religious figures in recent Nigerian history, followed by allegations of his flogging of his worshippers without restraint, and even bathing some church members with petrol and then setting them on fire. To date he has remained under police custody awaiting trial on these alleged criminal acts.

The Sokoto Caliphate, founded during the Fulani Jihad in the late 1700s and which was one of the most powerful empires in sub-Saharan Africa prior to European conquest and colonisation, has remained extant through the colonial and postcolonial periods, though with reduced power. The status of the Sultan of Sokoto is revered as the spiritual leader of Nigerian Muslims both historically and in contemporary times. For instance, the late Alhaji Muhammadu Maccido Abubakar

III, the 19th Sultan of Sokoto, was not only hailed as *Sarkin Musulumi* (Commander of the Faithful) and spiritual leader of Nigeria's Muslims, but played a particularly prominent role in Nigeria's political and religious life. Not only was he the ruler of the Sokoto Emirate, the title also gave him the primacy among all Nigeria's Emirs, by virtue of descent from Othman Dan Fodio, founder of the Sokoto Caliphate. His religious vocation was underlined by the fact that he was president-general of the Nigerian Supreme Council for Islamic Affairs (NSCIA), the highest institutionalised Islamic body in Nigeria.

But Islam has also produced its own controversial religious icons. Sheikh Abubakar Gumi (1922–1992) was one such figure in the twentieth century. He was vehement in his criticism of politics and governance in Nigeria and internal developments within Islam. He was known for his volatile commentaries, which were widely believed to have heightened religious tensions. Gumi stood apart from other Muslim icons such as Ibrahim Zakzaky and Yakubu Yahaya, who refused to recognise the state of Nigeria on grounds that its laws were not Islamic. The critical attitude displayed by Gumi towards Sufism and his writings against the Qadiriyya and the Tijaniyya were crucial elements in the later establishment of the Izala-society.

Abubakar Mujahid, who broke away from Zakzaky, led a more radical Muslim faction in the north – known as the Ja'amutu Tajidmul Islami, the Movement for Islamic Revival. Neither Ibraheem Zakzaky nor Abubakar Mujahid held political office in Nigeria, but both resolutely maintained disdain for the power elite that rules Nigeria. Mohammed Marwa Maitatsine was another Islamic scholar who led a fringe Islamic group that started in Kano in the late 1970s and operated throughout the 1980s. He was renowned for his controversial interpretation of the Qur'an. With its own mosques and antagonistic teaching to established Islamic and societal leadership, its main appeal was a large following of marginal youths, unemployed migrants, poverty-stricken urban dwellers, and those who felt that mainstream Muslim teachers were not doing enough for their communities. As Maitatsine's following increased in the 1970s, so did the number of confrontations between his adherents, and the police. He and several of his followers were incarcerated on a number of occasions for alleged slander and public abuse of political authorities. He met his demise in 1980 in a face-off with Nigerian security forces during the Kano insurrection.

The coterie of charismatic leaders and celebrities, religious icons, spiritual entrepreneurs and charlatans is undoubtedly robust and dynamic. Many have invented religious empires endeared to the personality of the founder/leader, sometimes leading to their being dubbed as 'family businesses' or 'private enterprises'. Nevertheless, several existing religious organisations within Christianity and Islam, mobile and institutionalised as they may be, seem awash with a visionary myopia and have failed to learn lessons from the experiences of previous religious gurus. Many have ignored the problem of succession to leadership, the routinisation of charisma and bureaucratisation processes that will follow the demise of religious founders and celebrities. The lacunae created by the silence of appropriate legal provisions in constitutions, edicts, by-laws, memorandum and articles of association establishing such religious bodies often results in legal imbroglios and succession crises which challenge the post-charismatic fate and corporate existence of such religious entities.

The globalisation of Nigerian religious economy

Nigeria's religious dynamism must also be located within religious, political, socio-economic interactions and developments outside the immediate context of Africa (Adogame 2007, 2009b).

With growing revitalisation and internationalisation of indigenous religions, many Nigerians are beginning to appreciate their 'traditional' religions and to engage in both 'indigenous' and newer religious forms simultaneously. Indigenous Nigerian peoples have experienced something of a religious revival and have become concerned with the preservation of their religio-cultural heritage. Further, some communal rituals in commemoration of specific local divinities are becoming internationalised. These include the annual Yoruba Osun-Osogbo festival, the Eyo Festival in Lagos, the Igwe Festival in Benin City, the Argungu Fishing Festival in Sokoto, the Durbar Festival in Kano and Katsina, the New Yam Festival in Igboland, the Yakurr Festival and the Leboku rituals in Calabar. Today, these attract devotees and tourists from around the world, thus transforming these ritual events from ethnic-based ones to ones with an international audience and participation.

Migration is one significant avenue for the 'exportation' and commodification of the diverse Nigerian religious cultures and world views. Religion has become perhaps the second largest cultural export commodity beside crude oil. Thus, Nigerian migration is a significant ingredient in and consequence of globalisation. The mobility of this demographic group forms an integral part of the global phenomenon of international migration, serving as a viable instrument of religious and cultural expansion, identity and continuity. Thus, the global dimension of indigenous Nigerian religions is manifest in varied forms, being introduced to new geo-cultural contexts through migration, tourism, and with the utilisation of new communication technologies.

The Nigerian diaspora influences cultures in Brazil, Cuba, and Haiti, partly leading to the development of African-derived religions such as Santeria, Candomblé, Vodun, and Yoruba-Orisa traditions across the Americas. In 1981, an Act of Parliament in Trinidad and Tobago raised the Yoruba religion to the status of an official religion. The twentieth and twenty-first century proliferation of groups of Orisa practitioners outside of West Africa continues to attract millions of adherents of Yoruba and Santeria religious practices (Clarke 2004, 5). The growth of indigenous Nigerian religions in the US and Europe has been similarly characterised by the growth of virtual-based religiosity in which most Orisa and Ifa priests exist, operate and communicate through their internet websites with old and new clienteles as well as with the wider public.

While Nigeria is currently serving as a significant theatre for the dramatisation of Islam and Christianity, many Nigerian Christians and Muslims who have migrated to other parts of Africa and beyond have carried traits of their religious identities with them. The AICs and Pentecostal/Charismatic churches have increasingly taken to proselytising in North America and Europe, viewing the regions as 'new abodes' and promising 'mission fields' (Adogame 2005, 504). In fact, Nigeria can boast of producing the largest and most dynamic African immigrant religious and spiritual supermarkets in Europe and North America. Their impact is also hugely felt in Western, Eastern and Southern Africa where they are now described in some public circles as agents of a new religious colonisation. These comprise large and small groups existing as branches of mother churches headquartered in Nigeria; and others founded by Nigerian immigrants in the diaspora. Examples include the Redeemed Christian Church of God, the Winners Chapel, the Christ Embassy with headquarters in Nigeria, and the Kingsway International Christian Centre in East London. They all have huge Nigerian membership with pockets of non-Nigerians. The Embassy of the Blessed Kingdom of God for All Nations in Kiev, Ukraine, is a typical example of a Nigerian-led church with a majority non-Nigerian membership.

With the proliferation of Nigerian religions in virtually all parts of the world, Nigeria has become fully part of a global cosmos in religious terms. For instance, African (Nigerian) immigrant churches in Western societies, particularly Europe and North America, have assisted the renewed salience of Christianity (Adogame 2004). Within the framework of globalisation, the relevance of African (Nigerian) churches is not only located in the unique expression of African Christianity they exhibit, they also constitute international ministries and groups that have implications on a global scale. The significance of the 'exportation' of African churches, driven by a vision of winning converts, is that it offers a unique opportunity to analyse its impact at global levels. As part of an increasing phenomenon of what they term 'mission reversed' or 'remissionisation of Christianity to a secularised West', these African churches have systematically set out to evangelise the world.

In conclusion, the character of indigenous Nigerian religions in conditions of globality will continue to be determined and shaped by how and to what extent they negotiate continuity, identity, and change. A consideration of religious development in Nigeria must therefore be seen in terms of its relation and links with the local-global context, but also in how and to what extent it interrogates and negotiates wider external influences and global forces. In addition, the ways in which Nigerian diasporic religions are contributing to the enrichment and pluralisation of new geo-cultural and religious spaces becomes more and more significant. The diaspora setting provides a new space for the contestation, reinvention and shaping of religious ethos, polity, rituals and world views in the face of globality.

References

Adogame, A. 1999. Religion and economic development in Nigeria. *The Nigerian Journal of Economic History* 2: 22–45.

Adogame, A. 2004 The politicization of religion and the religionization of politics in Nigeria. In *Religion, history and politics in Nigeria*. ed. K. Chima and N. Ugo, 137–53. 2004. Lanham, MD: University Press of America.

Adogame, A. 2005. African Christian communities in diaspora. In *African Christianity: An African story*, ed. K. Ogbu, 494–514. Pretoria: University of Pretoria.

Adogame, A. 2007. Religion in sub-Saharan Africa. In *Religion, globalization and culture*, ed. P. Beyer and L. Beaman, 533–54. Leiden: Brill.

Adogame, A. 2009a. Fighting for God or fighting in God's name! The politics of religious violence in contemporary Nigeria. *Religions/Adyan, Journal of the Doha International Centre for Interfaith Dialogue* 1: 174–92.

Adogame, A. 2009b. Practitioners of indigenous religions in Africa and the African diaspora. In *Religions in focus: New approaches to tradition and contemporary practices*, ed. G. Harvey. London and Oakville, CT: Equinox.

Appleby, R. 2000. *The ambivalence of the sacred: Religion, violence and reconciliation*. Lanham, MD: Rowman and Littlefield.

Bouma, G. 2007. Religious resurgence, conflict and the transformation of boundaries. In *Religion, globalization and culture*, ed. P. Beyer and L. Beaman, 187–202. Leiden: Brill.

Bourdieu, P. 1986. Forms of capital. In *Handbook of theory and research for the sociology of education*, ed. J. Richardson. Westport, CT: Greenwood Press.

Brenner, L., ed. 1991. *Muslim identity and social change in Sub-Saharan Africa*, London: Hurst.
Clarke, K. 2004. *Mapping Yoruba networks: Power and agency in the making of transnational communities*. Durham, NC: Duke University Press.
Falola, T. 1998. *Violence in Nigeria. The crisis of religious politics and secular ideologies*. Rochester: University of Rochester Press.
Hackett, R., ed. 1987. *New religious movements in Nigeria*. Lewiston, NY: Edwin Mellen.
Hall, J. 2003. Religion and violence: Social processes in comparative perspectives. In *Handbook of the sociology of religion*, ed. M. Dillon, 359–84. Cambridge: Cambridge University Press.
Isichei, E. 1995. *A history of Christianity in Africa: From antiquity to the present*. London: SPCK.
Kalu, O. 2003. Experiencing evangelicalism in Africa: An Africanist perspective. In *Ghana in Africa and the world*, ed. F. Toyin. Trenton, NJ: Africa World Press.
Kalu, O., ed. 2005. *African Christianity: An African story*. Pretoria: University of Pretoria.
Kalu, O. 2008. *African Pentecostalism. An introduction*. Cambridge: Cambridge University Press.
Kukah, M. 1993. *Religion, politics and power in northern Nigeria*. Ibadan: Spectrum.
Olupona J., and T. Falola, eds. 1991. *Religion and society in Nigeria: Historical and sociological perspectives*. Ibadan: Spectrum.
Olupona, J. 2003. African religion. In *Global religions: An introduction*, ed. M. Juergensmeyer, 78–86. New York: Oxford University Press.
Olupona, J., ed. 2001. *African spirituality: Forms, meanings and expressions*. New York: The Crossroad Publishing Co.
Putnam, R. 1995. Bowling alone: America's declining social capital. *Journal of Democracy* 6, no. 1: 65–78.
Rosander, E., and Westerlund, D., eds. 1997. *African Islam and Islam in Africa: Encounters between Sufis and Islamists*. Athens, Ohio: Ohio University Press.

Nigerian elections and the neopatrimonial paradox: In search of the social contract

Darren Kew

Associate Professor, University of Massachusetts, Boston, USA

A review of a half century of Nigerian elections demonstrates the inextricable link between the Social Contract and election quality in the country. Ultimately, both must move forward if credible elections are to be sustained over the long term, for without a strong sense of public responsibility, power-holders are inclined to manipulate electoral systems to produce favourable outcomes. Nigeria initially enjoyed an 'ethnic contract' under which post-independence elites felt some obligation to care for the public interests of their ethnic constituents, but by the late 1980s the ethnic contract had largely given way to a more personal, neopatrimonial pattern of politics. Consequently, election quality has declined in every general election since 1993. As the 2011 elections fast approach, advocates of election reform must widen their scope to support the development of a viable political opposition that has an interest in credible elections and, ultimately, can help to build a national Social Contract.

Elections are the apex of the political cycle in Nigeria. They are so important, in fact, that political leaders have rarely allowed public preferences to get in the way of their preferred results.

Instead, Nigerians over the past 50 years have been regularly subjected to what are popularly called 'selections' – election outcomes that have largely been predetermined by elite backroom deals, or decided by massive rigging at polling sites and collation centres, violence and intimidation, or a combination of these factors. Poor elections were the signature events associated with the fall of Nigeria's first two republics; the Third Republic collapsed over an election annulment, and the nation's Fourth Republic has seen election quality decline since 1999.

Democratic systems rely upon elections to answer the fundamental question of who governs, to settle political disputes among elites, and to provide governments with legitimacy. Without credible elections, the public has little direct say in governance matters, and political leaders have less incentive to provide policies of interest to the impoverished majority. Credible elections, however, grow out of a relationship between elites and the public as much as elections structure that relationship. The essence of this relationship in a democratic context is an understanding known as the Social Contract: the public gives its loyalty and support to the individuals currently controlling the government in exchange for the government providing order and policies that reflect the broader interests of the public at large (Rousseau 1968; Rawls

1999, 2001). Consequently, elections are the most basic political process allowing for the protection and expression of the Social Contract, but the development of credible elections also depends to a degree upon the pre-existence of some recognisable form of Social Contract. Without an organised public demanding clean elections – a sign of the prevalence of Social Contract expectations – election improvements are dependent upon the interests of political elites.

Unfortunately, over the five decades since Nigeria's independence, the nation's elites have shown declining interest in clean elections. This decline has mirrored a deeper trend since 1960 that has undermined the Social Contract: a shift from traditional ethnic sources of political loyalty and organisation to a more personalised politics known as neopatrimonialism, the 'big man' or 'godfather' structure of patronage politics. After the volatile ethnic politics of the First and Second Republics, Nigerian elites built extensive networks across ethnic lines during the 1980s and 1990s, which over the last decade of the Fourth Republic have produced a remarkable level of stability at the federal level. This rogues' peace, however, bought by massive corruption and rent distribution through patronage pyramids nationwide, has exacerbated tensions at the state and local levels and produced an increasing number of political officeholders with little interest in credible elections. Civil society groups have fought this trend over the years, but the balance of resources is stacked heavily against them.

A brief review of a half century of Nigerian elections will demonstrate this inextricable link between the prevailing pattern of politics regarding the Social Contract and election quality. Progress or decline on one half of the ledger will raise or drag down the other, but ultimately, both must move forward if credible elections are to be sustained over the long term. Election reform efforts in the past have overwhelmingly focused on improving the technical capacity of the election system, without sufficient attention to the Social Contract side of the equation. As the 2011 elections fast approach, advocates of election reform may have a chance to widen their scope and lay the groundwork for sustained progress in 2015 and beyond.

The ethnic contract and insecurity

Given the centrality of elections to democratic governance, their role in the polity is deeply influenced by the dominant patterns of political development at the time, just as elections may affect those patterns in a reciprocal fashion. Nigeria approached independence in 1960 under the thumb of British imperialism, which had stitched together a host of societies that had charted largely independent paths until the late nineteenth century. From the outset, this created a bifurcation in Nigerian political life that was common to other African colonies that Peter Ekeh called the Two Publics, in which individuals navigate between two different moral realms in society. Because the Nigerian state was an imposed, exploitative, alien (British) creation, neither the Nigerian public nor its elite inheritors of the state at independence felt any deep connection or loyalty to it. Consequently, the state was viewed as an amoral realm where different or no traditional values applied, such that the state could be utilised for narrow, sectional goals or looted without being immoral. Corruption could even be seen as patriotic, if it meant taking the funds from the colonial overlord to assist one's community. In the traditional realm, on the other hand, long-standing moral standards remained in effect, where notions of accountability, personal integrity, and the public good continued to hold sway (Ekeh 1975, 91–112).

This bifurcated society thus created a divided Social Contract. The state, particularly in regard to the national government of Nigeria's federation, held little attachment and was viewed as a separate moral realm from traditional norms. These were reserved for the ethnic polity, which were soon organised into ethnic political parties vying for control of Nigeria's three federal units (known as regions until 1967), each generally corresponding to one of the nation's three largest ethnic groups: Hausa, Yoruba, and Igbo, who constituted two-thirds of the population (Sklar 1963). One of the nation's great independence leaders, Chief Obafemi Awolowo, summed up this orientation toward traditional polities at the time succinctly: 'Nigeria is not a nation. It is a mere geographical expression. There are no Nigerians in the same sense as there are English, Welsh, or French. The word Nigerian is merely a distinctive appellation to distinguish those who live within the boundaries of Nigeria from those who do not' (Awolowo 1947, 47–8).

Consequently, Nigeria became independent in 1960 with a largely *ethnic* Social Contract, or an ethnic contract. Each of the ethnic majorities had a party associated with group interests: the Northern Peoples Congress (NPC – Hausa), Action Group (AG – Yoruba), and the National Council of Nigerian Citizens (Igbo – NCNC). Most political leaders demonstrated a palpable sense of responsibility to the members of their ethnic groups and provided an expansive array of social policies within their ethnic homelands in exchange for their members' support (Diamond 1989). Education, healthcare, economic infrastructure, and other public works grew dramatically under the First Republic (1960–1966), and the three (four after 1962) regional governments are widely seen as some of the most responsive governments that Nigeria has ever had.

The ethnic contract was not, however, the sole factor structuring political outcomes in the years just prior and subsequent to independence. Class divisions were clearly a major force cutting across ethnic lines, buttressed by progressive political parties and a growing trade union movement. The pro-independence NCNC scored significant electoral victories in the Yoruba-majority Western region in the colonial legislative elections in 1951 and 1954, while the Northern Elements Progressive Union (NEPU), a left-leaning party with strong support among the Northern working class and traditional commoners (*talakawa*), also showed growing influence. An NCNC–NEPU leftist alliance had the British colonial administration sufficiently concerned, in fact, the British actively worked against it by encouraging the NPC organisation in the North and an AG ethnic strategy in the West to portray NCNC as an Igbo party (Usman 2001; Dudley 1982; Sklar 1963).

The growing popular sense of an ethnic contract combined with British meddling and politicians playing the 'ethnic card' set out to undermine class and other possible cross-cutting factors for social organisation. Ethnicity became the primary social category for political mobilisation and ethnic-based political parties came to dominate the regions. As ethnicity became the primary vehicle for political competition, it set off a dynamic common to many postcolonial African states that I call the *ethnic security dilemma* (Kew 2005). Much like the security dilemma of Realist political theory, the ethnic security dilemma sees ethnic groups perceiving a growing threat from other ethnic groups as they gain more control over the state. This creates an incentive for other groups to mobilise to control the state, making everyone else increasingly insecure. Each ethnicity thus perceives a growing need over time to increase its power in order to control the state and protect its interests, exacerbating the insecurity of the others. If one group or stable coalition cannot achieve mastery fairly quickly, then ethnic competition can escalate rapidly to violence.

Such ethnic competition and insecurity undermined class-based organisation and reinforced the ethnic contract, particularly for the majority Hausa, Yoruba, and Igbo communities, who quickly dominated their regional governments and moved to challenge each other over control of the federal government. Development within their respective regions strengthened the hands of the ruling parties at the federal level, so that the NPC, AG, and NCNC all engaged in rapid expansion of economic infrastructure and other public goods in the regions. Thus, both the ethnic contract and competition among the ethnic parties worked in favour of improved governance outcomes in the First Republic.

The early elections

The two general elections held for the First Republic period reflected these trends of the ethnic contract and insecurity. The first, in 1959 as a prelude to independence, saw the NPC win a plurality with 134 out of 312 seats in the British-style parliamentary system (see Appendix A). NPC, AG, and NCNC won control of their regional legislatures as well. In order to form a government, the NPC turned to the NCNC as a coalition partner, which surprisingly abandoned its progressive alliance with NEPU and joined the government, leaving AG to lead the opposition.

Increasingly caught in the escalatory logic of the ethnic security dilemma, however, NPC soon embarked upon a policy of 'northernisation', seeking to solidify its position within the Northern Region ('one North') and at the federal level by redistributing resources from the more economically advanced southern regions (Falola and Heaton 2008). NPC also seized upon a 1962 crisis in the Western legislative assembly to jail Chief Awolowo (head of the AG), split the AG, and carve the Midwest Region out of the Western Region, diminishing effective opposition to its rule. Upheaval in the West continued as government corruption increased, and the NPC embarked upon a range of tactics to ensure its dominance in the next election: manipulating the census and voter registration exercises, inflating voting results in its constituencies, intimidating opposition, falsifying ballots, and other forms of rigging that would become the gold standard for later election malfeasance. Recognising at last the NPC's drive for hegemony, the NCNC joined what remained of the AG and NEPU in the United Progressive Grand Alliance (UPGA) for the 1964/1965 general elections. NPC sharp tactics, however, assured it of an outright majority of 162 out of 312 seats, plus the support of an additional 36 seats from coalition partner the Nigerian National Democratic Party (NNDP), consisting primarily of AG defectors from the 1962 crisis.

The deadlock escalated through 1965, and the two coalitions turned to the military for leverage in their dispute, only to discover that the military had its own solutions in mind, beginning with the first coup in January 1966. This exacerbated the ethnic security dilemma, leading to civil war the following year, followed by an extended period of military rule until 1979.

Unlike the British, however, the military appeared less interested in determining who succeeded them, and established a fairly credible election commission (FEDECO) to oversee the 1979 contest to usher in the Second Republic. Energies were focused instead on developing a new federal constitution modelled on the United States, with a strong presidency, bicameral legislature, and 19 constituent states (Oyediran 1979). In fact, the military showed little interest in the structure of the political parties, such that the leading First Republic parties largely resurfaced under new names, but with some important differences. The NPC re-emerged as the National Party of Nigeria (NPN), absorbing some of its Western NNDP allies from the First Republic alliance and in the Niger Delta region as well. AG became the Unity Party of Nigeria (UPN) and regained its lock on the Yoruba southwest, while the NCNC structure became the Nigerian People's Party (NPP) and NEPU returned as the People's Redemption Party (PRP). One new party, the Great Nigerian People's Party (GNPP), splintered from the NPP and formed its base among northeastern minority groups, particularly in Borno State, created in 1976.

Consequently, the ethnic security dilemma that brought down the First Republic was largely replicated in the Second Republic (Joseph 1987). After winning the presidency in 1979 and pluralities in both houses of the National Assembly (see Appendix A), where it formed an initial alliance with the NPP to pass legislation, the NPN resumed its drive for national dominance. This drive ultimately forced the other parties, including the NPP, into a progressive alliance against the NPN. As mutual suspicions increased, massive rigging from all the parties then marred the July/August 1983 elections, with NPN out-rigging them all and scoring itself massive majorities in both houses of the National Assembly and comfortably returning NPN President Shagari to power. Within months, however, the military seized upon massive public outrage at the election to take power on 31 December 1983.

The shift to neopatrimonialism

The ethnic contract remained largely intact through the short-lived Second Republic, as the parties sought to channel development policies and patronage to their ethnic bases, particularly at the state level, where social policies were again expanded (Ayeni and Soremekun 1988; Joseph 1987). Two important dimensions, however, had changed since the First Republic and began to undermine the foundations of the ethnic contract. First, the expanded number of states in the federation gave greater access to the nation's many political minorities, forcing the parties to expand their bases in order to compete nationally and at the state level (Suberu 2001). Although the First Republic parties had built coalitions with ethnic minority parties in other regions, in the Second Republic the main political parties sought to bring these minorities *within* their core structures. This created greater incentives for party leaders to bargain ethnic differences within the party to some degree of mutual satisfaction, producing the beginnings of policies that could have more national interest, and prompting greater expectations of a national Social Contract (Horowitz 1991).

A second important change was that, by 1979, Nigeria had established itself as an oil rentier state with a centralised economy dominated by the presidency. Thirteen years of military rule under Generals Yakubu Gowon, Murtala Muhammed, and Olusegun Obasanjo had strengthened the federal bureaucracy under what was to become the new presidency. In addition, the 'commanding heights' of the economy were placed under federal control in the hope that this would promote more equitable distribution of national resources (Forrest 1995). Consequently, when

Nigeria's burgeoning oil industry began to enjoy the massive revenues from the oil shocks of the 1970s, mind-boggling profits poured into federal coffers. Soon, the individuals in key government posts were managing huge budgets, corruption jumped, and many of these individuals – both military and civilian – became fabulously rich.

By the time of the Second Republic, therefore, we see a pattern of personal enrichment setting in, first with powerful ministers such as Transport Minister Umaru Dikko, but also spreading to other echelons of the bureaucracy and tiers of government. As the political parties began to expand for electoral reasons beyond their ethnic bases, these oil-enriched individuals began to build networks of supporters within and across ethnic lines through the distribution of patronage.

In this way, the ethnic contract began to give way to a more personal pattern of politics known as neopatrimonialism. Often called the 'Big Man' or 'godfather' syndrome, neopatrimonialism creates personal loyalty networks in a pyramid fashion beneath the central benefactor, who gives patronage downward in the network in exchange for loyalty upward (Bratton and Van de Walle 1997; Joseph 1987; Pitcher et al. 2009). Ethnicity thus gives way in intra-elite relationships to a simpler 'cash-and-carry' clientelism, such that ethnicity is not as divisive a force at the national level as in the First Republic, but at the cost of heightened corruption. This is the paradox of neopatrimonialism: it buys a measure of political stability among elites, but at the expense of the Social Contract, or in the case of Nigeria after independence, the ethnic contract. As elites grow richer off state largesse, their networks expand, creating mutual interests across cultural divides that dampen elite conflicts but demand more cash to maintain the networks. This need for cash creates greater incentives for corruption and less interest in providing real development policies for the public, and eventually even for one's narrow ethnic constituents.

Ethnicity remains the primary category of political mobilisation in Nigeria, and elites may still play the 'ethnic card' in public disputes, but among elites themselves far greater room and willingness to bargain and to reach mutually acceptable deals has developed. By the fall of the Second Republic, personal interests began to take on far more importance to elites than ethnic interests, with complex multi-ethnic relationships possible, greased with the vast oil wealth available.

The Third Republic and Abacha's feint

Although the coup that swept General Muhammadu Buhari to power at the end of 1983 took an aggressive stand against corruption, with high profile prosecutions of Second Republic figures like Umaru Dikko, Buhari's heavy-handed regime was replaced after 20 months by General Ibrahim Babangida in 1985. Thus the shift to neopatrimonial politics gained momentum, as Babangida proved more personal and corrupt than any of his predecessors, utilising an extended transition to a Third Republic as a means to prolong his stay in office. Babangida further centralised power in federal hands by creating more states and local governments, thus diluting their powers and making them more dependent upon federally-distributed oil revenues (Olowu 1991). He also personalised this dependency by routing much of the available patronage through the presidency, which he spread liberally to extend his network of clients (Diamond et al. 1997). Emblematic of this neopatrimonial decline was the disappearance of the $12 billion Nigeria earned during the 1990–1991 oil 'boomlet' from the Gulf War. Babangida put the earnings in a special 'dedicated' federal account, ostensibly in order to protect it, but by the time General Sani Abacha seized power, the funds had vanished entirely, and no one was ever identified as culpable, much less prosecuted.

During this same period, the price of oil fell dramatically while Nigeria's debts rose. Per capita incomes, which in 1980 stood at $1,000, dropped to $250 by the 1990s as local non-oil industries collapsed. At the same time, Babangida imposed a structural adjustment programme that imposed austerity across the nation's fragile public service infrastructure. Beset from above and below, most Nigerians fell into deep poverty, such that by 2006 the World Bank estimated that 70% of Nigerians lived on less than a dollar per day, and 92% lived on less than two dollars.

In this environment of extreme poverty, the influential individuals who had access to state largesse grew even more powerful in relative terms than in the Second Republic or earlier. The bonds of the ethnic contract soon frayed and, for many elites, broke altogether, such that they had little interest in constituencies outside their immediate support networks. Just as the public at large became less useful to elites, it grew more atomised under military oppression – as civil society organisations were hounded and/or co-opted – and demoralised under creeping impoverishment. Real public policies, such as the drives for public education in the First and, to some degree, Second Republics, fell to a trickle and most economic activity centered on winning government contracts, which companies were increasingly not expected to fulfill so long as kickbacks were provided.

Nonetheless, Babangida's complex game of keeping the country busy with an extended democratic transition programme while he stayed in office required that he actually implement a measure of credible decisions in that transition. One of the most important was the establishment of a fairly credible National Electoral Commission (NEC) under the leadership of Humphrey Nwosu. In addition to gaining the reputation of being a generally neutral umpire in election contests, the NEC also experimented with a new method of voting aimed at preventing rigging known as Option A4. This method had voters meet within a designated time frame on election day and line up behind the party standard for which they wished to vote, and then a single count of all the votes would be taken in plain sight of the community in question. Option A4 was controversial in sacrificing ballot secrecy for transparency in the counting, which provided the public and party observers a way to hold NEC accountable, but also raised fears that voters could be intimidated or face reprisals if they dissented from the local majority. Nonetheless, the election results produced by Nwosu's NEC over the 1990–1993 period of the Third Republic remain viewed as some of the most reliable and respected in Nigeria.

In addition to NEC, Babangida also implemented another innovation that was far more controversial. He imposed a state-funded two-party system of the Social Democratic Party (SDP) 'a little to the left' and the National Republic Congress (NRC) 'a little to the right' on the nation's politicians, forcing them to join one or the other party (Badejo 1997). Although Babangida clearly intended and used the two-party frame to out-manoeuvre the nation's powerful political networks, it had the unintended effect of continuing the move toward multi-ethnic parties begun under the Second Republic. The NRC generally absorbed key elements of the old NPN structures, which had already expanded to the southwest and added supporters in the Niger Delta and southeast. The SDP, on the other hand, built a rainbow coalition from the remaining Second Republic networks – UPN, NPP, GNPP, and PRP – and made inroads into parts of the 'core North' that was the NPN base. In effect, SDP largely recreated the progressive alliances that had come together in the dying days of both the First and Second Republics to challenge the conservative NPC and NPN, which the NRC generally inherited and expanded upon. The result was that the Third Republic enjoyed two truly national parties that transcended ethnicity, religion, and region (Osaghae 1999, 233–9).

National Assembly and gubernatorial elections in 1992 confirmed that neither party had a lock on any particular region in the country (see Appendix A). The SDP had comfortable majorities in both houses of the Assembly, but the NRC took a slight edge in the number of governorships in the country. As the final stage in the transition process approached with presidential elections scheduled for late 1992, however, Babangida prevaricated. Intense speculation on his motives still rages, but the self-proclaimed 'evil genius' has yet to give a full public answer. Perhaps hoping to set up the conditions to have himself transformed into a civilian president like Ghana's Jerry Rawlings, Babangida delayed the presidential contest until 12 June 1993, and some confusion persisted until the last minute as to whether the election would hold even then.

NEC, however, went ahead with what may well be Nigeria's most credible national election to date, declaring SDP's Moshood Abiola the victor. Abiola had put together an appealing Yoruba–Kanuri presidential–vice presidential ticket, both of whom were Muslim, and barnstormed the country in an unprecedented national campaign, outpolling his opponent even in his home city of Kano. The confusion as to whether or not the election would hold dampened voter turnout to approximately 20%, but Abiola still emerged with an impressive victory and a public mandate.

Days later, however, Babangida seized upon a questionable court challenge to Abiola's victory to annul the 12 June election. The nation erupted in protest, forcing Babangida out of office two months later. As a last manoeuvre, rather than handing over power to Abiola, who had fled the country, Babangida created a transitional government headed by businessman Ernest Shonekan until new elections could be held in February 1994. Without popular legitimacy and with the economy in freefall, however, Shonekan's government could not stabilise the country, and General Sani Abacha was able to topple the interim government without a shot in November 1993.

General Abacha quickly dismantled the entire structures of the Third Republic, including the SDP and the NRC. He jailed a number of their leaders, including Abiola himself when he returned to Nigeria in 1994 to claim his mandate as president, a year too late. Abiola would later die in custody under suspicious circumstances, just as it appeared he would be released in 1998. With Abiola safely in jail, Abacha instituted his own extended transition programme in 1995, following a similar process to Babangida's.

The elections held under Abacha's transition programme were local government contests in March 1997 and state assemblies in December 1997, which had dismally low turnouts – probably less than 5% on average – as voters made clear their antipathy toward another military managed process with uncertain ends. State and National Assembly elections held in April 1998 had such low turnouts that the junta cancelled the results. Abacha had registered five political parties in 1996, none of which included prominent politicians from the pre-existing networks. When all five of these endorsed him as their presidential candidate in 1998, reducing the August

1998 presidential election to a referendum, the true objective of the transition process became clear (Lewis et al. 1998).

By the end of the Abacha years, the neopatrimonial pattern of politics was well rooted in the polity. Years of military machinations and predatory largesse had left little of the ethnic contract at the local level, as political networks centred on powerful individuals and coalitions of these networks sought to gather resources and bide their time until the military allowed them a shot at office. The old AG/UPN structures persisted through the Yoruba cultural association *Afenifere* and the NCNC/NPP structures were preserved to some extent by the pan-Igbo association *Ohaneze Ndigbo*, but within several years both groups would be largely abandoned in favour of personal networks. With no Social Contract, Nigeria approached the twenty-first century with a massive social gap between the overwhelmingly poor majority – roughly 92% of the entire population – and a tiny elite with little sense of obligation to provide public goods outside their loyalty networks.

The Fourth Republic

Abacha's unexpected death in June 1998, probably at the hands of his own generals,[1] prevented a major confrontation over his planned referendum that summer and brought Nigerians into the streets to celebrate. His successor, General Abdulsalami Abubakar, implemented a rapid transition programme that installed a new Fourth Republic less than a year later in May 1999.

Abubakar came to office over a military that was as deeply divided as the nation after nearly 15 years of Babangida's and Abacha's game play. Some officers expected their turn at the top, while others wanted a return to professionalism. Others feared prosecution for excesses during military rule. Consequently, the military needed a political party and a president friendly to its interests, to sooth these fears and to keep potential coup artists at bay. In addition, the new president had to be from the southwest to appease the Yoruba leaders who were threatening secession over Abiola's trampled mandate.

The first problem was solved later that year when a coalition of some of the nation's most powerful neopatrimonial networks came together to form the People's Democratic Party (PDP). Largely devoid of ideology, the PDP was little more than an alliance of convenience among the oligarchs sitting atop these personal networks from across the nation, particularly the northeast, Middle Belt, Niger Delta, and the southeast Igbo region. Most of these individuals had worked closely with military governments in the past and had grown rich from their association, and thus were seen as largely safe for the exiting military officers. Each was expected to 'deliver' his state or states during the forthcoming elections. Moreover, their networks of supporters collectively ran across the nation, creating a massive multi-ethnic party even larger than the Third Republic's SDP or NRC.

PDP leaders quickly realised that they needed to address the problem of a presidential candidate acceptable to the military. Thus the choice narrowed to an ex-military officer of Yoruba descent (to appease the southwest) who could also command some confidence among Northern interests, who had long been in power. Indeed, only one man appeared to fit these criteria, and the PDP soon nominated as its flagbearer former military head of state Olusegun Obasanjo, a Yoruba who won

Northern appreciation after he handed power to Shehu Shagari in 1979 despite a court challenge from the Yoruba runner-up, independence leader Obafemi Awolowo.

Initially, General Abubakar seemed inclined toward a two-party system like Babangida. He instructed the new Independent National Electoral Commission (INEC) to hold local government elections in December 1998, and to register only those parties that could win 5% of local government seats in 24 of the now 36 states. This rule ensured that only the PDP would sail over without question.

One other party also managed to clear the mark, the All Peoples Party (APP). APP was an amalgamation of the five Abacha parties, with particular strength in the northwest, northeast, and the Middle Belt states of Kwara and Kogi, where the Second Republic governor Olusola Saraki still maintained his powerful network. Like the PDP, APP had no real ideology and served primarily as a holding company among its powerful founders. A third party, the Alliance for Democracy (AD), was an outgrowth of *Afenifere*, the Yoruba cultural organisation that had preserved some of the AG/UPN structures of the southwest. As a primarily ethnic party, however, the AD only fared well in the six southwestern Yoruba states in the local elections and did not meet the registration threshold. The AD soon entered frantic merger negotiations with the APP, and Nigeria looked poised to have another two-party system. Surprisingly, however, the INEC decided to recognise the AD as a third party. The public reason given was to appease the southwest over its loss of Chief Abiola's mandate and to offer voters greater choice, but the fact that this move also divided opposition to the PDP was clear.

The INEC then moved quickly to organise state assembly elections in January 1999, and National Assembly, gubernatorial, and presidential elections on two dates in February 1999. Through the sheer size of its networks, the PDP performed as expected: winning 21 of the 36 governor seats, 23 state assemblies, comfortable majorities in both the House (214 out of 360) and Senate (63 out 109), and gaining retired General Obasanjo the presidency with 62% of the vote with 52% voter turnout. The APP won nine governorships in its strongholds of the northwest, northeast (Borno and Yobe), Kwara, and Kogi, with 77 House members and 26 Senators. The AD took only the six Yoruba-majority states of the southwest, 20 Senate seats and 69 House contests (see Appendix A).

The election, however, was tarnished by a host of irregularities or outright fraud in much of the federation, and former US President Jimmy Carter, who observed the election, left early in protest and refused to endorse it. The Niger Delta states were rigged outright – many local governments reported an impossible 100% voter turnout – while the Igbo southeast was almost as problematic, such that approximately a third of the state totals (primarily PDP strongholds) were largely fictional. Another third of the states across the north and the Middle Belt were 'comfortably corrupt', such that many of the contests at the ward level were reasonably competitive, but a number of wards or rural local governments were most probably rigged heavily in one direction in order to push the favoured party candidate comfortably over the winning total. The last third of the states, in the southwest and pockets of the north, were generally competitive and saw totals reported that most likely reflected public preferences (Kew 1999).

Although President Carter quite reasonably saw questionable outcomes in roughly two-thirds of the federation as making the election unacceptable, most of the international community took its cue from Nigerian civil society monitors and the public at large, who were willing to live with the outcome in order to get the military out of power. In addition, President Obasanjo's election appeared to reflect the public's wishes, although his margin of victory would have likely been less had real contests been held in the fraudulent and 'comfortable' states. Given the dominance of the presidency in the political system, local and international observers alike were inclined to embrace his win with 'irregularities' and overlook the outright farcical elections in the Niger Delta, southeast, and elsewhere at the lower echelons of government.

President Obasanjo took office in May 1999, promising an ambitious reform agenda, including the repair of the INEC. The US, Britain, UN Development Programme, and other international donors and election experts such as the International Foundation for Electoral Systems (IFES) assisted INEC financially and technically to develop strategy and infrastructure for reform. Yet, Obasanjo did little to alter the pattern at INEC, and withheld funds for the 2003 election until only six months prior to the contest. Party primaries and internal democracy were also discussed, but never addressed. In late 2002, the Supreme Court ruled INEC's restriction of political parties as unconstitutional, and the number of new parties expanded dramatically thereafter.

President Obasanjo did not have a neopatrimonial network upon assuming office. In fact, he had spent much of the Abacha years in jail, accused of plotting a coup, and the PDP leaders had brought him out of retirement because of his credentials (and demographics) and put him into office. One of the largest oligarch networks in the PDP was led by Abubakar Atiku, who became vice-president in 1999 and was given a substantial role in managing the economy and privatisation policies. Some of Atiku's supporters encouraged him to replace Obasanjo as president in the PDP convention prior to the 2003 elections, which the vice-president appears to have seriously considered before giving way at the behest of Obasanjo. The two men reconciled to win a second term in 2003, but the president did not forget or forgive, and soon moved to build a personal network of his own.

With little reform at the INEC, the 2003 elections thus followed a similar pattern as 1999 (see Appendix B). Since the president withheld INEC funds until the last minute, the commission was forced to rush through with minimal preparations, strengthening the hand of the local political networks seeking to compromise INEC state offices and minimally-paid ad hoc staff hired just for election day activities at the ward level and polling booths. In addition, nearly all office holders now enjoyed the power of incumbency, which the governors in particular used to their benefit. In the end, 2003 produced roughly the same level of credibility as 1999: a third of states enjoying competitive elections, a third 'comfortably corrupt', and a third (again in the Niger Delta and southeast) completely rigged (Kew 2004).

The most startling change occurred in the southwest, where many of the AD governors had grown deeply unpopular for their lack of performance. Obasanjo, who had lost his home region in the popular vote in 1999, allegedly struck a deal with AD leaders that the PDP would not put up more than a token fight in the southwest state elections if the AD did not nominate a presidential candidate. After the time expired for presidential nominations, Obasanjo publically declared that he had never agreed to such a deal, and the PDP spared no expense in the southwest. The unpopularity of the AD governors and the gerontocratic AD leadership overall combined with a measure of 'comfortable' PDP corruption in a number of localities to sweep the PDP into five of the six Yoruba state offices. The AD collapsed into infighting and managed only to retain the governorship in Lagos.

Obasanjo swept back into office with virtually the same victory ratio as 1999: 62%. The PDP saw its number of governorships and assemblies swell to 28 out of the 36 states, while its majorities in the House and Senate topped up slightly. The APP (now ANPP after a merger) retained most of its 1999 states, but lost Kwara and Kogi from the defection of the Saraki machine to PDP, and Gombe as well. The ANPP gained Kano in a stunning upset, however, bringing its total to seven states.

Even when the APP and AD controlled 15 states together over 1999 to 2003, they never formed a viable opposition coalition, except to field a joint presidential candidate in 1999, former Secretary to the Government of the Federation, Samuel Olu Falae. Obasanjo deftly invited both the APP and AD to join him in a 'unity government' after taking office, which undermined their nascent coalition and reduced their criticism of his government. No coherent opposition leadership emerged, and thereafter, APP and AD went largely separate ways. The AD voiced occasional criticism of PDP policies, but both the AD and APP preferred to negotiate with the PDP over national legislation and policy. Since none of the parties had strong ideological orientations, individual members were open to bargaining and offers of patronage. In fact, the strongest opposition to President Obasanjo came from within his own party, which instigated impeachment proceedings against him in 2002 over his refusal to honour the budget. Once the AD lost five of its six governorships in 2003 and the ANPP lost control of two of its states, the opposition grew even quieter. It was joined in 2006 by one additional party, All Progressives Grand Alliance (APGA), which the Supreme Court ruled had won the 2003 gubernatorial election in Anambra. The opposition was also undermined by the explosion in political parties after 2002. By 2007, over 40 political parties were on the ballot, creating a dizzying array of choices and a two-foot long ballot paper for the nation's many illiterate voters to navigate.

President Obasanjo emerged from his 2003 victory determined to gain control of the PDP by building his own neopatrimonial network and to thwart the political ambitions of Vice- President Atiku. His first plan was to amend the constitution to remove the two-term limit on the presidency. Public outrage, civil society organising, and Atiku's assistance all moved the Senate to reject the amendment in 2006. Obasanjo then used a combination of state largesse and the threat of prosecution from the anti-corruption commission to wrest control of the PDP from Atiku and other opponents. The vice president and a small splinter group were ultimately forced from the PDP into a new party formed with the remainder of the AD, called the Action Congress (AC). Hounded by Obasanjo at every turn, Atiku and the AC were never able to mount a serious campaign outside of Lagos and several urban centres.

As a final effort to prolong his stay in office, Obasanjo set the conditions for a disastrous election in 2007, in the hope of provoking a crisis that would allow him the opportunity to declare a state of emergency.[2] As a backup, Obasanjo made himself the head of the PDP's Board of Trustees, from where he hoped to control his handpicked successor, Governor Umaru Yar'Adua of Katsina State, whose chronic health concerns were certain to be a debilitating factor. To cement the plan, Obasanjo made Maurice Iwu, a pharmacologist with minimal election experience, the chairman of the INEC. Iwu soon wasted commission resources on an expensive high-technology voters' registration and vote collation scheme that never functioned properly, and erected a series of obstacles to prevent civil society oversight. The INEC was reduced to a marketplace, with candidates accusing Iwu of auctioning offices to the highest bidder where President Obasanjo had not predetermined the outcome.[3]

Appendix B demonstrates the farcical results the INEC announced the day after the elections, despite the logistical impossibility of the commission having tallied the results so quickly. The full extent of how arbitrary the INEC results were can be seen when compared to opinion polls taken just before the election. Appendix B subtracts the Afrobarometer[4] pre-election polls of the gubernatorial candidates from the actual INEC results, demonstrating that 28 of the 36 states had official gubernatorial figures that were over 20 points different than what they had been predicted to earn shortly before the election. For instance, the Bayelsa governor topped the charts by scoring 81 points higher in the official results than the opinion polls had predicted. Yar'Adua himself also scored roughly 30 points higher than expected. Reports flooded from across the nation that polling stations never opened, or where they did open, a host of irregularities were recorded. INEC clearly announced arbitrary figures that fit with the predetermined PDP sweep, allowing the opposition to retain several states for appearance purposes – or where opposition parties were too strong to dislodge, such as Kano and Lagos. Recognising the scam, however, neither civil society nor the Nigerian public at large took the bait to revolt, and Obasanjo was forced to leave office in disgrace.

President Yar'Adua thus took office in 2007 under a cloud of illegitimacy. Local and international observers alike condemned the 2007 election as a farce, and in the coming months the courts would overturn 10 gubernatorial races alone, most requiring election reruns that Iwu's INEC again handed to the PDP. Yar'Adua's own position was in doubt until the Supreme Court, in a split 4–3 decision, upheld his election in December 2008.

Like President Obasanjo before him, President Yar'Adua did not have a national support network and had been placed in office by the powerful mandarins of the PDP. Yar'Adua promised to make election reform a priority, but first set out to gain control of the party, using the familiar neopatrimonial tactics of patronage and the threat of corruption inquiries to bring the politicians in line. He did establish an Electoral Reform Committee in 2008, which released a report whose recommendations were largely endorsed by key civil society groups, but his administration rejected most of them.

What remained of the opposition largely collapsed after 2007. ANPP lost more seats in the 2007 elections, and saw three of its governors decamp thereafter to the PDP, leaving it clinging only to Kano and Borno. A PDP splinter party, the Progressive Peoples Alliance (PPA) won two governorships in the southeast, but saw one of them return to the PDP in July 2009. Courts later awarded the governorship of Edo to the AC and Ondo to the Labour Party (LP), bringing the total number of opposition-controlled states to a mere seven, split among four different parties.

President Yar'Adua's health difficulties soon escalated, forcing him to seek foreign medical care for several lengthy absences from the country, the last attack incapacitating him in November 2009 until his death in May 2010. Vice-President Goodluck Jonathan of the Niger Delta state of Bayelsa then assumed the presidency, promising election reform of the thoroughly discredited INEC, but also seeking to gain control of the PDP and retain his office in the 2011 elections.

Analysis: A reluctance to let the public speak

Some debate still remains over whether or not the British went so far as to alter the results of Nigerian elections in the 1950s. Regardless, they clearly used the resources of government to favour the NPC, whom the British deemed as more favourable to their interests than any other party. The very structure of the federation, with the North controlling half the population and nearly two-thirds of the land, all but ensured that a dominant Northern party would control Nigeria itself (Suberu 2001). Consequently, although the 1959 election was perhaps technically competent, in the sense that outright rigging was marginal, the precedent was set from the dawn of Nigerian independence of manipulating the election environment in order to achieve results that favoured the interests of the power of the day.

The NPC soon took this trend to the next logical step of outright electoral malfeasance by 1964, perfecting an array of rigging tactics – manipulation of the census and voter registration, underage and ghost voters, results fabrication and so on – that set the trend for subsequent election contests. The NPN replayed this scenario in 1983, inviting the military to set back democratic progress for nearly two decades for a second time.

Consequently, from the beginning, elections were seen by power holders as too important to allow them to function correctly. Where possible, incumbent parties that had the ability to alter outcomes in their favour would do so, sometimes discreetly, as in the case of the 'comfortable' corruption in 1999 and 2003, or blatantly, as in the farcical 2007 elections, the Niger Delta in 1999 and 2003, or the massive rigging done by all sides in 1983 as the NPN outdid its opponents.

To some extent, the problem is structural. In the First Republic, the logic of the ethnic security dilemma fed an overriding NPC fear of southern domination, leading it to pursue its destabilising 'northernisation' policy that set off intense ethnic competition that made justifying election rigging into a matter of cultural survival. These ethnic fears persisted into the Second Republic as well, but by then the bloating of state coffers with oil rents had added a new and more personal financial incentive to rigging. As poverty rose and social and economic infrastructure collapsed in the 1980s and 1990s, control of elections became an even greater matter of personal survival, since pubic office brought access to state largesse and losing office left politicians with few alternatives. Consequently, they soon adopted a zero-sum perspective on winning, which justified increasingly egregious tactics to ensure favoured electoral outcomes, such that on the eve of the 2011 contest the use of political thugs, gangs, and militias had grown widespread.

The most credible post-independence elections – 1979, 1993, and perhaps a third of the states in 1999 and 2003 – had several factors in common. In the first three, the military was exiting power and had some interest in maintaining a neutral, professional image. In addition, to some extent in 1979 and clearly in 1999, the military was reasonably sure that a sympathetic party would win a relatively open contest. Parties had less time to compromise election structures in the 1979, 1993, and 1999 contests as well.

The one factor that all four credible contests shared, however, was that they were all characterised by vigorous opposition parties. The 1993 election – likely the most credible contest thus far – saw two fairly equal, national parties competing across the federation and keeping each other in check. In 1979 four major but divided parties challenged the NPN across much of the country as well. The states where credible elections did hold in 1999 and 2003, such as Kano and Lagos, saw generally balanced opposition parties facing off and policing each other's more egregious tendencies. Conversely, as the NPC, NPN, and PDP grew more dominant in subsequent elections, the outcomes plummeted in quality, culminating in the largely fabricated results of 2007. More than any other domestic political actor, viable opposition has an interest in clean election outcomes. Moreover, opposition parties need a mobilised public in order to balance the power of incumbents, which creates an incentive for opposition to promise policies in the public interest in exchange for support – the beginnings of the Social Contract. The African countries providing better governance and, increasingly, development, such as Ghana, are characterised by having well-organised political opposition (Kew 2005).

To be sure, viable opposition is not the only piece of the solution for credible elections. Nigerian opposition parties have not always upheld democratic principles. Opposition alliances in 1964 and 1983 turned to the military to resolve their struggles with the NPC and NPN, and opposition parties massively rigged the states they controlled in 1983, and in some instances in 2003 and 2007 in a 'fight fire with fire' response to the PDP. Even the competitive elections in Kano and Lagos in 2003 were backed up with arsenals of fuel cans, with which the ANPP and AD planned to make these cities burn if the PDP and INEC refused to honour their electoral mandates. In addition, the last four years have seen a growing number of opposition governors and other office-holders willing to cross carpet to the PDP out of their own personal interests.

Underpinning Nigeria's foundering opposition has been the deeper problem of the dwindling Social Contract. The ethnic-based Social Contract of the First Republic ensured that political leaders at least sought to provide solid development policies to their respective ethnic constituents. Both the First and Second Republic regional and state governments thus provided major expansions in the provision of public goods and were far more responsive to constituent needs than their Fourth Republic successors have been.

As the ethnic contract faded in the 1980s, it was not replaced with a national Social Contract. Instead, the neopatrimonial pattern took root, severing elite relationships with and accountability to their constituents, such that personal interests are the central driving force of politics, greased with the vast oil wealth available. On some issues that involve great public interest, elites may still feel obligated to show a public face of concern for ethnic group interests or for clear public preferences. This was particularly evident, for instance, in the movement to block Obasanjo's efforts for a third term. The overwhelming amount of time, energy, and resources, however, are increasingly directed to the maintenance of neopatrimonial networks and moving their oligarchs into higher office, where more resources are available.

This simpler form of clientelism among the oligarchy has facilitated the rise of the vastly multi-ethnic PDP at the centre of power, and its expansion since 1999. For this reason, the past 10 years have seen far less destructive or debilitating intra-elite ethnic conflict at the national level than the First and Second Republics, as the PDP (and ANPP and AC later) has great incentive to work out ethnic compromises within the party. By this measure, the PDP has overseen the most stable decade of Nigerian politics since independence, with GDP growth rates averaging 6% and the non-oil sector growing over 8.5% from 2006 to 2008 (*The Economist* 2007). Yet this elite sharing of the 'national cake' at the federal level has intensified state and local competition, as local elites fight harder to control local resource channels and move up the chain. Here they have been far more willing to stoke ethno-religious sentiments in their political battles, igniting local versions of the ethnic security dilemma. The result has been that ethno-religious conflict at the state and local level has been far more intense over the last 10 years than in the previous republics, with Human Rights Watch (2004) having calculated 10,000 deaths by 2003 alone.

Relative stability at the national level through cash-and-carry neopatrimonialism has, however, come at the price of decreasing election quality and rising militarism on the part of elites. The 2007 election was such a farce that many elites now see the only way to gain office as a combination of financial inducements, relationships with powerful 'godfathers', and military muscle. Worryingly, more politicians are turning to thugs to 'secure their mandate', and Niger Delta militants have been hired as military advisors in other parts of the federation (Asuni 2009).[5]

This suggests that the stability of clientelism among the elites of the last 10 years may have reached its limits. The number of challengers seeking to enter the centre circle of patronage may have outstripped the capacity of the oligarchy to absorb them or block them out. More disturbing is the rising militarism among the elite, which unchecked could lead to widespread localised violence and perhaps invite a devastating military coup.

While neopatrimonialism can spiral downward toward state collapse, its accenting of personal interests also raises the constant possibility that new elite coalitions may form. The National Assembly, for instance, has proven less beholden to the executive than in the Second Republic, with PDP legislators instigating impeachment proceedings against Obasanjo three times and refusing to grant him a third term. The recent flood of opposition politicians crossing the carpet to the PDP is another example of this fluidity, suggesting that the flood could easily shift back in the other direction under the right circumstances. Consequently, this raises some hope that the PDP may break, perhaps over President Jonathan's election ambitions in 2011, such that a disgruntled group of governors and other oligarchs may join an opposition party or coalition.

Civil society has largely been divided since 1999 over whether to work with the government or to take a more aggressive stance. Since the 2006 third term debate, however, civil society has seen an increasing number of organisations decide to 'return to the barricades', particularly once President Yar'Adua rejected the recommendations of his own Electoral Reform Committee in 2009. Many groups are now moving to be in place to document violations and to protest the outcomes if necessary. This may also strengthen the hand of a viable opposition coalition, should it emerge. Moreover, civil society is an essential player in the restoration of the Social Contract, and the lack of civil society alliances with political parties in recent years has been a sign of the absence of a Social Contract.

Together, viable political opposition backed by rigorous civil society involvement are essential ingredients for creating the thickly dispersed balance of power necessary to build the Social Contract, demand credible elections, and move democratic consolidation forward. Broad-based, progressive opposition coalitions formed at the end of both the First and Second Republics, and the stillborn Third Republic were poised to be governed by the inclusive, left-leaning SDP, balanced by the conservative NRC. The PDP behemoth has so far undermined such a coalition or inclusive opposition party in the Fourth Republic, but the tenuous, patronage-based neopatrimonial relationships of its members holds open the prospect of splinter groups forming.

As President Jonathan took office following the death of President Yar'Adua in May 2010, prospects for election reform looked bleak. Maurice Iwu ended his term as INEC chair in disgrace, leaving the commission bankrupt and shot through with patronage relationships from powerful politicians across the country. Some of the groundwork for another fraudulent election in 2011 was already in place, and as the president's ambition to be elected in 2011 became clear, it seemed that he too would have a powerful incentive to ignore the public's right to vote.

Strikingly, however, President Jonathan has made repeated commitments at home and abroad to election reform, and in June 2010 he nominated Professor Attahiru Jega, a former chairman of the radical Academic Staff Union of Nigerian Universities, ASUU, for INEC chair. Jega assumes office with enormous credibility as a former union leader against the military, experience in election management and political science, and a reputation of incorruptibility, fairness, and rigour. Given the strong role of the INEC chair in managing the commission, this one move suddenly opened the possibility that the 2011 elections might be better than 2007 or perhaps even surpass some of the better elections of the past.

Professor Jega is, however, surrounded by the sharks of the neopatrimonial political machines. Some INEC commissioners and state representatives are open PDP members, while many of the INEC staff are compromised. Moreover, the voters register is incomplete. All of these reforms will take time and funds that may not be sufficient in order to turn the system around for 2011, perhaps leading to the last minute confusion that allowed local neopatrimonial networks to take advantage, as in the 1999 and 2003 contests. At the least, however, Jega will have a better chance to run credible election reruns if the same high number of 2011 contests are overturned by the courts as in 2007, and prospects for a reformed INEC by 2015 look even better.

Much will depend upon the choices President Jonathan makes in trying to stay in office beyond 2011. If he allows Professor Jega to run credible elections, and if sufficient opposition to Jonathan's candidacy provokes defections from the PDP, then Nigeria may enjoy the birth of a new Social Contract upon which a viable opposition movement can flourish and demand improved governance. If, however, Jega's efforts are thwarted and the president follows the pattern of his predecessors of building massive personal patronage networks, Nigeria will continue down the neopatrimonial spiral toward drift, decay, and possibly, dissolution.

Notes

1. Nigeria's major dailies reported a month after Abacha's death that papers were found on his desk that indicated he was ready to sack all of the service chiefs. See, for instance, *The Guardian* (Lagos), 15 July 1998. For other speculation, see Mudiaga Ofuoku, 'Abacha's last days', *Newswatch*, June 1998. http://www.onlinenigeria.com/abacha_last_days.asp.
2. Interviews with PDP leaders, 15 August 2007; 8 November 2007; 12 January 2008.
3. Interviews with AC leaders, 20 January 2010; ANPP leaders 25 January 2010.
4. See http://www.afrobarometer.org/access.html.

5. Also supported by author's interviews with two Nigerian conflict resolution organisations, 14 January and 1 March 2009.
6. Adapted from Richard Sklar (1963, 36).
7. Adapted from Diamond (1989, 227).
8. Richard A. Joseph, (1987, 125–7).
9. Richard A. Joseph, (1987, 125–7).
10. Richard A. Joseph, (1987, 125–7).
11. Adapted from Toyin Falola and Julius Ihonvbere, (1985, 220–1).
12. Adapted from Toyin Falola and Julius Ihonvbere, (1985, 220–1).
13. Adapted from Toyin Falola and Julius Ihonvbere, (1985, 220–1.
14. All 1991–1993 election results are from Diamond et al. (1997).
15. 1999 results from *The Guardian* (Lagos), February 24.
16. From Kew and Lewis (2008, 363–413).

References

Asuni, J. 2009. Understanding the armed groups of the Niger Delta. New York: Council on Foreign Relations Press.

Awolowo, O. 1947. *Path to Nigerian freedom*. London: Faber and Faber.

Ayeni, V., and K. Soremekun, eds. 1988. *Nigeria's second republic.* Lagos, Nigeria: Apapa.

Badejo, B. 1997. Party formation and party competitition. In *Transition without end: Nigerian politics and civil society under Babangida*, ed. L. Diamond, A. Kirk-Greene, and O. Oyediran. Boulder, CO: Lynne Rienner.

Bratton, M., and N. van de Walle. 1997. *Democratic experiments in Africa*. Cambridge: Cambridge University Press.

Diamond, L. 1989. *Class, ethnicity, and democracy in Nigeria*. Syracuse: Syracuse University Press.

Diamond, L., A. Kirk-Greene and O. Oyediran, eds. 1997. *Transition without end: Nigerian politics and civil society under Babangida*. Boulder, CO: Lynne Rienner.

Dudley, B. 1982. *An introduction to Nigerian government and politics.* Bloomington, IN: Indiana University Press.

Ekeh, P. 1975. Colonialism and the two publics in Africa: A theoretical statement. *Comparative Studies in Society and History* 17: 911–2.

Falola, T., and M. Heaton. 2008. *A history of Nigeria*. Cambridge: Cambridge University Press.

Forrest, T. 1995. *Politics and economic development in Nigeria*, 2nd ed. Boulder, CO: Westview.

Horowitz, D. 1991. Making moderation pay: The comparative politics of ethnic conflict management. In *Conflict and peacemaking in multiethnic societies*, ed. J. Montville, 451–75. New York: Lexington Books.

Human Rights Watch. 2004. *Nigeria's 2003 elections: The unacknowledged violence*. New York: Human Rights Watch.

Joseph, R. 1987. *Democracy and prebendal politics in Nigeria: The rise and fall of the second republic*. Cambridge: Cambridge University Press.

Kew, D. 1999. *Democrazy–Dem Go Craze, O*: Monitoring the 1999 Nigerian elections. *Issue: A Journal of Opinion* 27, no. 1: 29–33.

Kew, D. 2004. The 2003 elections in Nigeria: Not credible, but acceptable? In *Crafting the new Nigeria: Strengthening the nation*, ed. R. Rotberg. Boulder, CO: Lynne Rienner.

Kew, D. 2005. Building democracy in 21st century Africa: Two Africas, one solution. *Seton Hall Journal of Diplomacy and International Relations* Winter/Spring: 149–61.

Kew, D., and P. Lewis. 2008. Nigeria. In *Introduction to comparative politics: Political challenges and changing agendas*, ed. M. Kesselman, J. Krieger, and William A. Joseph. Boston: Wadsworth.

Lewis, P., B. Rubin, and P. Robinson. 1998. *Stabilizing Nigeria: Pressures, incentives and support for civil society.* New York: Council on Foreign Relations.

Olowu, D. 1991. Centralization, self-governance, and development in Nigeria. In *The failure of the centralized state: Institutions and self-governance in Africa*, ed. J. Wunsch and D. Olowu. Boulder, CO: Westview.

Dudley, B. 1982. *An introduction to Nigerian government and politics*. Bloomington, IN: Indiana University Press..
Oyediran, O. 1979. *Nigerian government and politics under military rule, 1966–79*. New York: St Martin's.
Pitcher, A., M. Moran, and M. Johnston. 2009. Rethinking patrimonialism and neopatrimonialism in Africa. *African Studies Review* 52, no. 1: 125–56.
Rawls, J. 1971 and 1999. *A theory of justice*. Cambridge, MA: Belknap Press.
Rawls, J. 2001. *Justice as fairness: A restatement*. Cambridge, MA: Harvard University Press.
Rousseau, J.-J. 1968. *The social contract*. New York: Penguin.
Sklar, R. 1963. *Nigerian political parties*. Princeton, NJ: Princeton University Press.
Suberu, R. 2001. *Federalism and ethnic conflict in Nigeria*. Washington, DC: US Institute of Peace.
The Economist, 7 November 2007.
Usman, Y. 2001. The misrepresentation of Nigeria: The facts and figures. http://www.nigerianbestforum.com/index.php?topic = 57524.0;wap2.
World Bank Development Indicators. 2006. http://web.worldbank.org/WBSITE/EXTERNAL/DATASTATISTICS/0,,contentMDK:20899413 ~pagePK:64133150 ~piPK:64133175~ theSitePK:239419,00.html

Appendix A: Nigerian elections 1959–2003

First Republic:

1959 Federal parliamentary election[6]

	Number of Seats	NPC	NCNC/NEPU Alliance	AG	Others
Total	310	134	89	73	14
Percent	100	43.2	28.7	23.6	4.5

Distribution of parliamentary seats after 12/64 and 3/65 elections[7]

	Number of Seats	NPC	NNDP	NCNC	AG	NPF	Independent
Total	312	162	36	84	21	4	5
Percent	100	51.9	11.6	26.9	6.7	1.3	1.6

Second Republic:

1979 General election, house of representatives[8]

	Number of Seats	GNPP	UPN	NPN	PRP	NPP
Total	449	43	111	168	49	78
Percent	100	9.6	24.7	37.4	10.9	17.4

1979 Senate election[9]

	GNPP	UPN	NPN	PRP	NPP
Seats won (out of 95)	8	28	36	7	16
Percent	8.4	29.5	37.9	7.3	16.9

1979 Presidential election[10]

		W. Ibrahim (GNPP)	O. Awolowo (UPN)	S. Shagari (NPN)	A. Kano (PRP)	N. Azikiwe (NPP)
Actual Vote	16,846,633	1.68 million	4.92 million	5.69 million	1.74 million	2.81 million
Percent	100	10.0	29.2	33.8	10.3	16.7
No. States won >25%	—	3	6	12	2	3

Requirements for victory: Plurality of popular vote, plus at least 25% of e vote in two-thirds (66.66% of the 19 states. Note that Shagari reached this level in just 12 of 19 states (63.16%); however, a favourable ruling by the Federal Elections Commission (FEDECO) ensured his victory.

1983 House of representatives election[11]

	Number of Seats	NAP	GNPP	UPN	NPN	PRP	NPP
Total	450[a]	—	—	33	264	41	48
Percent	100	—	—	7.3	58.7	9.1	10.7

[a]One seat added for FCT.

1983 Senate election[12]

	NAP	GNPP	UPN	NPN	PRP	NPP
Seats won out of 96[a]	0	1	16	61	5	13
Percent	0.0	1.0	16.7	63.6	5.2	13.5

[a]One seat added for FCT.

1983 Presidential election[13]

		Tunji Braithwaite (NAP)	Waziri Ibrahim (GNPP)	Obafemi Awolowo (UPN)	Shehu Shagari (NPN)	Hassan Yusuf (PRP)	Nnamdi Azikiwe (NPP)
Actual Vote	25,454,967	.289 million	.641 million	7.91 million	12.05 million	1.04 million	3.53 million
Percent	100	1.1	2.5	31.1	47.3	4.1	13.9
No. States won (25%)	–	–	–	7	16	1	4

Requirements for victory: Plurality of popular vote, plus at least 25% of the votes in two-thirds of the 19 states.

Third Republic[14]

1991 State government elections:

	Total Gubernatorial Seats	Total State House Majorities*
SDP:	14	17
NRC:	16	11

*Two of the State Houses of Assembly were evenly split between the SDP and NRC.

1992 National assembly and senate elections (total seats):

	National Assembly	Senate
SDP:	276	38
NRC:	317	53

1993 Presidential elections (annulled by the military):

	Percentage of popular vote	States won (out of 30)
SDP (M.K.O. Abiola):	58	19
NRC (Bashir Tofa):	42	11

Fourth republic:

1999 State Gubernatorial and house of assembly elections (out of 36)[15]

	Governors	House of assembly majorities
PDP	21	23
APP	9	8
AD	6	5

1999 National assembly elections

	Senate (out of 109)	House (out of 360)
PDP	59	206
APP	29	74
AD	20	68

1999 Presidential election

	Percentage of votes cast
PDP (Olusegun Obasanjo)	62.78
APP-AD alliance (Olu Falae)	37.22

2003 State gubernatorial and house of assembly elections (out of 36)[16]

	Governors	House of assembly majorities
PDP	28	28
ANPP	7	7
AD	1	1

2003 National assembly elections

	Senate (out of 109)	House (out of 360)
PDP	76	223
ANPP	27	96
AD	6	34
Others	–	6

2003 Presidential election

	Percentage of votes cast
PDP (Olusegun Obasanjo)	61.94
ANPP (Muhammadu Buhari)	32.19

Appendix B: 2007 Election Results

Legitimacy Deficit

Difference between opinion poll and vote

ZONE		PDP	ANPP	AC	APGA	PPA
nc	Benue	16	7	-4	0	
nc	FCT					
nc	Kogi	24	22	-23	0	
nc	Kwara	45	-8	-2	0	
nc	Nasarawa	0	8	-8	0	
nc	Niger	14	0	8	0	
nc	Plateau	-20	0	23	0	
ne	Adamawa	42	-19	3	0	
ne	Bauchi	25	-16	-8	0	
ne	Borno	-8	20	2	0	
ne	Gombe	61	-30	3	0	
ne	Taraba	29	-23	-2	-2	
ne	Yobe	16	-27	5	0	
nw	Jigawa	36	-46	8	0	
nw	Kaduna	41	-23	-3	-1	
nw	Kano	25	-10	-3	0	
nw	Katsina	17	-10	2	0	
nw	Kebbi	57	-45	0	0	
nw	Sokoto	44	-36	0	0	
nw	Zamfara	0	25	0	0	
se	Abia	2	-7	0	-3	PPA
se	Anambra	50	2	-31	-1	Now APGA
se	Ebonyi	55	-15	0	-20	
se	Enugu	59	-4	-6	-27	
se	Imo					Now PPA
ss	Akwa-Ibom	37	-6	-3	-2	
ss	Bayelsa	81	-20	-12	-10	
ss	Cross-River	43	-12	-7	-2	
ss	Delta	47	-1	-11	-1	
ss	Edo	30	0	27	0	
ss	Rivers	54	-25	-12	-1	
sw	Ekiti	31	8	20	0	
sw	Lagos	13	-4	41	-1	
sw	Ogun	24	1	-11	0	
sw	Ondo	30	0	-40	-2	
sw	Osun	43	-4	17	0	
sw	Oyo	34	29	-8	0	
TOTAL		36	-6	-3	-2	

28 States over 20 points difference btw poll and INEC

Epilogue - Nigeria: Unity in Diversity at Fifty[i]

Axel Harneit-Sievers
Director, East Africa/Horn of Africa Regional Office, Heinrich Böll Foundation

I am delighted and honored to be here in Lagos today. I have been following Nigerian political debates since the 1980s – and sometimes I have had the opportunity to participate a little, here and there. What has always impressed and fascinated me is the way Nigerians discuss Nigeria: the intensity of the debates, the excitement involved, and also the peculiar mix of both - desperation and hope – that always comes up. It is difficult to find anybody discussing Nigeria in a cool, disinterested manner; debates about Nigeria are almost always hot, sometimes red-hot. I am happy that we'll have the opportunity today to engage once more in such a debate, on a sophisticated level, and with illustrious participants.

Naturally, an independence anniversary, and especially a 'Golden Jubilee', is an opportunity for stock-taking. One may look at achievements over the last half-century, or compare expectations then with realities today. I want to contribute 'my own 50 kobo' to this debate, as a friend of Nigeria who has been as excited and as frustrated about the country's path as Nigerians themselves.

I want to speak about 'Unity in Diversity at Fifty', employing a phrase that has been used and misused many times but – I believe – is still relevant. I am asking: What holds the country together, despite its diversity and the numerous conflicts resulting from it? I will address politics, economy, and what I call (for want of a better term) culture.

A colonial (faulty) design and its federal solution

First, politics and structures. This much is known: The very fact of Nigeria existing in its borders today, and with a high degree of internal diversity, is merely a result of the colonial past. The 'amalgamation' of 1914 which brought Nigeria into existence, combined three major colonial territories with very diverse histories and cultures. And even these smaller units were heterogeneous in many respects. Their concrete shapes resulted, more often than not, from accidental and hazardous acquisitions, rather than from a very systematic policy of colonial acquisition and expansion. No doubt, Nigeria - its boundaries, and the combination of people and cultures Nigeria comprised - was artificial. But which of the more than 50 other countries in Africa is not?

Realizing this artificialness, the Pan-Africanists of the colonial and early post-colonial days drew the conclusion that those boundaries had to be done away with, to be

[i]Introductory remarks at the Public Discussion of the Special Issue of the Journal of Contemporary African Studies on 'Nigeria at Fifty: A Nation In Narration' hosted by Heinrich Boll Foundation, held at the Protea Hotel, Ikoyi, Lagos, October 9, 2010.

replaced by a continental project. But in practice, more local and regional political interests of emerging political elites prevailed, and perhaps the interests of the colonial powers that were just about to leave to 'divide and rule' Africa. (However, it is important to note that Britain, at critical moments from the 1940s to the 1960s, always strived to keep Nigeria as one entity.)

The amalgamation, the colonial boundaries and their transformation into the boundaries of the independent state, for better or worse, were a historical fact to live and work with. Nigerians have often complained about this fact, and continue to do so. But *most Nigerians, for most of the time,* accepted them as the framework to work with. It needed very severe experiences of mistreatment – the killings of Igbo in the North in 1966, the decades of neglect of people in the oil-producing areas – to make Nigerians seriously ask for secession. Beyond those extreme examples, people usually complained in order to re-negotiate the system. Obafemi Awolowo's famous description of Nigeria, in 1947, as a 'mere geographical expression', did not lead him to advocate breaking up the country; instead, he was merely looking for better political arrangements do deal with the situation. The search for such arrangements has been going on ever since.

The federal system, as we know it, is very much a product of the evolution of independent Nigeria, and I regard it as one of its major achievements. It needed the tragedy of the Civil War to bring it about: to change the unwieldy structure of three regions, inherited from colonialism (with each region dominated by an ethnic majority group, while including many minority groups; and with the regions fighting against each other, as well as internally), into something that gave more representation and autonomy to minorities, while at the same time breaking up the monolithic, and formerly overwhelming, large ethnic blocs by allowing smaller – sub-ethnic, more localized – interests to emerge and gain relevance within them.

I will limit myself to a few remarks on the federal system. The federal system stands at the core of Nigeria's survival as a nation state after independence. It balances interests and manages Nigeria's ethnic, regional and even religious diversity, with reasonable success.

Federalism in Nigeria has its problematic sides: It has been massively affected (distorted and corrupted) by Nigeria's political culture (i.e. the way how politics is being done) and also by Nigeria's oil dependency. It is likely the most distribution-oriented federalism in the world, and perhaps its greatest problem, in the long run, lies in the fact that it tends to perpetuate and even increase and exacerbate the very diversity it tries to manage: It creates parochial identities and even divided concepts of citizenship under the pretext of 'indigeneity'.

But for all its numerous problems, a federalist structure appears to be the only realistic option to come to terms with Nigeria's diversity and keep the country united. The impact of a break-up of the country, and the costs it would have for many of its citizens, appears all too frightful to be considered seriously as an alternative. On the other hand, a higher degree of centralization (it already existed - under federal guise – during military rule) did not achieve greater national cohesion. Instead it created tension and deferred hatred – and we saw those trends exploding right after the political opening with the return to democratic and civilian rule in May 1999. Thus, the further development and refinement of the federal system deserves all creative thought and all the support we can give it.

Political independence, economic (oil) dependence

I now turn to economics. It is often stated today that Nigeria, in 1960, had a better starting position than some South East Asian countries which later on saw dramatic economic progress, while Nigeria – except for the shiny oil boom decade of the 1970s – fell behind dramatically. This is an undeniable truth, one that begs the question of why Nigeria did not capitalize on its apparent advantage.

The colonial heritage is worth considering here. British colonialism had organized Nigeria as an economy dependent on agricultural exports, with a very limited degree of economic integration, sectorally as well as inter-regionally. But since about the late 1940s, agricultural exports were doing really well, and by the 1950s, still under British rule, Nigeria took first steps to expand the industrial and manufacturing sector. Thus, the economic foundations around 1960 were not bad, by early post-colonial standards of the time.

Critics have argued that the government was not radical enough (as against Ghana under Kwame Nkrumah, for example), pursuing a course all too friendly towards foreign economic interests, especially the British. But before Nigeria could seriously become what those critics have called a 'neo-colonial' dependent economy, the oil boom arrived. It created something very different: an oil-dependent economy that had little in common with either the colonial structures or the 'neo-colonial' order of other African countries.

For some years, it appeared that oil would make everything possible: the expansion of infrastructure and education, a state-managed accelerated industrialization programme, the politics of indigenization, a strong role in international affairs (remember a Nigerian foreign minister's call to acquire nuclear weapons?). In reality, however, agriculture declined, imports and debts rose, Nigeria became a nation of middlemen traders, forwarders and contractors; corruption exploded while many of the grand industrial schemes never really took off. By 1982, the party was over; while poverty rose rapidly, long and painful years of structural adjustment followed.

Today, it is obvious that the oil boom of the 1970s constituted a singular, unique opportunity for Nigeria – not only to break with the colonial past, but also to build something new. This opportunity was largely wasted. Today, we know that it is not enough to view this as merely the (moral) fault of individual, misguided political leaders, military or civilian. It was not even merely their wrong policies. Today, we understand what happened as a systemic issue known as the 'resource curse'. Though the term was coined much later, it describes well what happened (in Nigeria perhaps only more radically than elsewhere): a system whereby volatile oil rents dominate the economy and tend to damage all other economic sectors; and a system where politics primarily revolves around sharing the oil income, resulting in both: massive corruption and sharp political conflict. In short: only countries with the best structures of governance survive an oil boom without major damages and are able to use the oil income for long-term development. Nigeria does not belong in this category. It continues to suffer from the resource curse syndrome until today, even though economic and governance reforms since the late 1990s have brought some improvements (and even rapid economic development in certain sectors). The outcome has been the failure of the Nigerian state to deliver positive social goods, for example basic services and security, to its citizens.

Oil has had very ambivalent impacts on unity and diversity in Nigeria.

- On the one hand, oil money – while not bringing development to Nigeria – has helped to create a national elite. Its minimum joint interest – to put it bluntly – consists in sharing the oil revenue, which only works as long as the country remains united. The federal order (with its mechanisms of electoral politics and revenue allocation) provides the necessary institutional framework. Of course, sharing the oil money still remains competitive, and is thus not without conflict. The incumbent People's Democratic Party (PDP) has become the most important forum for political actors to negotiate these issues – and in this sense, the PDP, for better or worse, has become a truly national party, a 'voice of unity' often in a rather perverted form.
- On the other hand, oil production is concentrated in a small part of the country, in a minority area that was politically marginal for most of Nigeria's post-independence history. For decades, this massive imbalance allowed whomever was in power in Lagos or Abuja to take the oil money (and run) away. This has changed since the late 1990s, and decisively so over the last 5 years, largely as a result of economic warfare by militant actors in the Niger Delta. Thus the Nigerian federal system has reached its limits in handling 'diversity' if it is combined with deep-seated experiences of marginalization, provoking aggressive self-assertion.

Unity and diversity in (political) culture

My final point is about culture. Much of the discussion around 'unity' and 'diversity' in Nigeria takes a top down approach – focusing on the institutions required to manage diversity in order to maintain unity (especially the federal order) and on issues of the political system (parties, leadership, governance). The *Journal of Contemporary African Studies* special edition presented today is a good and very valuable example.

All this is highly relevant, of course – but it may not be enough. Instead, I want to suggest that we should also use the opportunity of the independence anniversary (and of this discussion) to once again look at the actual foundations of unity within Nigeria's diversity.

While, historically, Nigeria may be an artificial construct, its political elite (or at least, most of them) are its main beneficiaries. They also carry the main responsibility to make it work, and make it work better. Still, Nigeria would be even more in danger if it were merely a project of its political elites. I emphatically believe that it is not just that.

Around the time of independence, it was perhaps correct to describe Nigeria as a product of an 'amalgamation without integration', implying that colonialism had done (or allowed) little to achieve substantial social and economical integration of the country. Fifty years later, this claim no longer rings true. Cities have grown beyond recognition. Migration has brought millions of Nigerians to live and work in areas outside of what they (or the idea of 'indigeneity') may regard as their ethnic 'homes'. Economic linkages between these cities and the countryside, especially trading networks, have multiplied. Living together in towns is not always easy, and conflicts are easily exploited by warlords who mobilize communities against each other. Still, it is worthwhile to view and analyze Nigeria's urbanization not merely as a source of conflict and violence (as done so often). Rather, urbanization may also be looked at as a success story of national integration, *in most areas, most of the time*. The unity of the country (fragile and contested as it may appear at times) is a precondition and a fundamental resource for every Nigerian, not only for the political elite, but also for millions of poor people in search of livelihoods. To them, Nigeria remains a large country providing many options and opportunities, even if their expectations often remain unfulfilled. Sometimes this failure is due to competition from others. But more often and more systematically, it is due to the failure of government to provide the right framework within which Nigerians can live, work and prosper.

In the first decades after independence, symbols of national unity were primarily state-sponsored, such as festivals, impressive government buildings, army parades (and even a museum displaying the bullet-ridden car of a former head of state). Most of these state-sponsored symbols of national unity became hollow over time, not least due to their misuse by successive military regimes. Today, they have been overtaken by products of the 'culture industry'; in everyday life, Nollywood and Nigerian pop music bring (not only young) people together - throughout the country and even beyond. There is integration, indeed.

Finally, I want to revisit an observation I made at the beginning about how Nigerians debate Nigeria. These debates do not merely take place on the comment pages of newspapers, but also in beer parlours, at churches and mosques, and also in many of the products of the culture industry just mentioned. In a way, the very fact that there is a virtually perpetual talk about Nigeria – much of it critical in character – seems to keep people united: There is a sense of common concern (and even ideas about a common destiny – and how the country should be governed) in many of the most damning statements about the reality of the country. Some Nigerian talk about Nigeria displays 'unity in complaint' (or even 'unity in misery'). May I suggest that, as long as Nigerians talk about (and criticize) the country, Nigeria remains relevant for them, keeping them together?

Index